IMAGES
of America

PINNACLE PEAK

I0806270

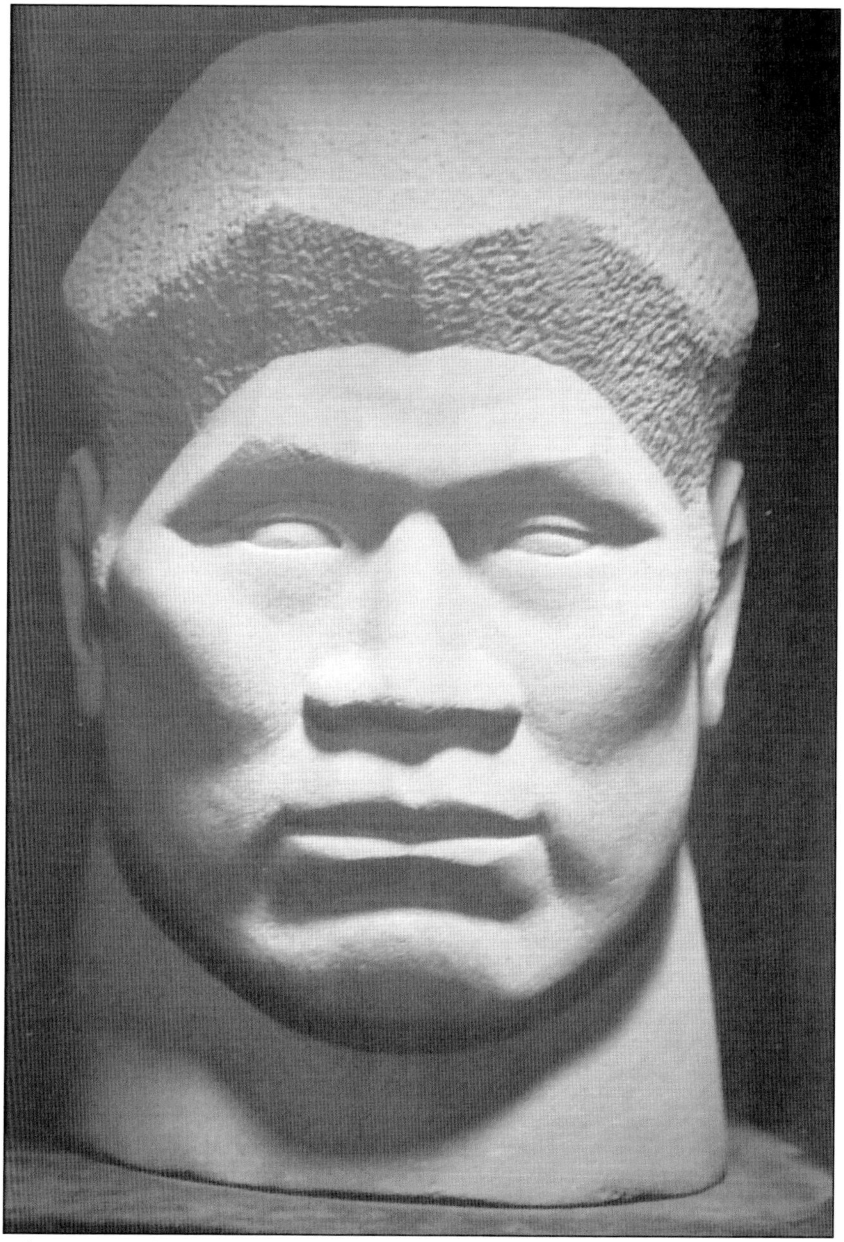

This sculpture, *Apache Warrior*, was created by Mathilde Schaefer Davis. She trained at the Art Institute of Chicago, studied with European sculptors, and was one of the artists at the Scottsdale Craftsman Building in Scottsdale, where she had the first pottery kiln in Arizona. Mathilde and her husband, Lew Davis, were among the artists who lived near Pinnacle Peak in the 1950s. (Courtesy of Liz Stapleton Ogden.)

ON THE COVER: It does not snow often on Pinnacle Peak, and it is an event when it does. This photograph of Bruce Barnett and his horse was taken in the early 1970s on one of those special snow days. Barnett sang at Greasewood Flat for tips. Greasewood Flat is approximately a mile from Pinnacle Peak. (Courtesy of Joyce Eller.)

IMAGES
of America

PINNACLE PEAK

Les Conklin and the
Greater Pinnacle Peak Association

ARCADIA
PUBLISHING

ISBN 978-0-7385-7984-9

Published by Arcadia Publishing
Charleston, South Carolina

Printed in the United States of America

Library of Congress Control Number: 2011920847

For all general information, please contact Arcadia Publishing:
Telephone 843-853-2070
Fax 843-853-0044
E-mail sales@arcadiapublishing.com
For customer service and orders:
Toll-Free 1-888-313-2665

Visit us on the Internet at www.arcadiapublishing.com

To my wife, Judy, for her support and incredible patience and to those individuals and organizations that have worked to preserve our community's natural environment

Contents

Acknowledgments

The Greater Pinnacle Peak Association (GPPA) began in 1977 as the Greater Pinnacle Peak Homeowners Association (GPPHA). Since its founding, members have advocated and worked tirelessly to preserve the environment, heritage, and quality of life in the North Scottsdale Sonoran Desert. Our community would be a very different place without their efforts.

I am indebted to the staff, editorial contributors, and advertisers who have enabled the GPPA to publish *A Peek at the Peak* (*The Peak*) as a complimentary community service since 1983. *The Peak* has been a key source of information for this book. I am especially indebted to former editors Liz Stapleton Ogden, Don Schoenau, and Nancy Lucas. Liz was the founding editor of *The Peak* and researched and wrote about Pinnacle Peak's past. Don Schoenau and Nancy Lucas published invaluable articles based on their conversations with local old-timers.

I also want to thank my editor at Arcadia Publishing, Jared Jackson, for his expert guidance. Thanks to Arcadia authors Doug Sydnor and Joan Fudala, who is the master of Scottsdale history. Also thanks to the following individuals who provided access to their collections and granted permission to reproduce images from those collections: John Loleit, of the City of Scottsdale's Pinnacle Peak Park; Dr. Arleyn Simon, of Arizona State University; Donna Ropp, of the Desert Center; Dana Braccia, of the Scottsdale Public Library; JoAnne Handley, of the Scottsdale Historical Society; Marv Dickson, of Pinnacle Peak Patio; Joyce Eller, on behalf of the Cavalliere family; Katchinas Bill McMorris and Robert Owens, and Erik Filsinger, of the Arizona Mountaineering Club.

There are several people who have paved the way for this book through their photography, writing, and love of our area's history. Specifically, I wish to thank Michelle Anderson, Horst Berkner, Marty and Kathy Cambal, Bob Cappel, Ken Lew, Bob Mason, Len Marcisz, Ken Melnick, Howard and Carol Myers, Marg Nelssen, Maxine Rosenberg, and Ginger Schoenau for their contributions to preserving our community's environment and history.

In 1994, Scottsdale city manager Dick Bowers and Scottsdale mayor Herb Drinkwater provided the early support and guidance that fostered my interest in preserving local history and ultimately led to this book.

Images in this volume appear courtesy of *The Peak*, Creative Women of Pinnacle Peak (CWPP), Friends of Pinnacle Peak Park (FPPP), Friends of the Scenic Drive (FSD), the Rotary Club of Pinnacle Peak (RCPP), the Southwest Wildlife Conservation Center (SWCC), Arizona Research Institute/ Office of Cultural Resource Management (ARI/OCRM), and Library of Congress (LOC).

INTRODUCTION

It is 1983. Passengers are peering through their bus windows at Pinnacle Peak, one of central Arizona's most recognizable landmarks. The excited tourists are on their way to a famous Pinnacle Peak cowboy restaurant. The driver draws the passengers' attention to two men dressed in cowboy garb standing by the side of the quiet, lonely road. The men are waving for help. The driver pulls over and opens the door. The "cowboys," with six-shooters drawn and bandanas covering their faces, board the bus and shout, "This is a holdup!"

Since the long-gone days when tour companies routinely staged fake highway robberies, the popularity of Pinnacle Peak as a tourist destination has continued to grow. It has also become a coveted North Scottsdale residential area and home to 150-acre Pinnacle Peak Park, which welcomed its one-millionth visitor in February 2008. Most visitors are unaware of the remarkable natural and human history of Pinnacle Peak and the vibrant community that surrounds it. This book will focus on it's untold story.

Pinnacle Peak Mountain rises out of the Sonoran desert floor to an elevation of 3,170 feet. It is situated in the rich Sonoran Uplands at the north end of the McDowell Mountains. More than just a scenic spot, Pinnacle Peak's natural environment has supported human habitation for thousands of years.

Archeologists believe that archaic hunter-gatherers roamed the area from as early as 5000 BC until AD 600. Upland Hohokam resided in the region until approximately AD 1200. In 1988, Pinnacle Peak Village, a Hohokam settlement within two miles of Pinnacle Peak, was excavated and photographed.

In 1865, the US Army established Camp McDowell (later renamed Fort McDowell) approximately 20 miles from Pinnacle Peak. The camp's purpose was to provide protection for miners, ranchers, and settlers in central Arizona from various groups of native people, including the Tonto Apache and Yavapai peoples. The Army established a supply road connecting Fort McDowell with Fort Whipple near Prescott, Arizona. The road, traces of which can still be found, passed just north of Pinnacle Peak.

In the Arizona desert, no development can occur without an adequate supply of water. Three large-scale water-related projects contributed to the early development of Pinnacle Peak and neighboring areas. The Arizona Canal fostered the growth of the tiny farming community of Scottsdale, then a distant 20 miles south of Pinnacle Peak. Later, the construction of Bartlett and Horseshoe Dams created boom times for the tiny mining community of Cave Creek, approximately 13 miles northwest of Pinnacle Peak.

Interesting personalities have helped to create and build the foundation for today's Pinnacle Peak community. Edwin Orpheus Brown established a cattle ranch that grew to 44,000 acres. Kenyon Turner "K.T." Palmer built a homestead on the western flank of Pinnacle Peak in 1933. Decades later, after failing to find water in the Pinnacle Peak area, Palmer developed Arizona's first planned community, Carefree. Captivated by its beauty, artists settled near Pinnacle Peak. Adventurer and trader Don Pablo opened a western curio and antiques store in the remote desert at the intersection of two dirt tracks, today's Pinnacle Peak and Scottsdale Roads.

Late in the 1950s, colorful entrepreneurs opened cowboy venues in the Pinnacle Peak area, forerunners of Rawhide, Arizona's most popular attraction after the Grand Canyon. In the 1960s, after Scottsdale Road was paved, area residents installed plant identification signs along its northern reaches to protect the desert they cherished. A retired executive opened a golf course that used sand for greens. Cattle dramatically outnumbered residents.

In 1969, Jerry and Florence Nelson "struck it wet" when they drilled into a large aquifer not far from Pinnacle Peak. And the rush was on in more ways than one. As the 1960s gave way to the 1970s, 1980s, and 1990s, houses and golf courses began to replace vacant ranch land, residents continued to work to protect the natural environment, and the Pinnacle Peak area was annexed into the city of Scottsdale. Local organizations sprang up to protect the environment and encourage sensitive planning. As new master-planned communities were considered, members reviewed plans and disseminated information to property owners about development and preservation efforts. The master-planned communities approved during this period included Pinnacle Peak Plaza, Pinnacle Peak Country Club and its nine subdivisions, Troon Village, Troon North, Desert Highlands, Estancia, Legend Trails, Grayhawk, Terravita, and Winfield.

Development brought new conveniences. Paved roads replaced dirt tracks. Thanks to new water and telephone lines, residents no longer needed to haul water or drive five or more miles to make a telephone call. A new post office brought mail service to the area. A general store and then retail centers made it unnecessary to drive long distances for shopping.

The road construction and installation of water lines and other infrastructure brought by development also created new challenges for residents. Gun owners who enjoyed hunting and target practice in the open desert were angered by new regulations designed to protect residents and tourists. With no newspapers or magazines serving the area, Pinnacle Peak residents created their own publication to provide information about development projects, local activities, Sonoran plants and animals, and the ever-increasing number of stores and services.

Government leaders worked to enhance communication and understanding between "downtown" Scottsdale and the still remote northern neighborhoods. With the active participation of area residents and developers, ordinances designed to protect native plants, environmentally sensitive areas, and scenic roadsides were adopted.

In July 1995, the burgeoning community and its scenic landscape narrowly escaped disaster when a bolt of lightning struck the desert less than two miles from Pinnacle Peak. The mountain itself was spared, but the lightening strike caused the largest fire ever experienced in the Phoenix metropolitan area. The fire burned 23,000 acres east and southeast of Pinnacle Peak.

For many years, Pinnacle Peak was a secret destination for local equestrians, hikers, and rock climbers. In the 1970s, local residents began suggesting that a park should be created in the area. As growth continued to surge northward, those calls increased, and in 2001 after much public input and discussion, the City of Scottsdale opened Pinnacle Peak Park.

Most visitors to Pinnacle Peak Park enjoy the park's well-developed hiking trail. Many of the plant species and rugged desert landforms that the Hohokam observed can be seen and enjoyed from the trail. The 1.75-mile trail has a very smooth tread that is enjoyed by both equestrians and hikers. Experienced rock-climbing enthusiasts enjoy three climbing areas and a variety of routes within the park.

The park's interpretive signs and educational programs enable visitors to learn about the unique flora and fauna that live in the park and neighboring areas. Bobcats, desert tortoises, coyotes, chuckwallas, rattlesnakes, saguaro, cholla, and ocotillo are just a few of the plant and animal species found in the park and neighboring areas.

Like the eager tourists described in the opening paragraph, most people first come to Pinnacle Peak as visitors. Since the days of the prehistoric hunter-gatherers, the irresistible draw of the land and its wildlife has caused many to call Pinnacle Peak home. The beauty of the area led Scottsdale and its residents to create Pinnacle Peak Park and motivates us to work diligently to preserve the natural environment and heritage of this remarkable place.

One

Pinnacle Peak Beginnings

Pinnacle Peak is located approximately 25 miles northeast of downtown Phoenix, 20 miles north of downtown Scottsdale, and 13 miles southeast of Cave Creek and Carefree, Arizona. Rising out of the Sonoran Desert floor to an elevation of 3,170 feet, Pinnacle Peak's distinctive shape is recognizable from more than 25 miles away.

Situated in the Sonoran Uplands at the north end of the McDowell Mountains and enriched by slightly cooler temperatures, springs, and short-lived water sources from rain and rapidly flowing washes, Pinnacle Peak is the centerpiece of a rugged desert landscape. Pinnacle Peak and the neighboring foothills are dotted with saguaro, palo verde, mesquite, and cholla. The environment is harsh yet fertile and has provided habitats for many species of Sonoran wildlife since long before the arrival of man.

In *For Land's Sake: The Autobiography of a Dynamic Arizonan*, Kenyon Turner Palmer describes the 1933 discovery trip that motivated him to establish a homestead on the western slopes of remote Pinnacle Peak:

> The ironwood trees were in bloom, and seemingly for miles around there was nothing but ironwood trees. The morning light was just right. Back of all and forming the right background were the looming McDowell Mountains in varying shades of blue, with here and there a giant saguaro, highlighted in the sunlight. . . . For the first time I was thrilled by the Arizona landscape. Now, on this Sunday morning on a rough and rocky road . . . I experienced a conversion . . . I was overwhelmed with the desire to possess this land, to be a part of its beauty.

Reading Palmer's words, which were written so recently, it is easy to imagine the excitement of the first hunter-gatherers when they discovered the Pinnacle Peak area so long ago, before there was an Arizona, a Scottsdale, or a Pinnacle Peak Park. This chapter provides a glimpse of the pristine land prehistoric inhabitants discovered.

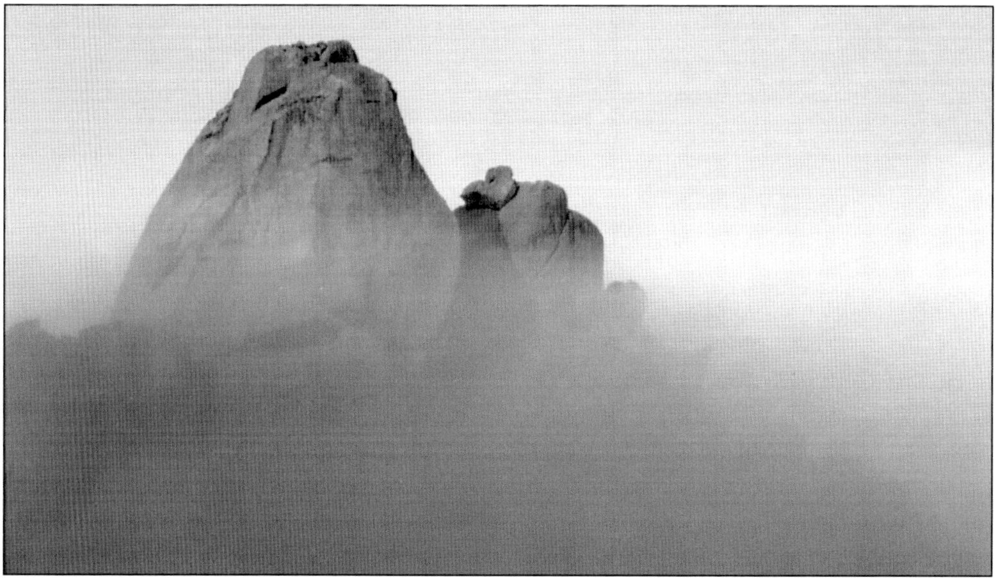

Looming out of the morning mist, Pinnacle Peak was formed about 18 million years ago as the result of tectonic plate movement. The pinnacle of course-grained granite that gives Pinnacle Peak its name has many large grains of pink to light-gray crystals and evolved from magma. (Courtesy of Kathy Mascaro.)

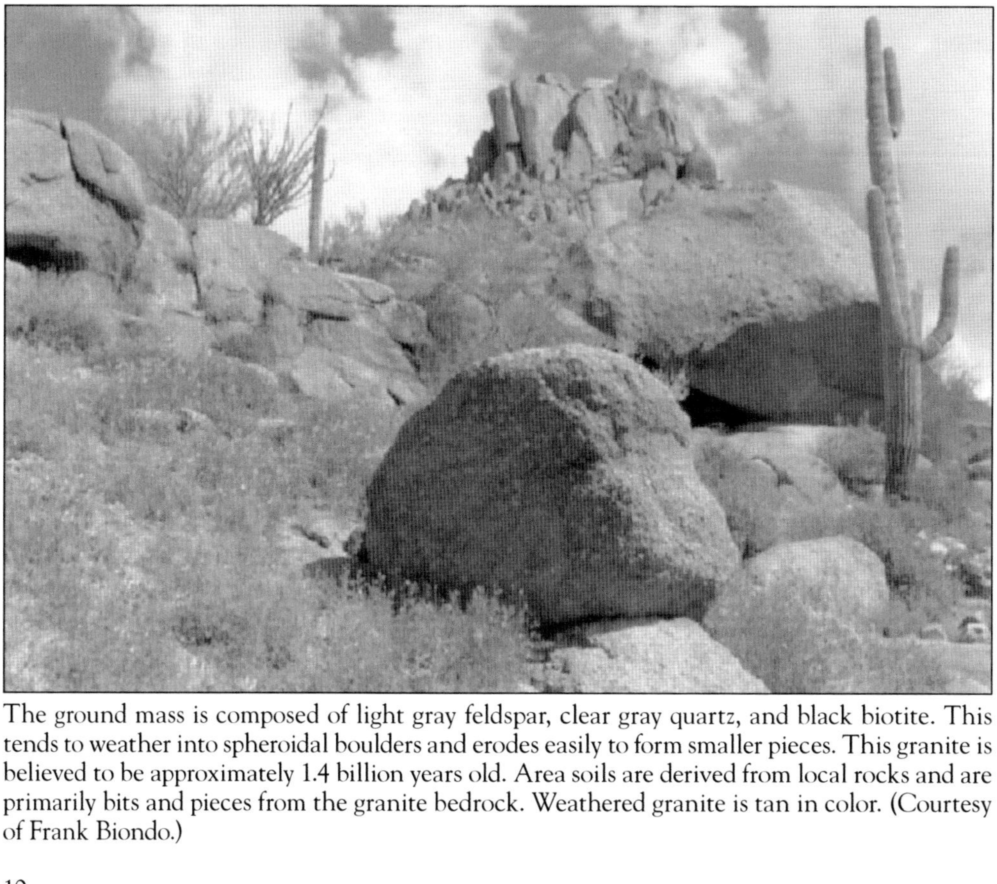

The ground mass is composed of light gray feldspar, clear gray quartz, and black biotite. This tends to weather into spheroidal boulders and erodes easily to form smaller pieces. This granite is believed to be approximately 1.4 billion years old. Area soils are derived from local rocks and are primarily bits and pieces from the granite bedrock. Weathered granite is tan in color. (Courtesy of Frank Biondo.)

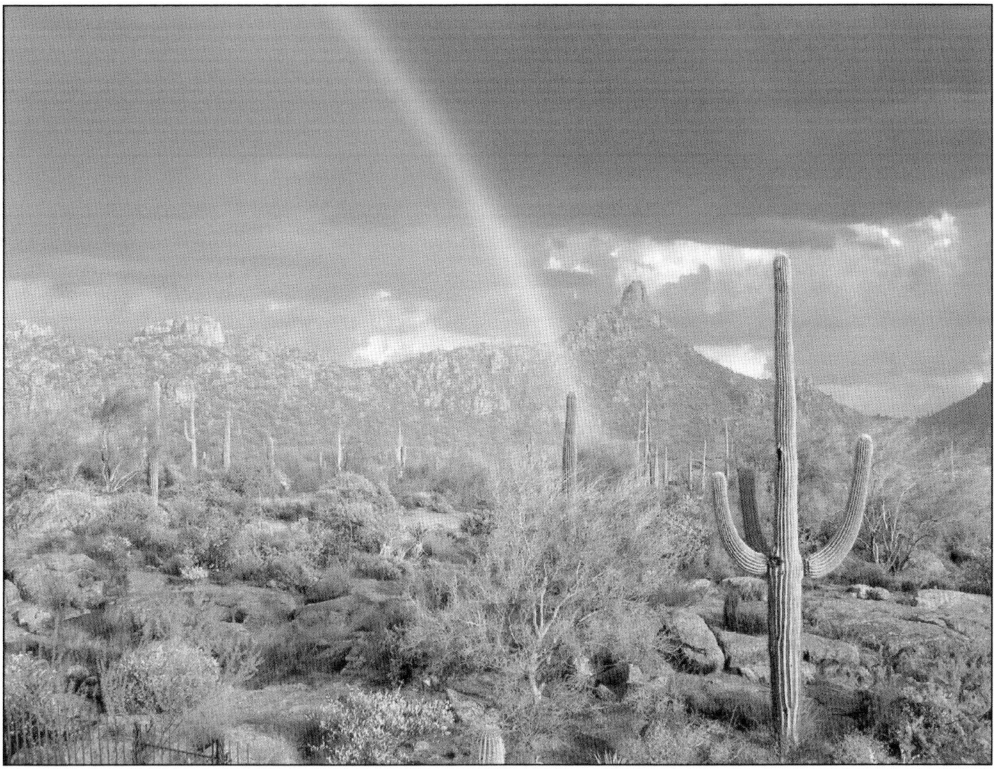

The Sonoran Desert is the only desert in the world with two rainy seasons. During the summer, compact monsoon-like storms originate in the Gulf of Mexico and arrive from the south. Clouds build along the Mogollon Rim to the northeast. Tropical storm cells sweep across the desert. Often, these brief but intense storms are followed by a rainbow. (Courtesy of Kathy Howard.)

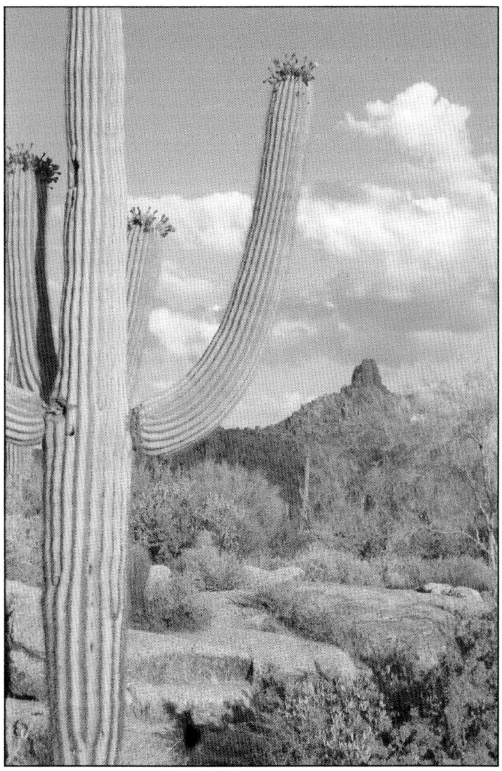

From December through March, winter storms last longer, cover more area, and produce a gentle rain. These storms originate in the Pacific Ocean and arrive from the north. In the winter, temperatures occasionally fall below freezing but only for a short period of time. Vegetation does not suffer from the mild freezes. During the summer, temperatures of 105 degrees Fahrenheit or higher can last for weeks and place considerable stress on flora. (Courtesy of Kathy Howard.)

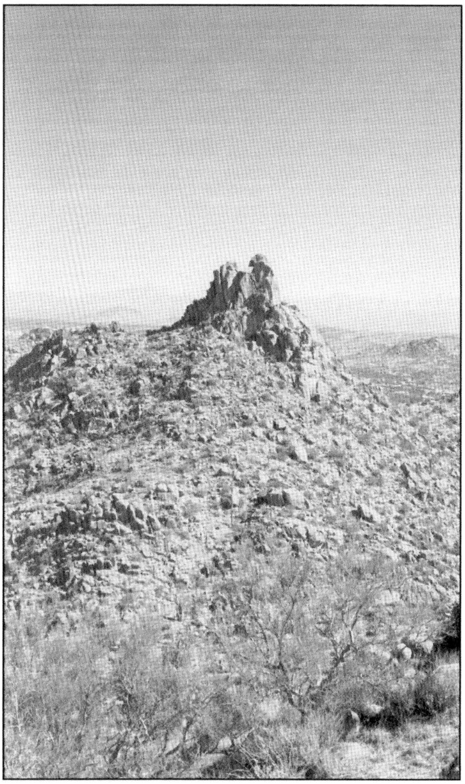

Pinnacle Peak's rugged landscape may seem forbidding and bleak, but it is home to many species of plants and wildlife that have adapted to the Sonoran Desert's harsh environment. (Courtesy of Howard Myers.)

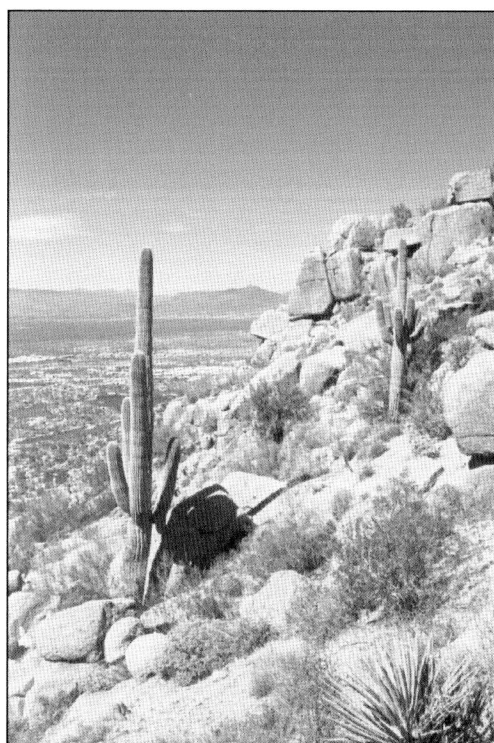

Looking west from the northern slope of Pinnacle Peak toward the large valley that contains the densely populated Phoenix metropolitan area, it is difficult to imagine the Valley of the Sun before the arrival of humans. (Courtesy of the City of Scottsdale.)

Many people are surprised to learn the number of different plant species that grow in the Sonoran Desert. In addition to cacti species, a plethora of native trees, bushes, and flowering plants grows throughout the different seasons. Like the saguaro, the agave is a source of food and water for many desert animal species. (Courtesy of Dennis Liddell.)

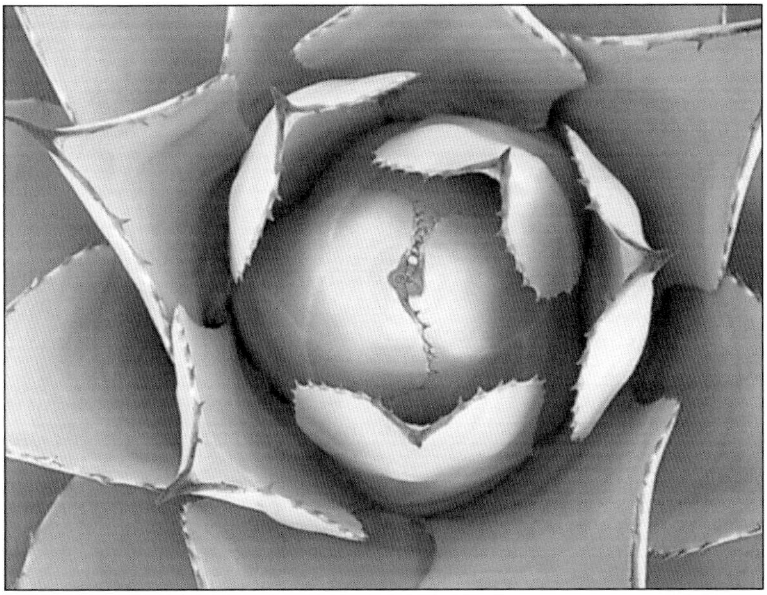

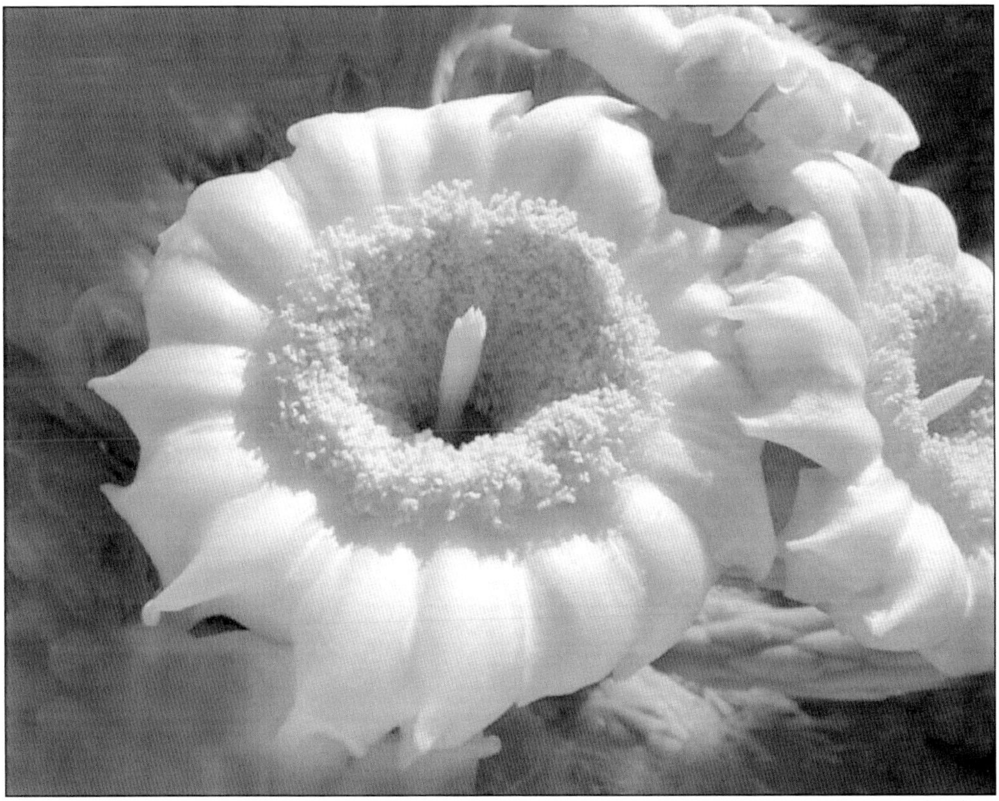

The saguaro blooms during the months of May and June. Its flowers attract bees and other insects during the day and bats and moths at night. Its pulp and seeds are a food source for birds, rodents, ants, and other insects, and the saguaro provides nesting sites for birds. A full-grown saguaro produces about 100 fruits per season. Indigenous people used the fruit and seeds as food. (Courtesy of Dennis Liddell.)

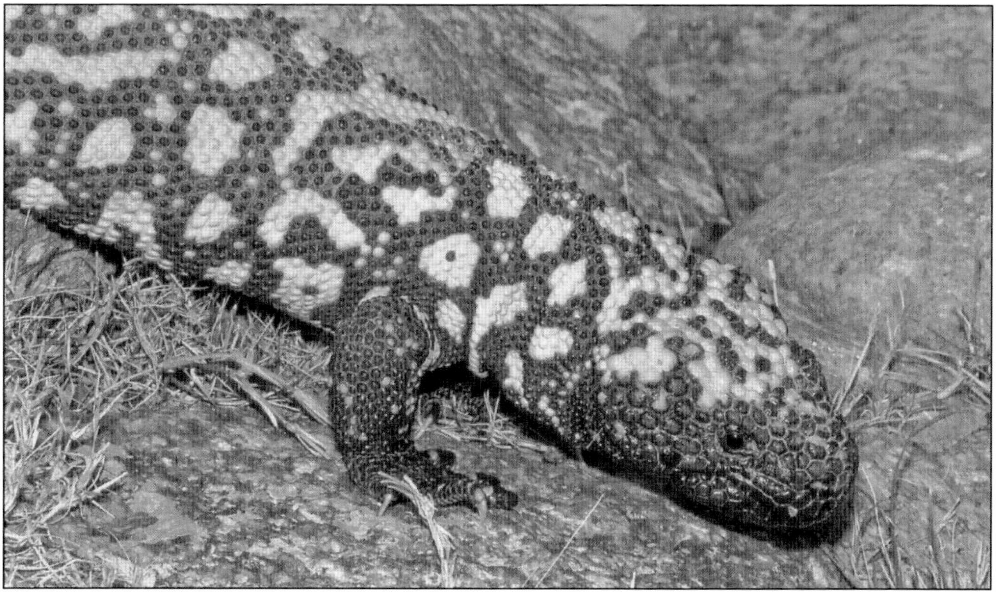

Just as wildlife depends on the existence of plants for survival, interdependence also exists between different species of wildlife. The slightest upset in the balance of nature can have wide-reaching effects on the ecology that inhabits the Pinnacle Peak area. Since the arrival of humans, the populations of Gila monsters has decreased. They are now on the US Fish & Wildlife Service Endangered Species list. (Courtesy of Bruce Houser.)

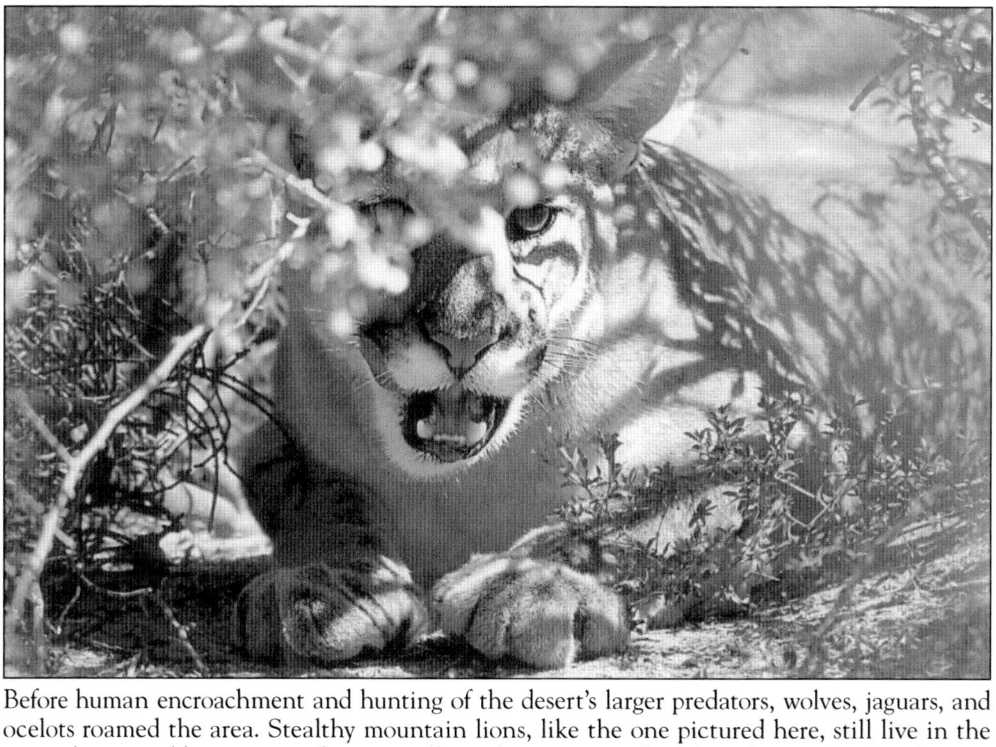

Before human encroachment and hunting of the desert's larger predators, wolves, jaguars, and ocelots roamed the area. Stealthy mountain lions, like the one pictured here, still live in the region but are seldom seen, as they typically prefer remote, rocky ridges that are far from human habitation. (Courtesy of SWWCC.)

During the winter, grazing mule deer and bighorn sheep were attracted to the Pinnacle Peak area by the available water supply. They were an important source of protein for the first Native Americans to migrate to the Pinnacle Peak area. (Courtesy of Kathy Howard.)

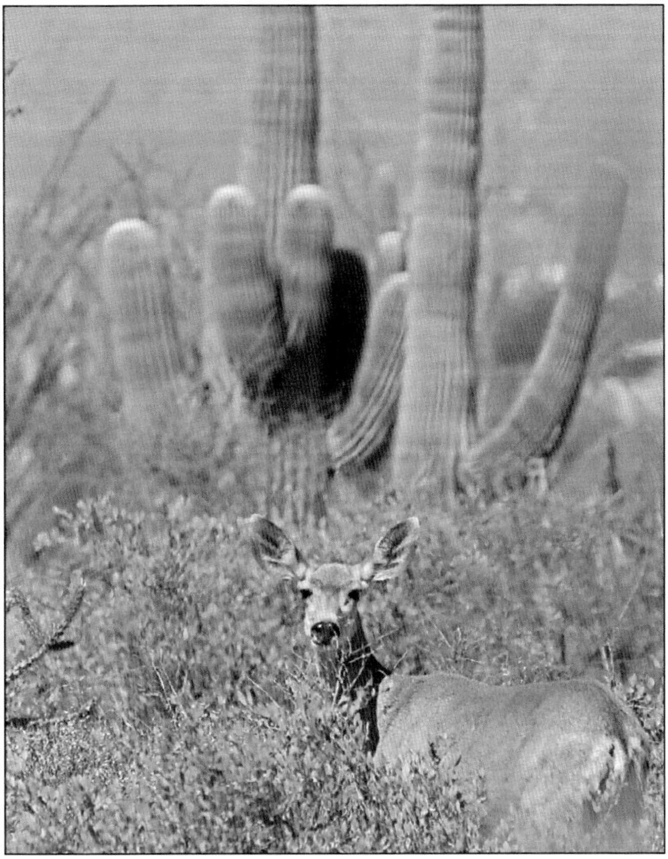

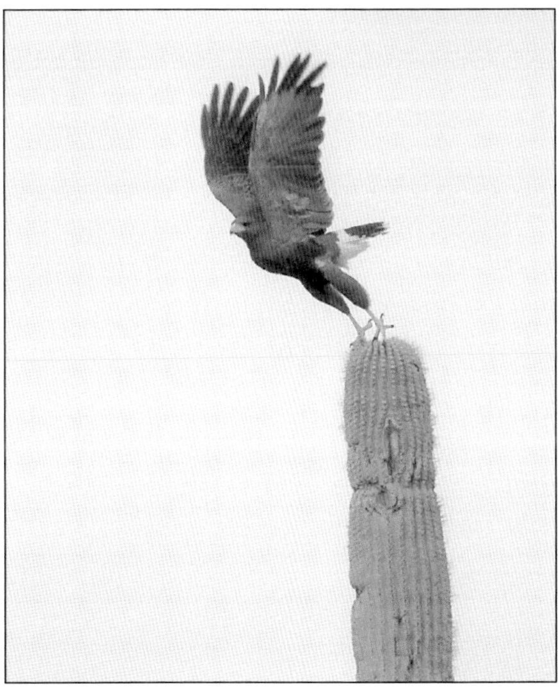

A variety of songbirds, quail, and mourning doves thrived on the plentiful supply of seeds and insects. Different raptors, including species of owls and hawks like the Harris hawk pictured here, preyed upon rodents, reptiles, and amphibians. Vultures often circled overhead searching for earthly leftovers. (Courtesy of Dale Howard.)

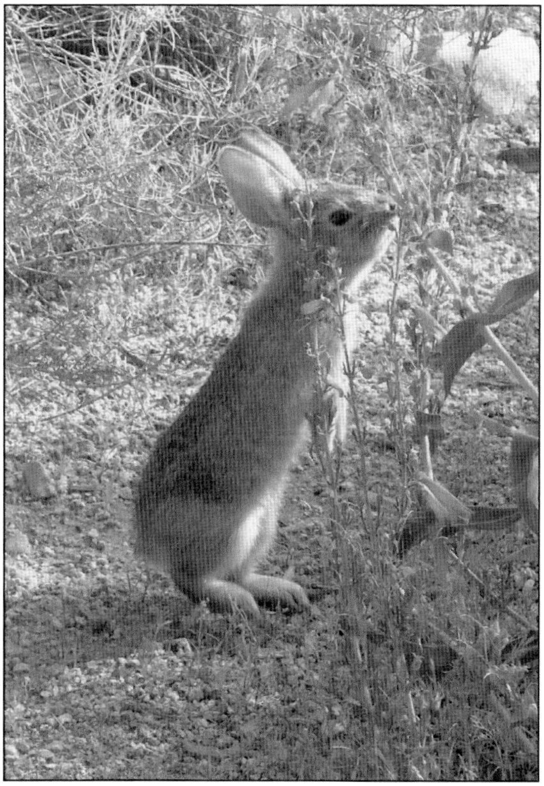

An assortment of gophers, mice, and other small rodents populated the pristine landscape. Jackrabbits and cottontail rabbits were common in the uplands. Rabbits, like the one pictured here, were an important food source for the Upland Hohokam people who settled in the Pinnacle Peak area. (Courtesy of Margit Kagerer.)

It is believed that bobcats, like the two pictured here enjoying the late afternoon sky at Pinnacle Peak Park, were living in the Pinnacle Peak area when the first hunter-gatherers arrived. (Courtesy of Bob Baile.)

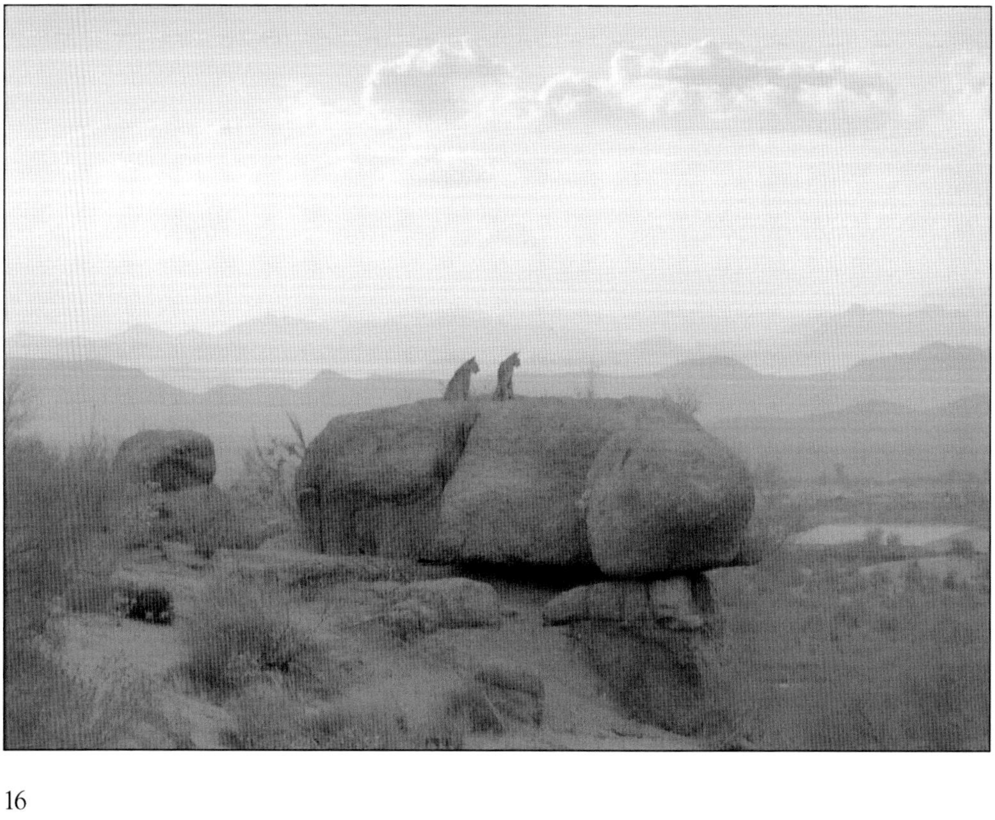

Two

Pinnacle Peak, Land of Native Peoples

The Native Americans of prehistoric times had to obtain their basic needs—food, drink, clothing, medicine, and shelter—from the desert. In the Pinnacle Peak area, they found the essential resources that included water, an abundance of vegetation, and wildlife.

The history of human activity at Pinnacle Peak and the surrounding region spans from prehistoric times to the modern day. Based on numerous studies, including those cited in *The Plants and Animals of Pinnacle Peak Park*, archaeologists believe that early groups in the area were archaic hunter-gatherers who roamed the area from the Middle Archaic period (5000 BC–3000 BC) to the Late Archaic period (AD 600). After the archaic hunter-gatherers, it is believed that the Upland Hohokam resided in the region until approximately AD 1200.

After the Hohokam, a group of hunter-gatherers known as the Yavapai moved through the area as part of the seasonal migration patterns that characterized their culture. Camping in the Pinnacle Peak and foothills area, the Yavapai utilized many of the village and rock-shelter sites previously used by the Hohokam and archaic cultures. The Yavapai were still traveling to this land when the US Army arrived in 1865.

Pinnacle Peak Village is an archeological site located 1.5 miles southeast of Pinnacle Peak. After excavating and studying the site, archeologists concluded that it could be among the largest and longest-occupied settlements in the northern periphery of the major Hohokam centers. These major centers were located on the Salt and Gila Rivers in the Valley of the Sun. The study is notable for another reason.

In the 1993 project report, Dr. Charles Redman, director of the Department of Anthropology at Arizona State University (ASU), wrote, "The Pinnacle Peak Village project is what I consider to be among the finest examples of cooperative effort among a private land developer, local avocational archaeologists, and professionals from ASU. Jerry and Florence Nelson, owners of the land, have demonstrated a serious concern for the preservation of these archeological remains and a responsible handling of data recovery versus development of the property." Unfortunately, many other archeological sites have been lost to development before they were studied.

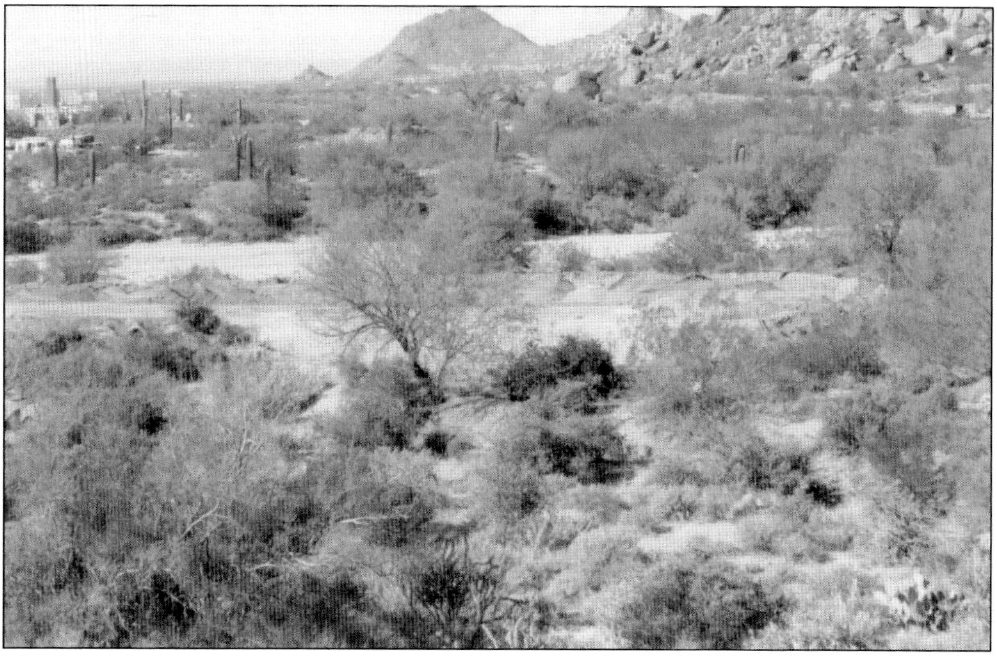

The Pinnacle Peak Land Company, owned by Jerry and Florence Nelson, was opening a new section for development at Troon Village. Workers digging a trench noticed a significant amount of broken pottery on the surface and curious changes of soil color in the trench. Work was stopped, and the Nelsons contacted ASU archeologists. This photograph shows the site prior to excavation. (Courtesy of the ARI/OCRM Collections.)

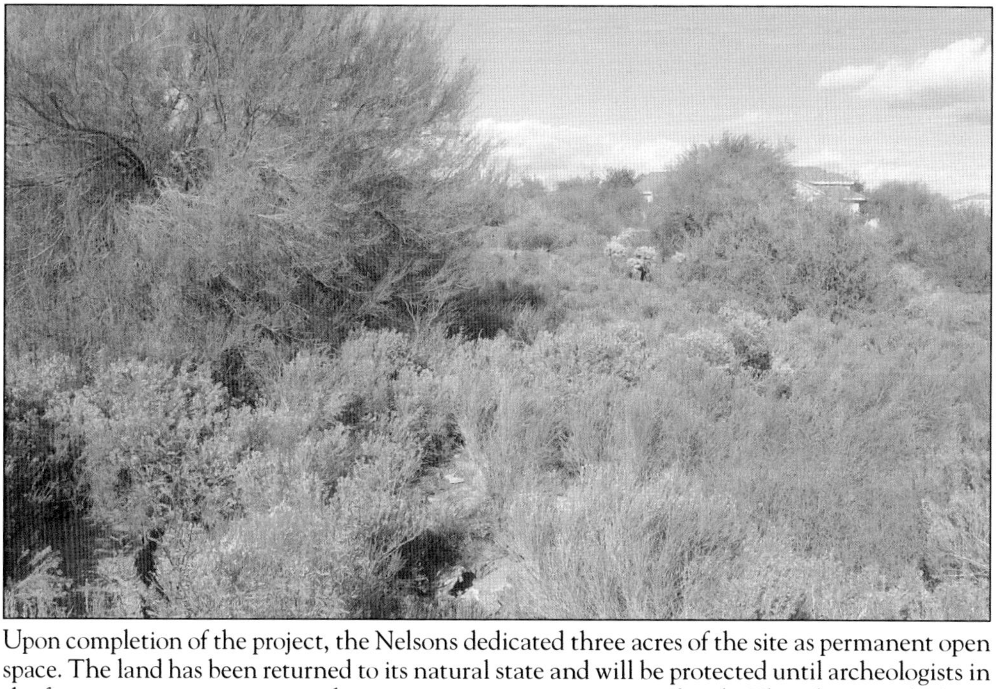

Upon completion of the project, the Nelsons dedicated three acres of the site as permanent open space. The land has been returned to its natural state and will be protected until archeologists in the future return to investigate the area using a new generation of tools. This photograph shows the site in December 2010. (Courtesy of Les Conklin.)

Initial research revealed that the site was formerly known as the Herberger site and that a limited archeological study had been conducted there in 1963 by an ASU graduate student. The site was one of several that ASU had studied in the area. The photograph shows the initial trench begun in 1987 and lengthened during excavations in 1988. (Courtesy of the Desert Center.)

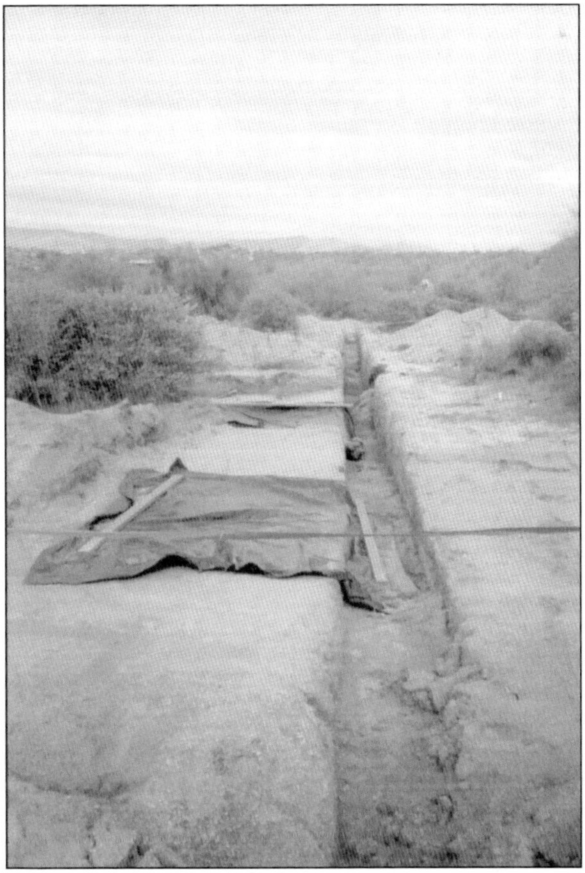

In January 1988, archeologists and more than 60 volunteers began the excavation of what was believed to be a prehistoric Hohokam village. ASU's Dr. Patricia Gilman was joined by members of the Desert Foothills and Phoenix chapters of the Arizona Archeological Association. This photograph shows a backhoe trench and exploratory excavations along its route. (Courtesy of the Desert Center.)

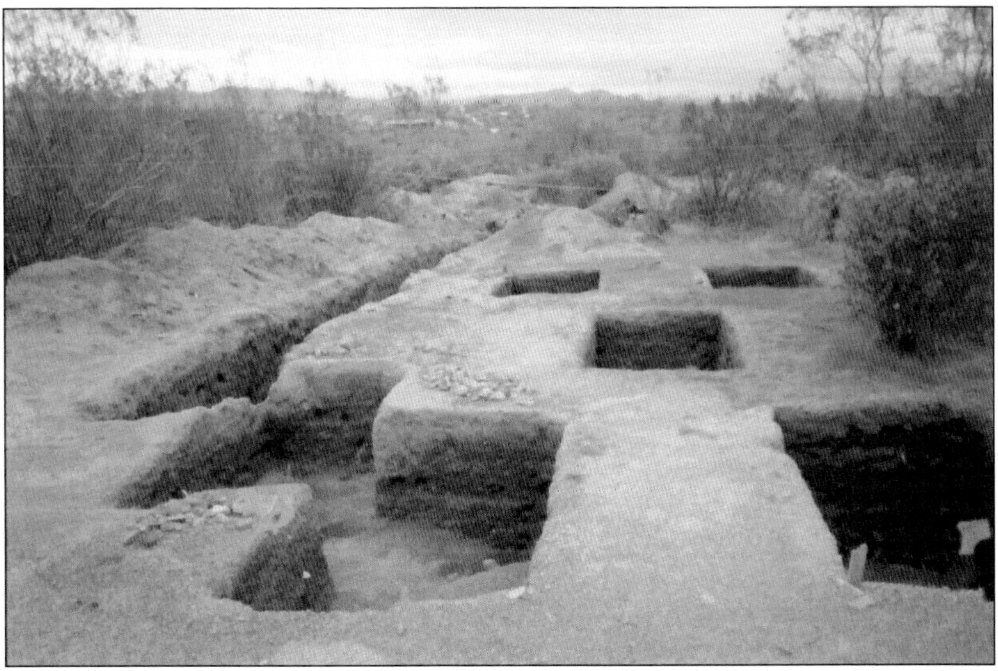

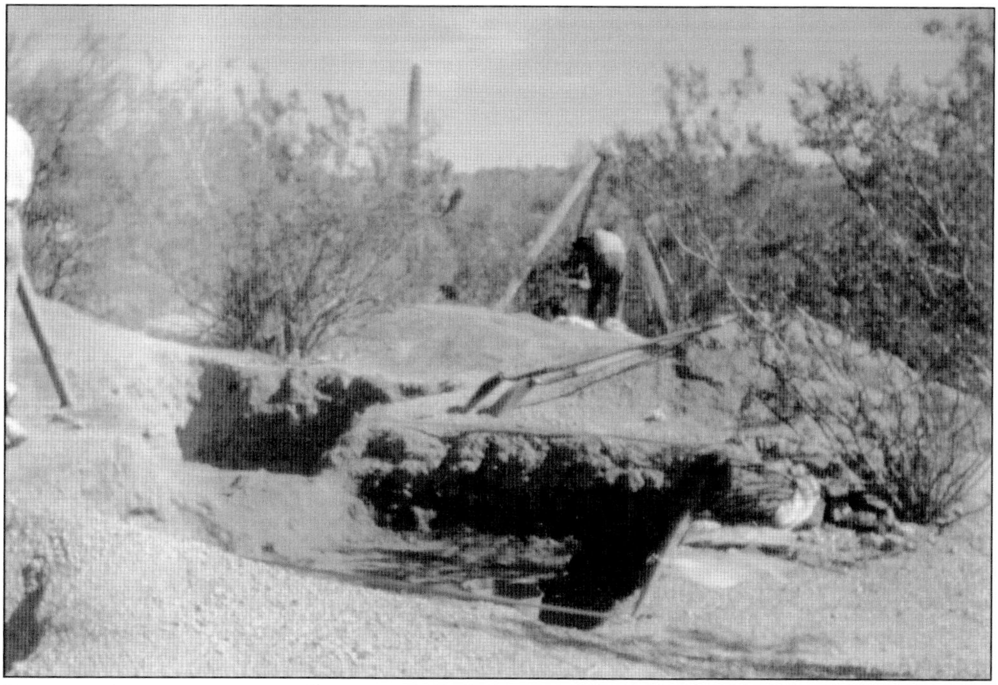

Seven pit houses were partially or completely excavated. Archeologists concluded that more than 100 pit houses, and perhaps as many of 200, existed at Pinnacle Peak Village, with perhaps as many as 25 pit houses in use at one time. Four trash mounds, out of an estimated 25, were sampled. (Courtesy of the ARI/OCRM Collections.)

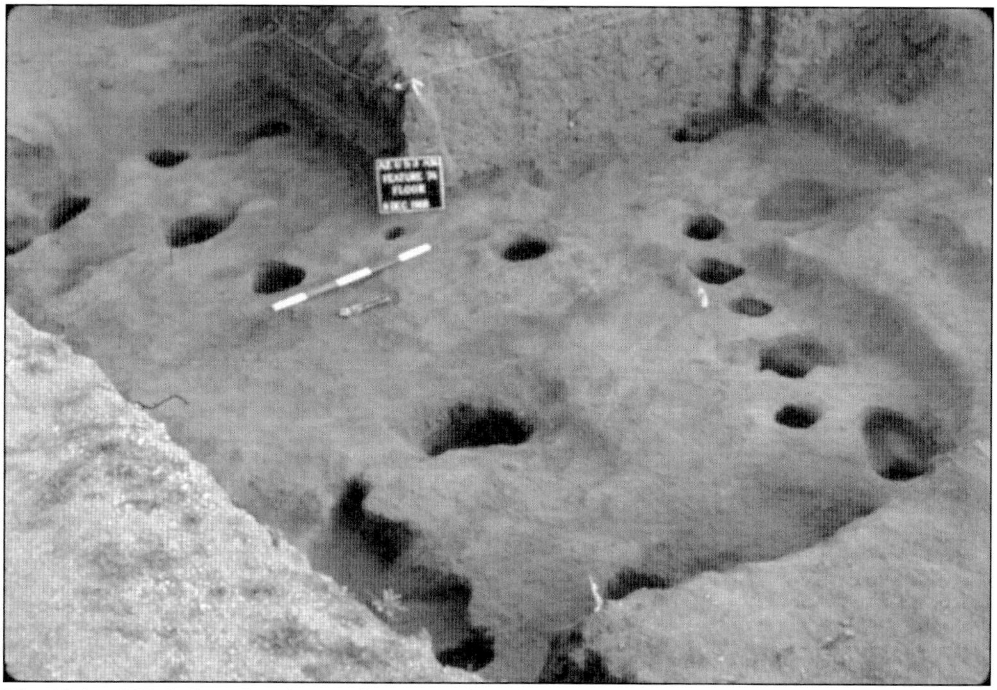

The Upland Hohokam lived in pit homes with walls and roofs of mud-caked brush. Locations of posts can be seen in this photograph. (Courtesy of the ARI/OCRM Collections.)

Archeologists concluded that the earliest occupation of the site was shortly after AD 300 and that the latest was possibly in the early AD 1400s. The peak population period was from AD 500 to AD 1150. Material from this hearth was submitted for archaeomagnetic dating. Occupation dates were also obtained through radiocarbon dating of burned roof beams and analysis of ceramics. (Courtesy of the ARI/OCRM Collections.)

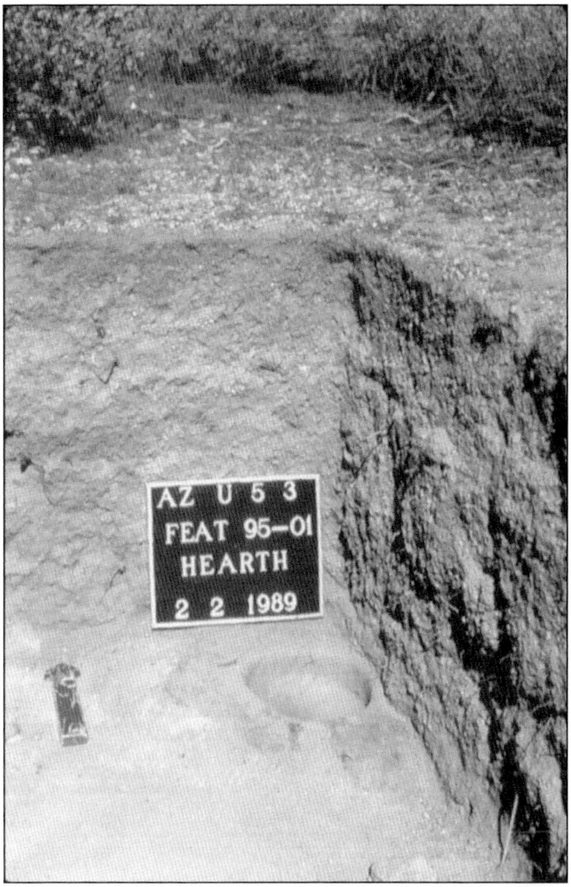

In this photograph, a tripod sifter is being used to recover artifacts near a pit house. The artifact density, both on the surface and within excavations, was quite high. Most of the artifacts were shards and pieces of chipped stone, but ground stone, shell, animal bone, plant remains, and a copper bell were also found. (Courtesy of the Desert Center.)

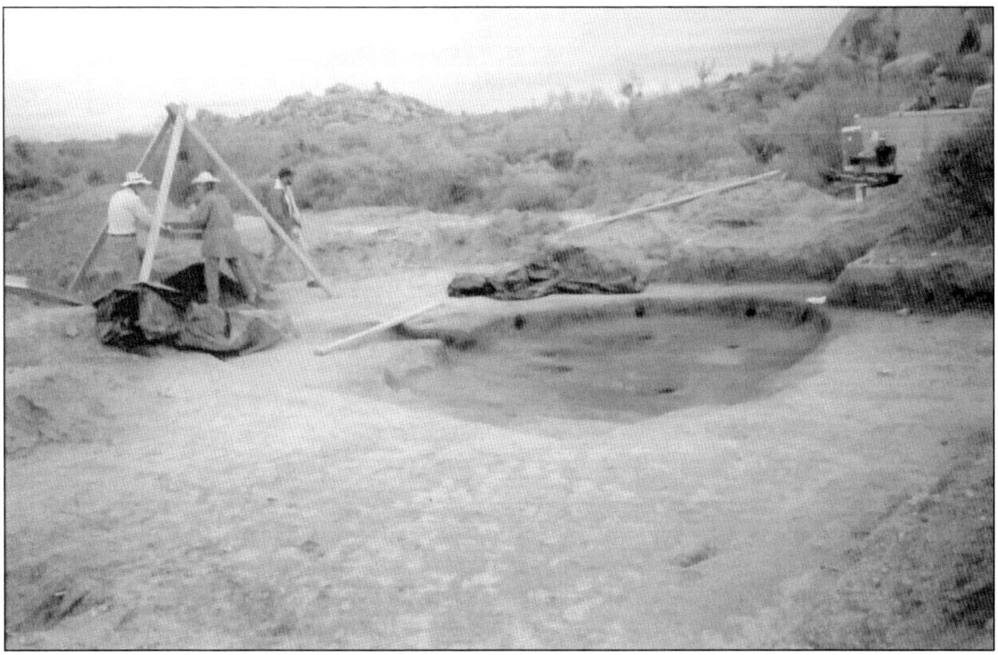

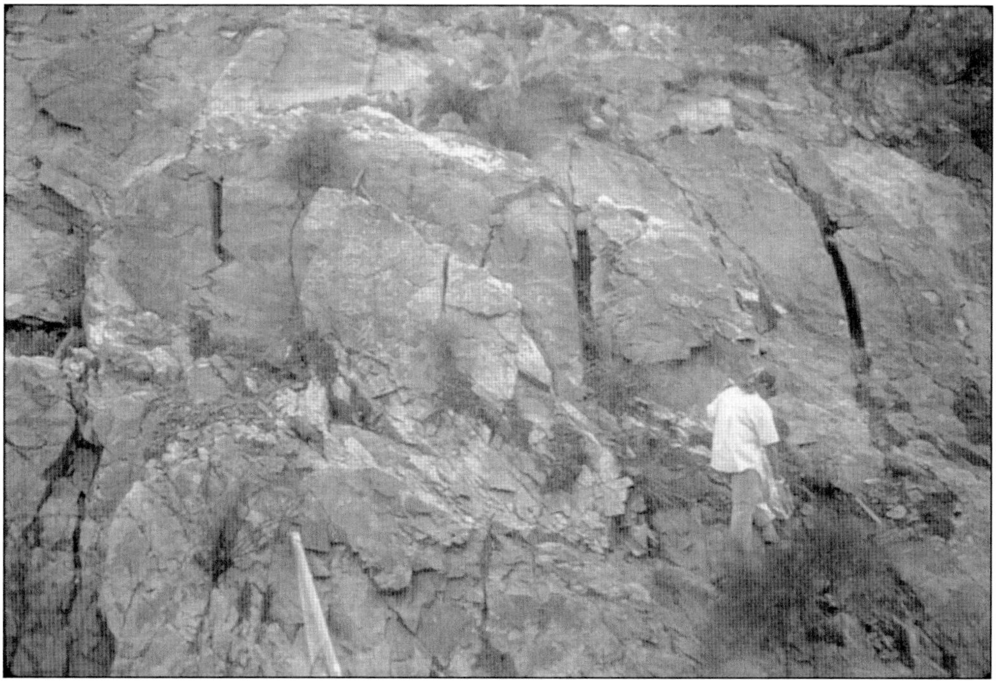

An archeologist examines a rock ledge near the Pinnacle Peak Village excavation site. Petroglyphs found throughout the Southwest showcase symbols created by prehistoric inhabitants, including the archaic and Hohokam peoples. (Courtesy of the ARI/OCRM Collections.)

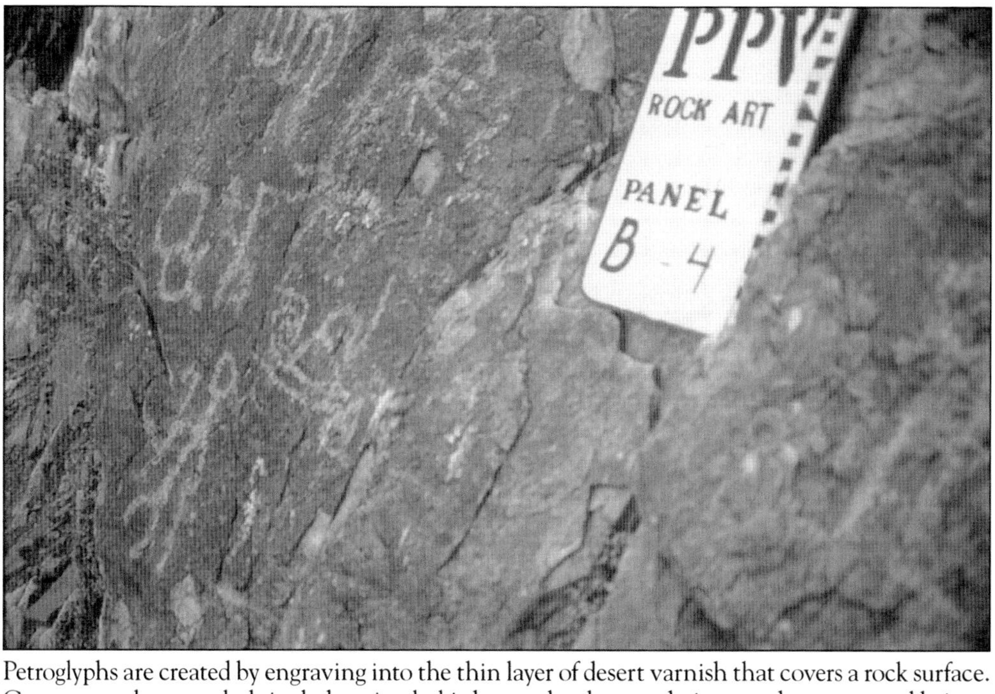

Petroglyphs are created by engraving into the thin layer of desert varnish that covers a rock surface. Common rock art symbols include animals, birds, people, abstract designs, and supernatural beings. Some petroglyphs may have been used to indicate migrations. Prehistoric rock art is protected by law, as are other Native American artifacts. (Courtesy of the ARI/OCRM Collections.)

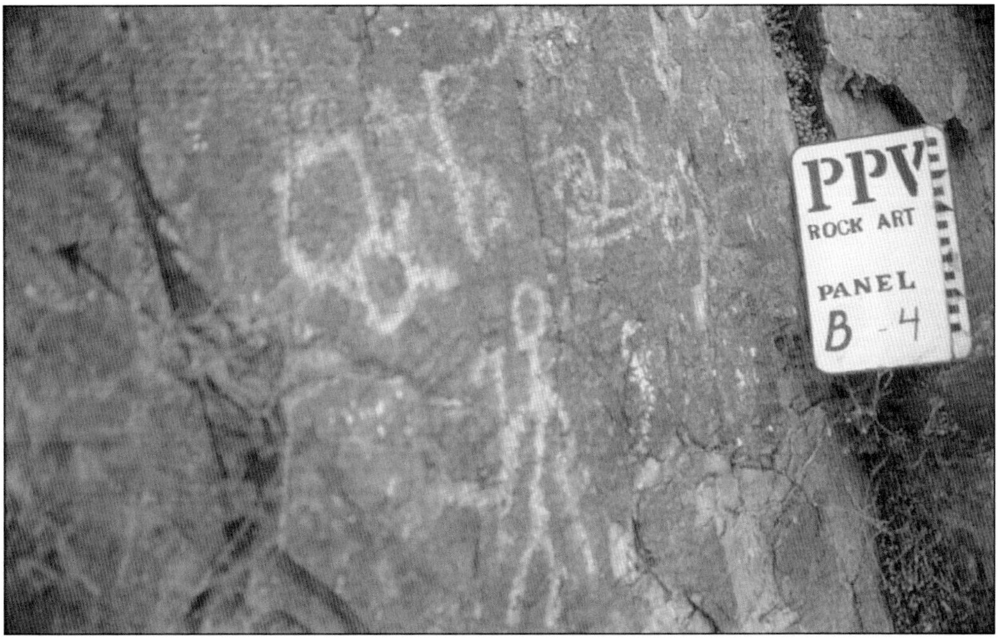

Archeologists and anthropologists cannot guarantee the artist's intended meaning of rock art symbols. There is evidence that some symbols have more than one meaning, even within a single culture. Rock art has been studied extensively. Several books (such as *A Field Guide to Rock Art Symbols of the Greater Southwest* by Alex Patterson) can be used to help interpret petroglyphs. (Courtesy of the ARI/OCRM Collections.)

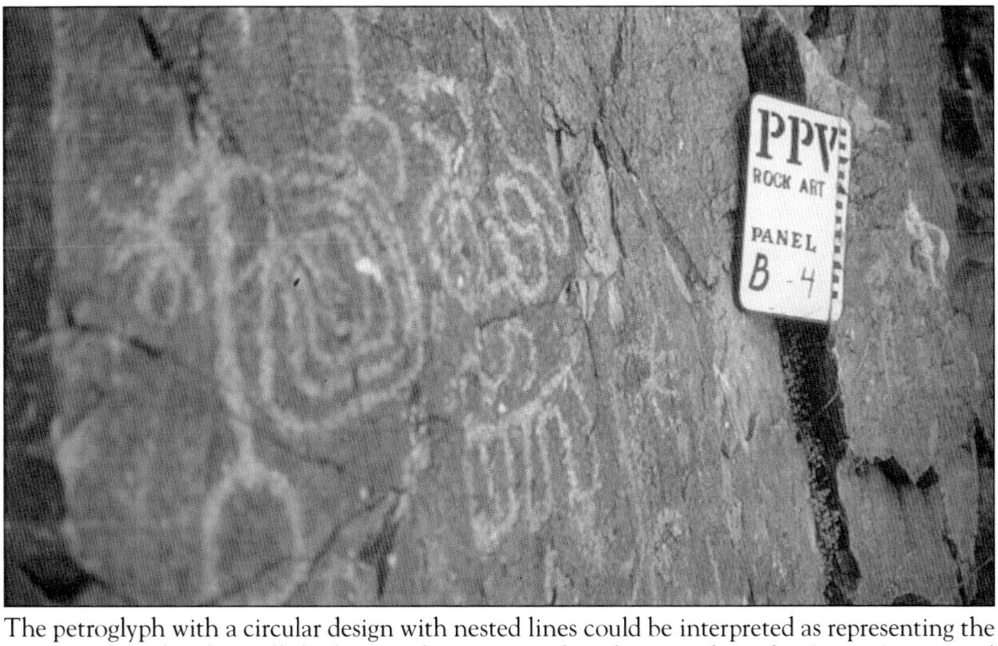

The petroglyph with a circular design with nested lines could be interpreted as representing the emergence myth, where all the lines and passages within the maze form the Creator's universal plan that man must follow on his road through life. The symbol is said to have essentially the same meaning for many Native American peoples in North, Central, and South America. (Courtesy of the ARI/OCRM Collections.)

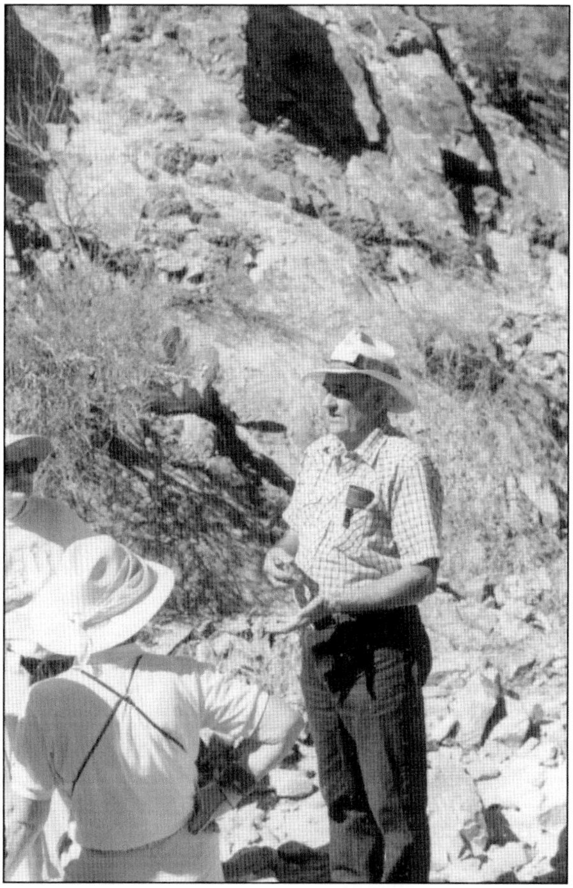

Approximately 3,400 residents and visitors attended a two-and-a-half-day open house held at the site in late March 1988. In this photograph, Lou Hagler presents information about the petroglyphs near the dig site. Hagler, a Pinnacle Peak resident and amateur archeologist, volunteered to work on the study. He had previously spent hundreds of hours looking for evidence of Native American habitation near Pinnacle Peak. (Courtesy of the Desert Center.)

Florence and Jerry Nelson and ASU sponsored the open house. In addition to learning about petroglyphs, guests heard lectures on archaeology and attended demonstrations on how the Hohokam made pottery, stone tools, projectile points, and bone awls. Other demonstrations focused on excavation, artifact cleaning, and pottery reconstruction. The event was widely covered in the local press. (Courtesy of the Desert Center.)

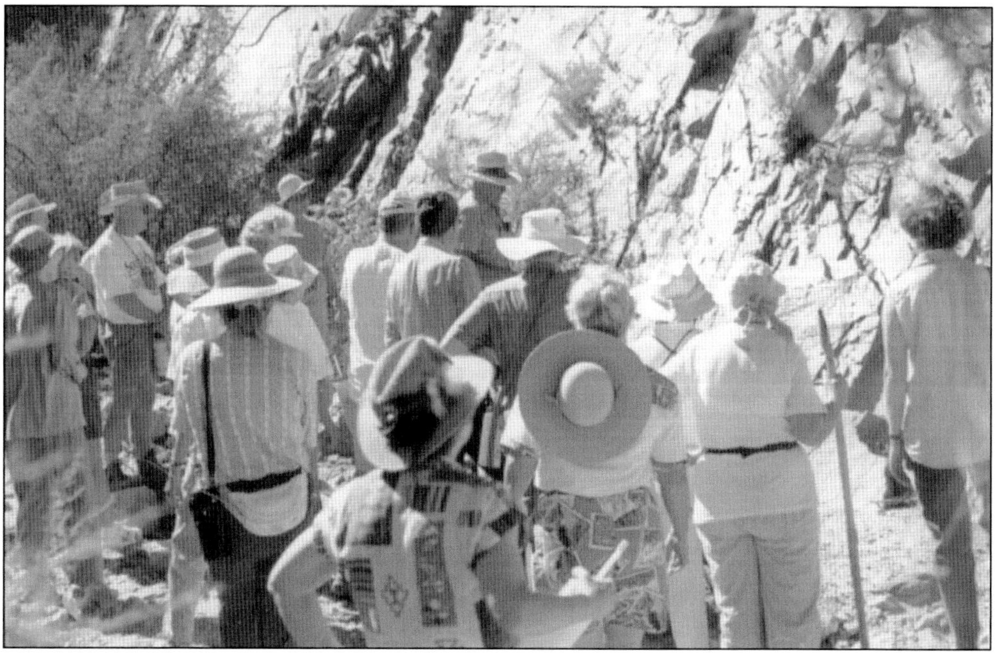

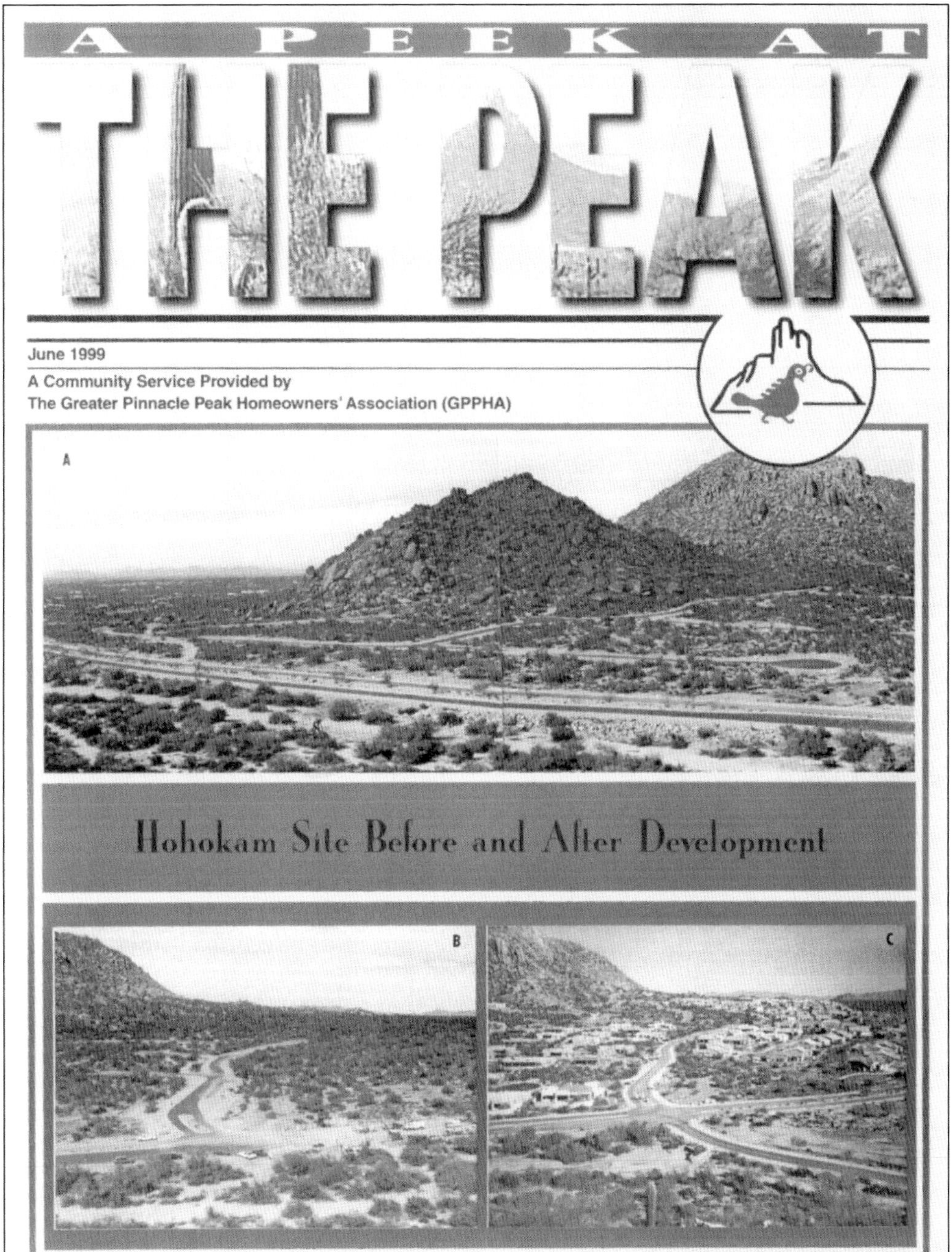

The June 1999 issue of *A Peek at the Peak* includes the article "Suburban Hohokam" by Lou Hagler. The cover features Hagler's photographs showing the area of the Hohokam village site. Photograph A (top) shows the site of the future Troon Country Club. Photographs B (bottom left) and C (bottom right) show the Hohokam site before and after development, respectively. (Courtesy of *The Peak*.)

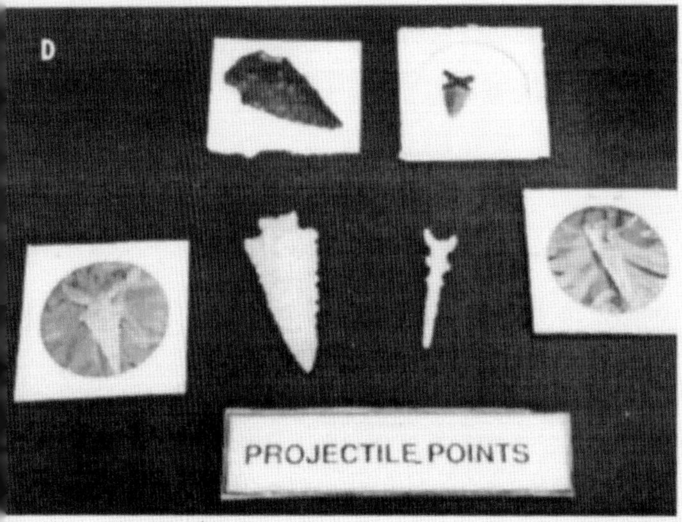

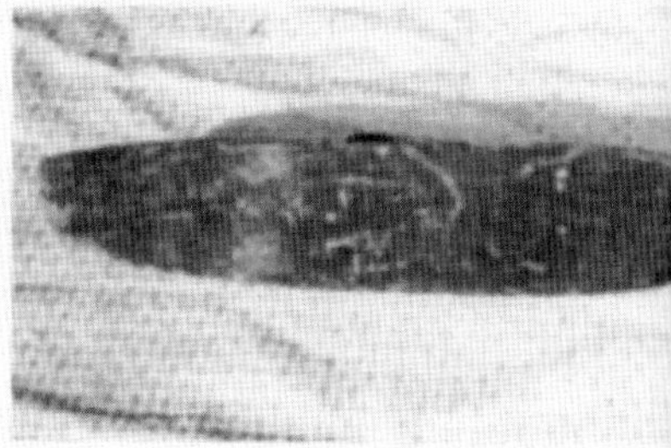

Hagler's article included exhibits of artifacts found in the Pinnacle Peak area. During the dig, arrowheads, chipped-stone knives, and many other projectile points were discovered. Obsidian, quartz, and chert were used to make the projectile points shown in Exhibit D (left). Only quartz was found near Pinnacle Peak. The chert likely originated from the Cave Creek area. Exhibit E shows a saw made of schist. It was used for cutting agave and yucca, butchering animals, and for cutting building posts. The unusually high number of stone knives found at the site indicates that large amounts of agave and other cacti were harvested and roasted. Other stone tools found at the site included hammer stones and stone axes. Many of the materials used to make the tools had been procured from outside sources including from the Verde River located 12 miles east of the site. (Courtesy of *The Peak*.)

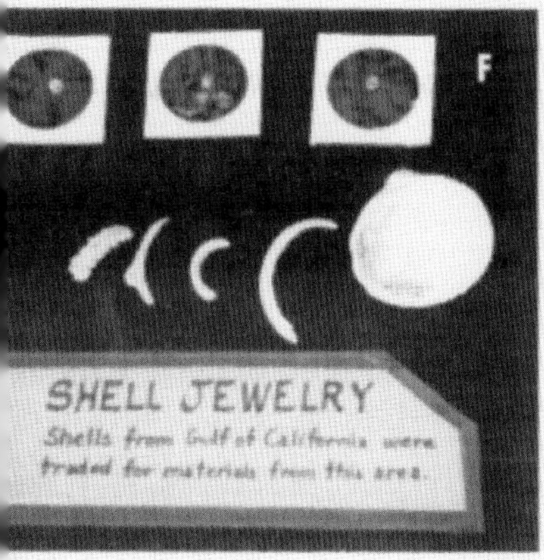

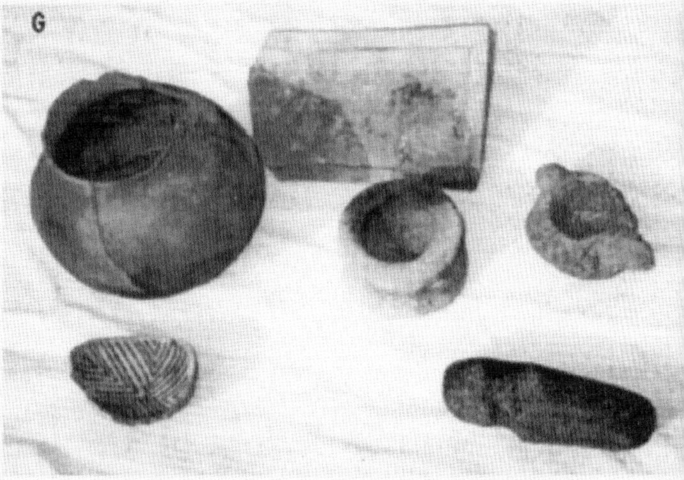

Exhibit F (left) is a display of shells from the Gulf of California and turquoise beads. Both were used to make rings, bracelets, and pendants. A complete shell pendant was found. Also recovered was a whole-shell ornament carved as a snake's head. The ornament appears to have been remade from a larger artifact. Shell was a prized ornament and is evidence of the existence of a widespread trade network covering large distances. Various articles from prehistoric Pinnacle Peak Village are shown in Exhibit G. Clockwise, from the top to the left, the items are a cooking vessel, paint palette, bird effigy, ax head, and ceramic scoop and in the center a stone cutter. A recovered copper bell, which was not included in Hagler's exhibits, created excitement among archeologists. The bell had an intact clapper and a loop for suspension at one end. The bell was believed to be a prized trade item from central Mexico. (Courtesy of *The Peak*.)

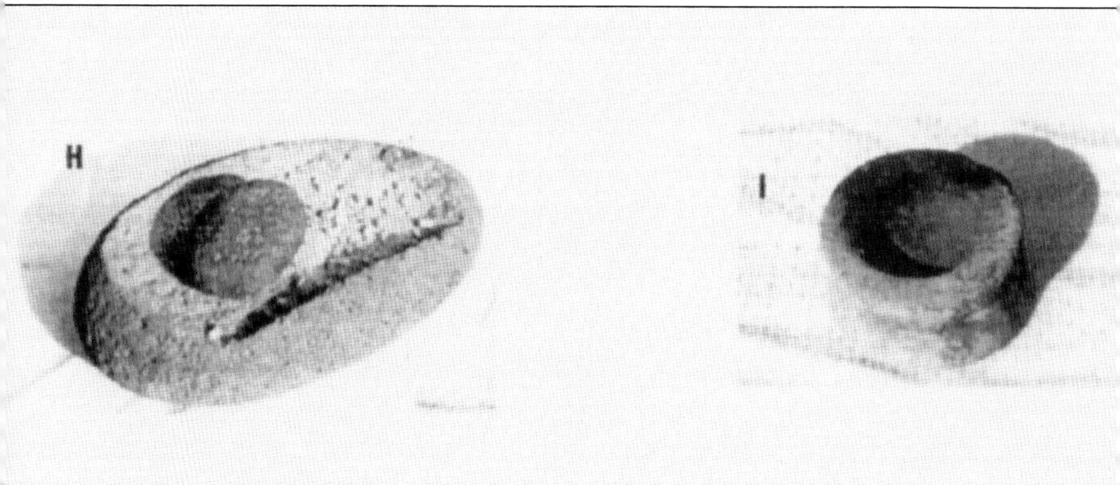

Exhibit H (left) is a stone used for grinding known as a metate. Chemical analysis of metates found at the site indicated that the stone was probably from a quarry near New River, Arizona, and was carried to the village site by traders. Exhibit I is a censer, a small stone utility bowl that was used for a variety of purposes including burning incense and grinding pigments. Archeologists recovered 26 jars, bowls, scoops, and censers. Given that only seven pit houses were excavated, experts considered this to be a surprisingly high number of vessels. (Courtesy of *The Peak*.)

Three

Early Development around Pinnacle Peak

Perhaps residents and visitors are fortunate that Pinnacle Peak's treasures remained essentially untouchable for so long. From 1500 to 1700, the Spanish dismissed central Arizona as *despoblado,* which Frances Carlson translates as "desert wilderness." More so than the fierce, nomadic Apache, the harsh desert environment convinced the Spanish to settle elsewhere. The Salt River and the arid landscape appeared to provide little chance of sustaining the conquistadores.

The organized settlement of central Arizona could not begin until 1865, when US soldiers established the first permanent Anglo settlement in the Salt River Valley at Camp McDowell, which is approximately 17 miles southeast of Pinnacle Peak. The soldiers came to protect America's newly acquired land and the small but growing frontier population from attack by the indigenous Native Americans.

Gold prospectors arrived in the vicinity of present-day Prescott in 1863, but fear of the Apache deterred exploration of the mountain ranges to the east. In 1870, soldiers built a supply road linking Prescott to Fort McDowell, thereby making it easier for prospectors and settlers to move east. In 1874, William Rowe made a significant gold discovery at Gold Hill. Rowe's discovery led to the establishment of Cave Creek in 1877. By the 1880s, a small community of ranchers and miners was living around Cave Creek, which was approximately 13 miles from Pinnacle Peak.

In 1867, Jack Swilling noticed the remains of systems of canals and irrigation trenches in the Salt River Valley. That December, Swilling began cleaning out a section of canals. Settlers saw the potential of providing crops and livestock to Camp McDowell and the mining camps. By 1870, the small settlement of Phoenix had risen from the dust of the Hohokam village abandoned hundreds of years earlier. Ranchers, miners, and gold rushers used the town as a transfer point for their goods.

In 1888, Winfield Scott and his wife made a down payment on a plot of land near the 40-mile-long Arizona Canal. Promoters believed the canal would bring agricultural riches to the area. The Scott family's purchase led to the establishment of the farming community of Scottsdale 20 miles south of remote, essentially untouched Pinnacle Peak.

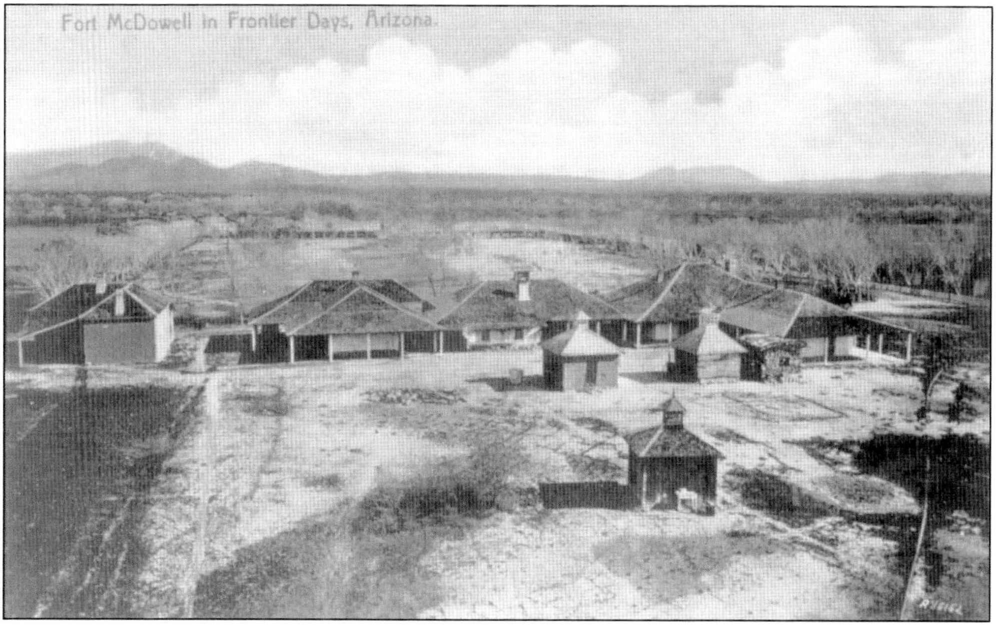

The US Army established Camp McDowell (later renamed Fort McDowell) to protect settlers from combative Indians in the surrounding mountains. Located at the confluence of the Verde and Salt Rivers, the installation commanded a number of the more important trails that served the Apache of central Arizona. The fort became an embarkation point for many military expeditions against the Apache. (Courtesy of the Arizona Historical Association.)

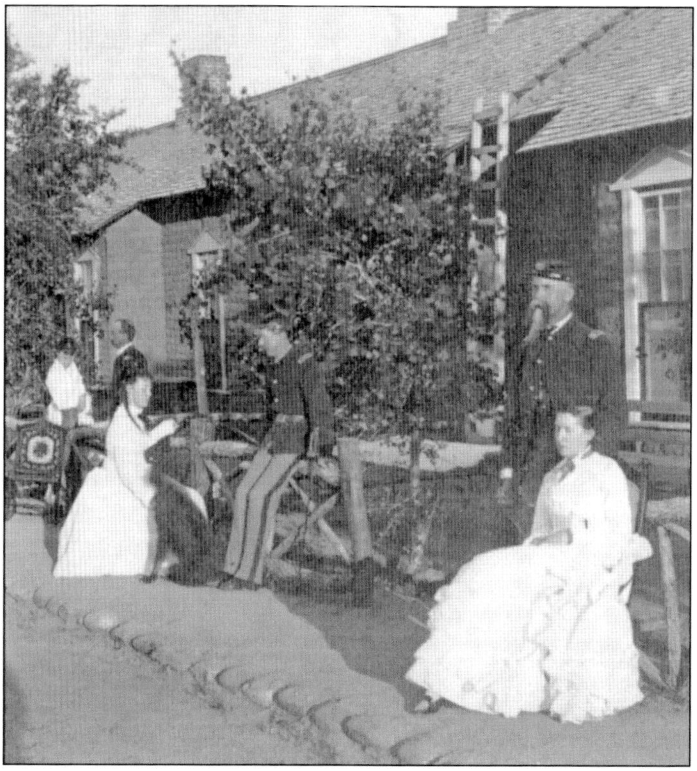

Some officers brought their wives and children to Fort McDowell. In this photograph, unidentified officers and their wives relax outside the fort's officer quarters. Army families endured a long, arduous journey to the remote fort and were faced with primitive conditions once they arrived. (Courtesy of the Arizona Historical Association.)

As they followed an Indian trail through the Cave Creek area in 1870, the Army built the first wagon supply road connecting Fort McDowell to Fort Whipple near Prescott, Arizona. The road was named after Col. George Stoneman, a Civil War veteran. Prior to the opening of the road, which became a main route of travel in central Arizona for 20 years, Fort McDowell suffered from acute supply shortages. (Courtesy of LOC LC-B813-1562 A.)

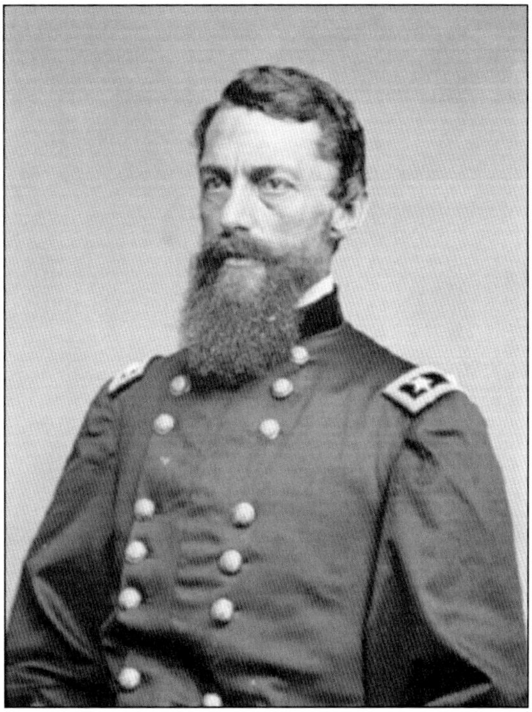

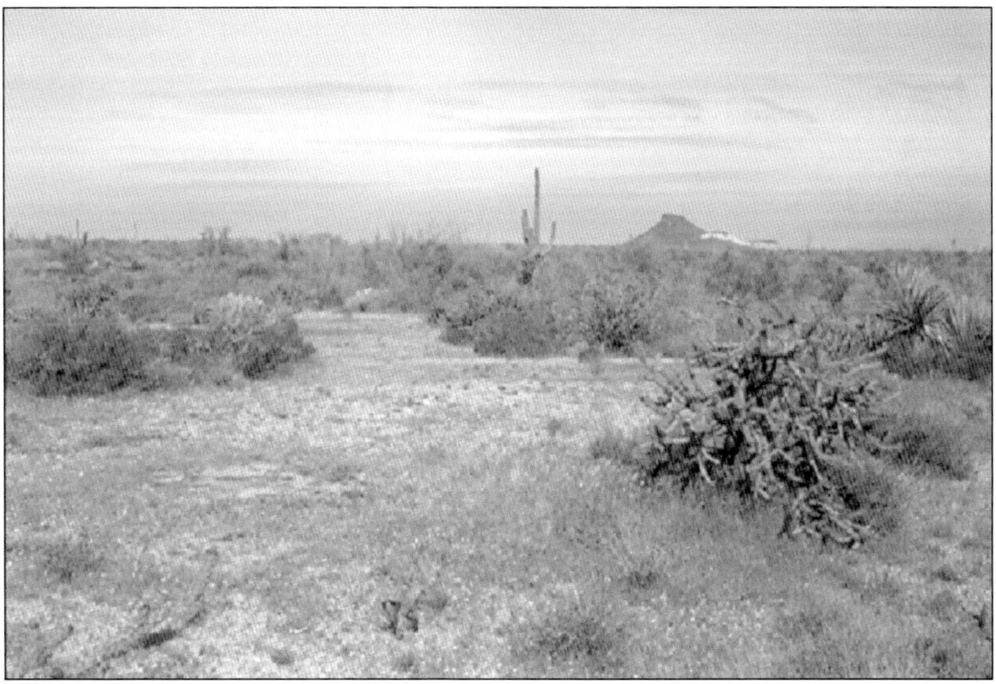

Traces of Stoneman Road still exist. It led northwest from Fort McDowell through today's McDowell Mountain Regional Park, passed just north of Pinnacle Peak near historic Brown's Ranch, and continued on to Cave Creek and a spring near present-day Rancho Manana. The Army used the road until 1890, when the fort became the Fort McDowell Indian Reservation. (Courtesy of Larry Levy.)

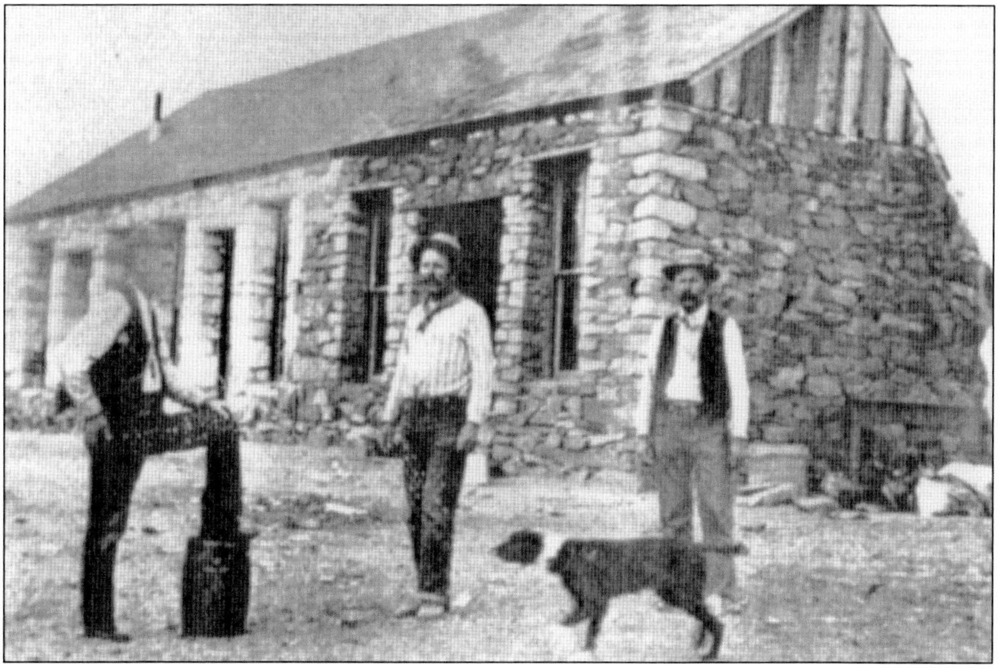

In 1874, gold was discovered northwest of Cave Creek on Gold Hill. The discovery was the catalyst for a gold rush. In 1877, Jeriah Woods built a home that he called Cave Creek Station. He kept a few cows, sold dairy products and beef to the mining camps, and supplied meals and firewood to travelers. Not too far from Cave Creek Station, Stoneman Road carried soldiers, freight wagons, and travelers. (Courtesy of the Cave Creek Museum.)

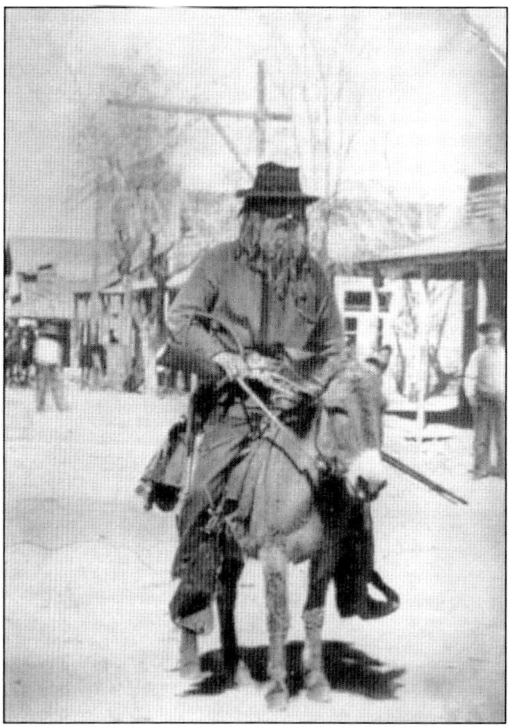

As the Apache became less menacing, prospectors followed Stoneman Road into unexplored land, including the Pinnacle Peak area and McDowell Mountains. Mines were opened in the McDowell Mountains. Kenyon Turner Palmer, who homesteaded near Pinnacle Peak beginning in 1933, found long-forgotten claim notices in Prince Albert tobacco tins—evidence of previous prospecting activity. This photograph from the 1880s is of a prospector known to Cave Creek residents as "Old Rackensack." (Courtesy of the Cave Creek Museum.)

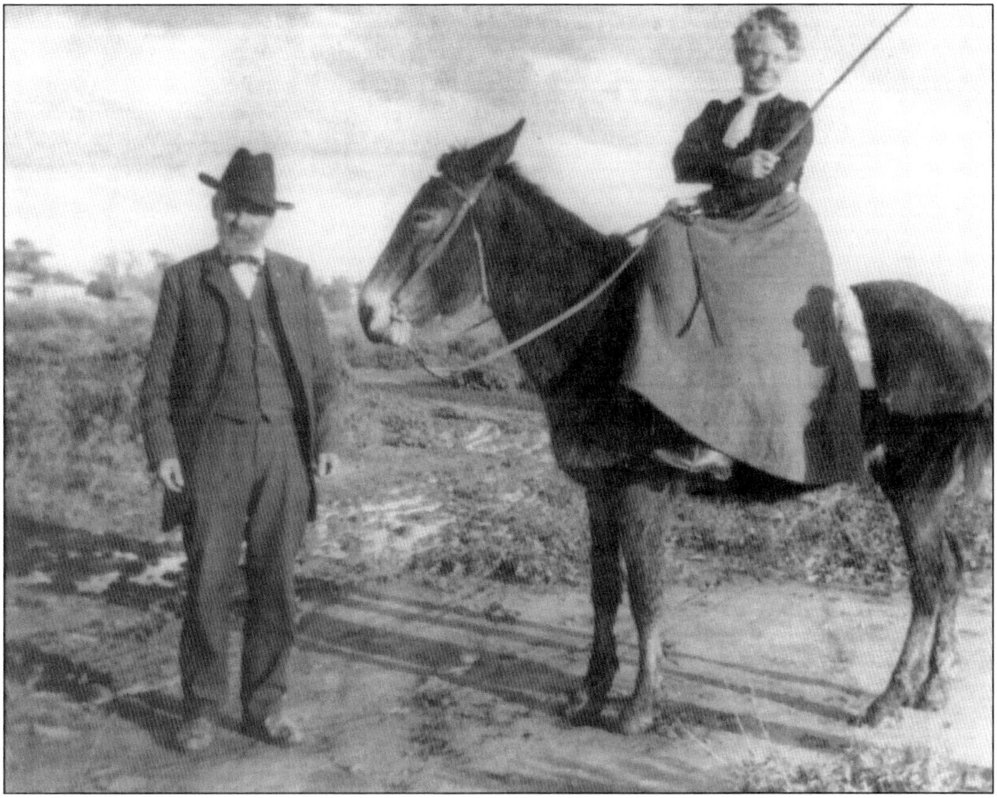

Chaplain Winfield Scott stands next to his wife, Helen, as they pose in 1900 with their retired army mule Old Maud. They purchased land for their homestead in Scottsdale in 1888 for $2.50 an acre. The location of the land, which was adjacent to the Arizona Canal, ensured access to water for irrigating future crops. (Courtesy of the Scottsdale Historical Society.)

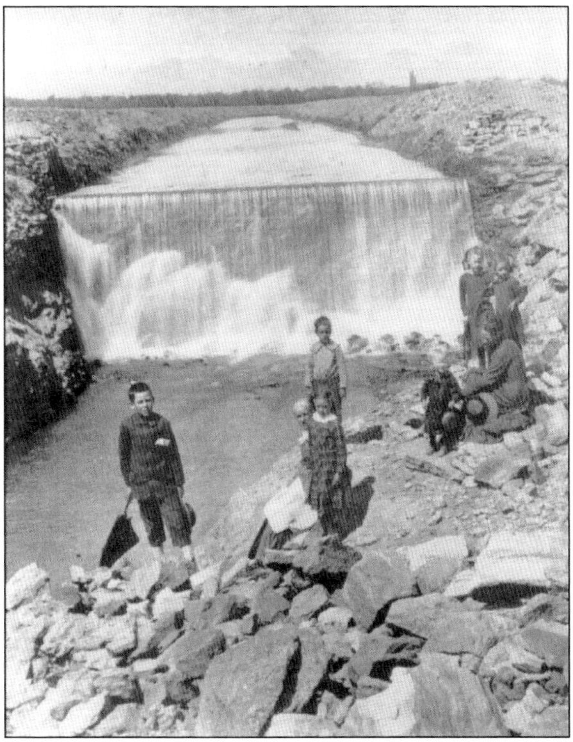

William J. Murphy founded Glendale and built the Arizona Canal, which runs through downtown Scottsdale on its way to New River. Construction of the canal began in 1883. This 20-foot waterfall was near the intersection of present-day Indian School Road and Fifty-sixth Street. The construction of the canal opened up new land for farming and enabled Scottsdale to grow. (Courtesy of the Scottsdale Public Library.)

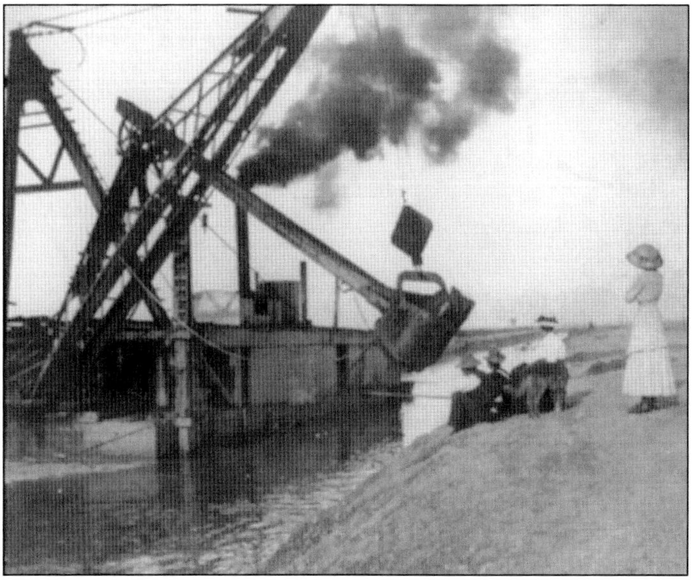

The Arizona Canal, which was completed in 1885, needed constant attention in order to keep water flowing to farms, ranches, and nearby homes of Scottsdale residents and other East Valley communities. Called "Cavie" for short, George Sidney Cavalliere, a welder by trade, and his wife, Mary Alice, moved to Arizona to maintain the dredging equipment shown in this photograph taken in 1908. (Courtesy of the Scottsdale Public Library.)

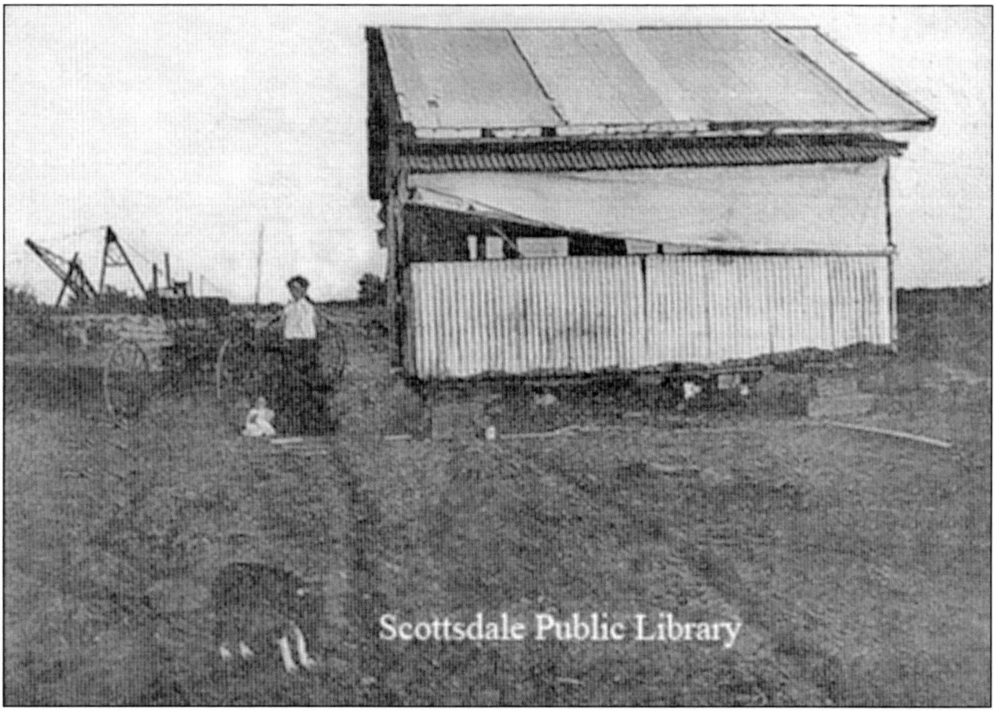

While working on the project, George Sidney Cavalliere and his family lived in this tin house that moved on sled rails as the dredging progressed. When the project was completed, they moved the house to the far southern edge of Scottsdale (on Brown Avenue at Second Street) and opened the town's first blacksmith shop. In this image, George Sidney Cavalliere's eldest daughter, Alice (left), and his wife, Mary Alice, stand next to their tin home. (Courtesy of the Scottsdale Public Library.)

In the 1800s, American settlers began using the Pinnacle Peak area for ranching and some prospecting. In 1916, Edwin Orpheus Brown, a Scottsdale businessman, established a ranch within sight of Pinnacle Peak. The ranch, DC Ranch, grew to 44,000 acres. His son Edwin Elsworth Brown ran a herd of 4,000 cattle in the area. (Courtesy of the Scottsdale Historical Society.)

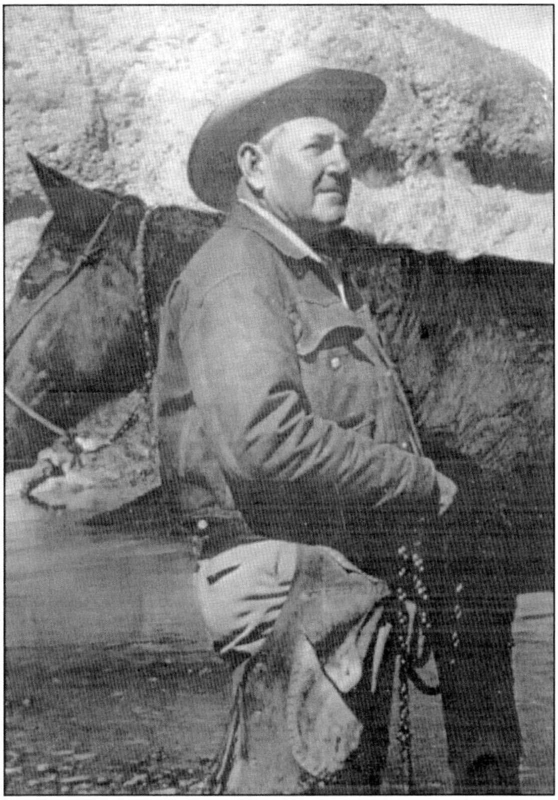

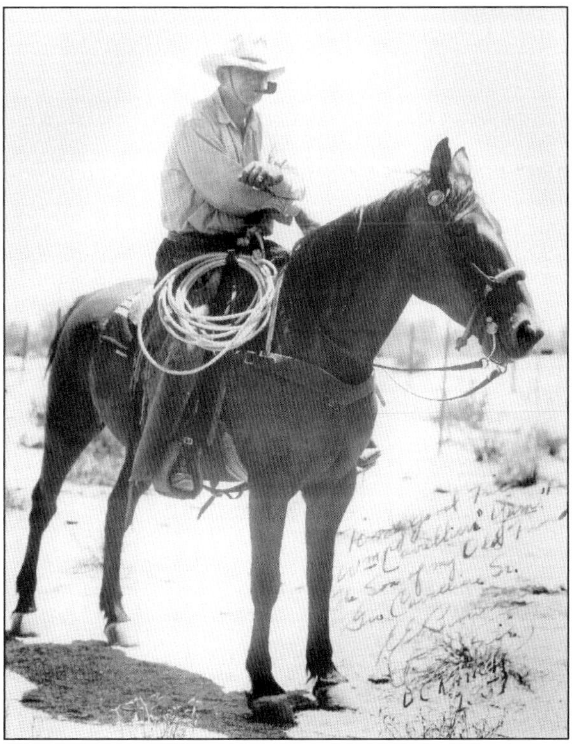

Reserved, dark-haired, and tall, Edwin Elsworth Brown, or "Brownie," was a quintessential cowboy. He ran a herd of 4,000 cattle and often worked with the cowhands riding, roping, and roaming the range all the while wearing a Colt .45 revolver. He is remembered for charging into a Scottsdale bar and causing a rousing celebration when a drought-breaking rain fell. (Courtesy of the Scottsdale Historical Society.)

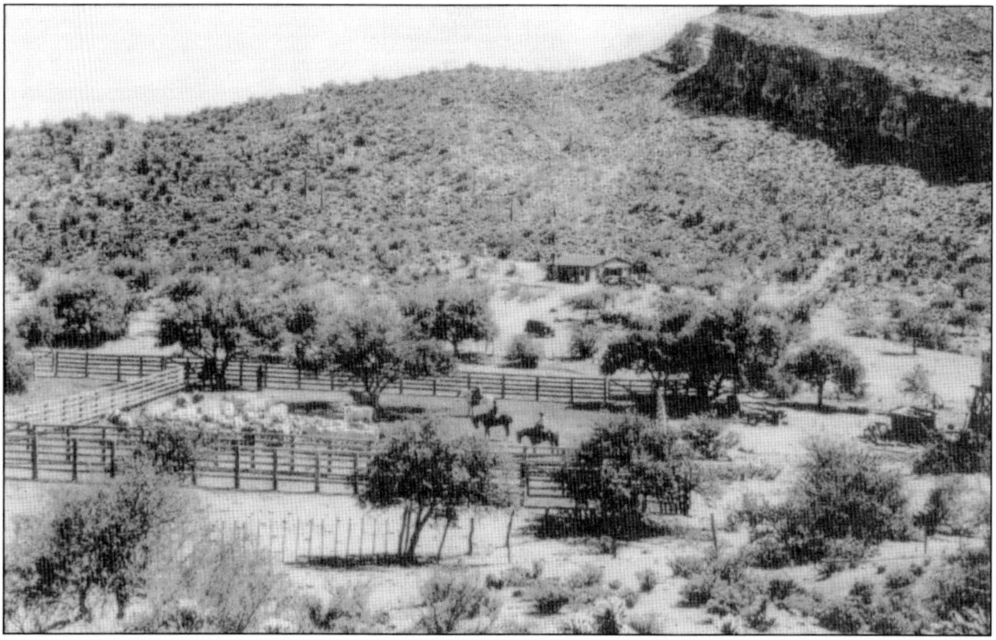

DC Ranch included upper and lower ranches. The latter, known as DC Ranch, was based south of Pinnacle Peak Road and east of Pima Road at the location of today's DC Ranch community. The upper ranch, which is pictured here, was known as Brown's Ranch and was located north of Pinnacle Peak and east of Pima Road. (Courtesy of the Scottsdale Historical Society.)

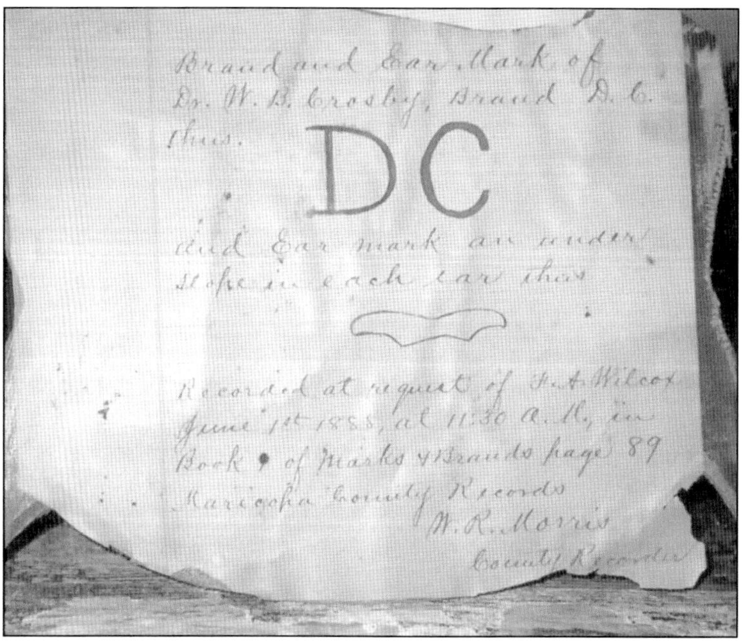

Brand and Ear Mark of
Dr. W. B. Crosby, Brand D. C.
thus.
DC
and Ear mark an under
slope in each ear thus
Recorded at request of F. A. Wilcox
June 1st 1885, at 11:30 A. M. in
Book 1 of Marks & Brands page 89
Maricopa County Records
W. R. Morris
County Recorder

The DC Ranch brand was first registered in 1885 and acquired by Edwin Orpheus Brown in 1917. The logo of today's North Scottsdale community DC Ranch is a stylized version of the brand. (Courtesy of the Scottsdale Historical Society.)

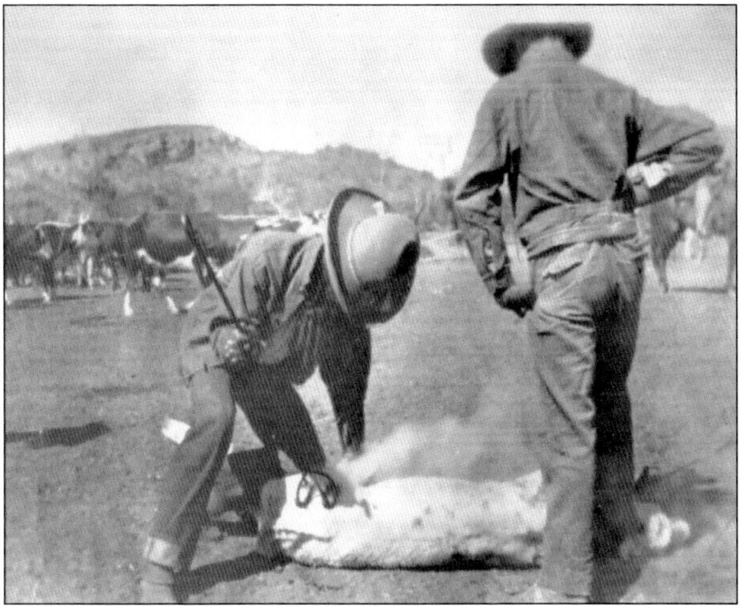

DC Ranch cowboys branded and butchered cattle, shoed horses at the ranch's blacksmith shop, jerked beef, and treated animals that were tangled with cholla cactus thorns. They showered standing under a bucket of water and ate the three *B*s: beef, biscuits, and beans. (Courtesy of the Scottsdale Historical Society.)

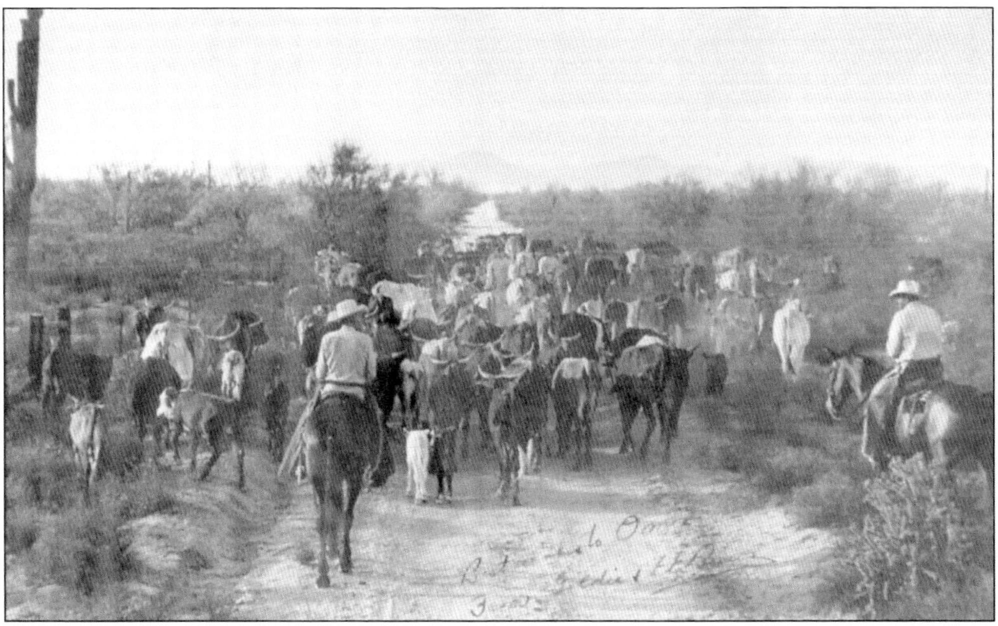

Until the 1950s, members of the Brown family and other cowboys drove DC Ranch beef cattle to market in Phoenix. Following dirt tracks across a vast open desert, it took two days to herd the cattle from Brown's Ranch to market. The cattle drive made an overnight stop at a way station near today's intersection of the Loop 101/Pima Freeway and Shea Boulevard. (Courtesy of the Scottsdale Historical Society.)

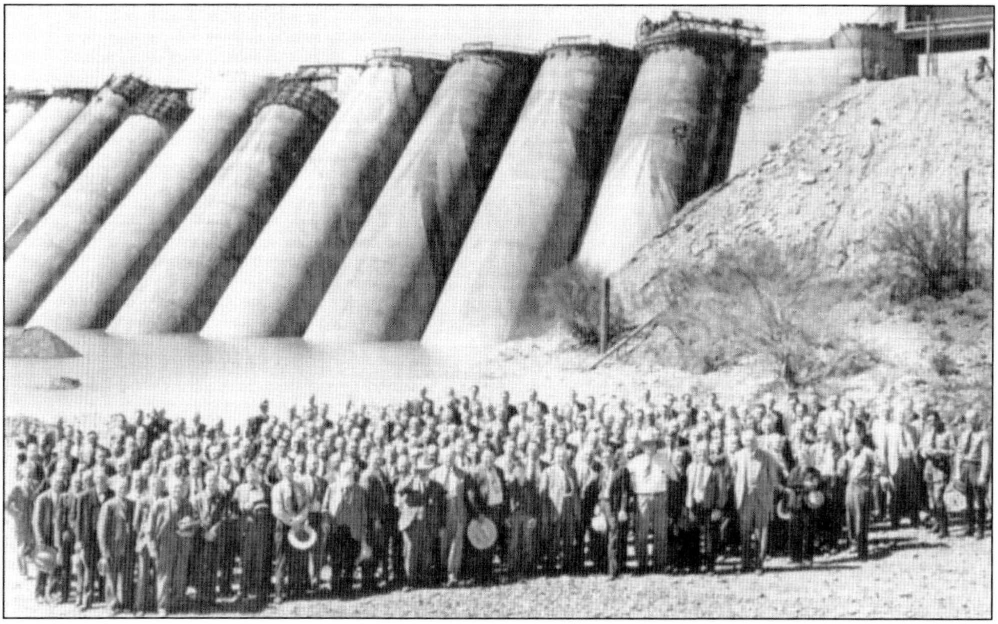

In response to the Great Depression, drops in crop prices, and farmer demands for a Verde River dam, the US Bureau of Reclamation constructed the Bartlett Dam between 1936 and 1939. Completed in only 1,000 days, it was the world's tallest multiple-arch buttress dam at the time. (Courtesy of the Cave Creek Museum.)

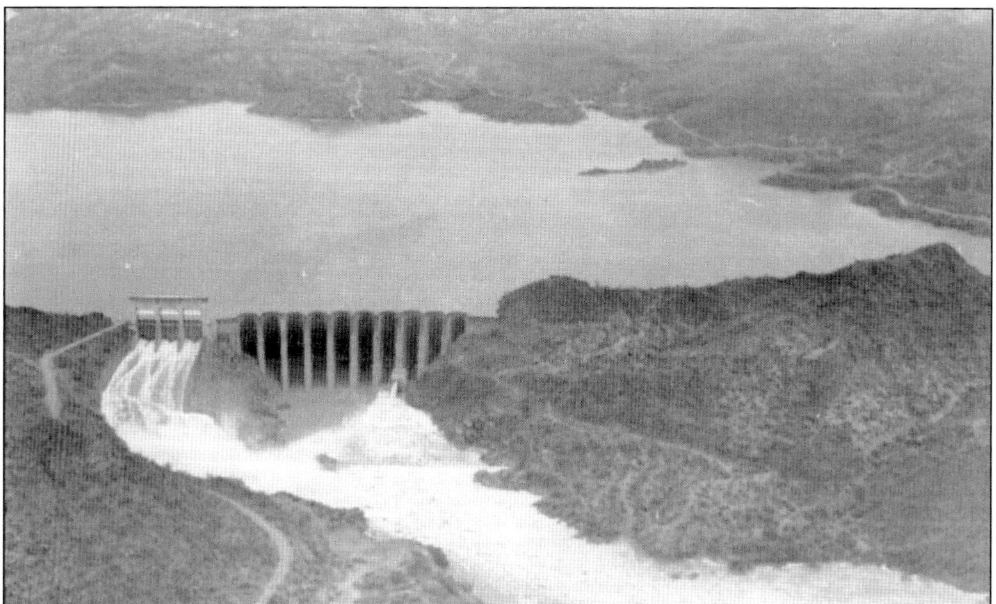

From 1944 to 1946, Horseshoe Dam was built. The Verde River, Bartlett Lake, and Horseshoe Lake provided some of the best fishing in Arizona and became favorites among fishermen and adventurous travelers. For some, the shortest route to the river and lakes was via a dirt track over the remote Reata Pass. (Courtesy of the Cave Creek Museum.)

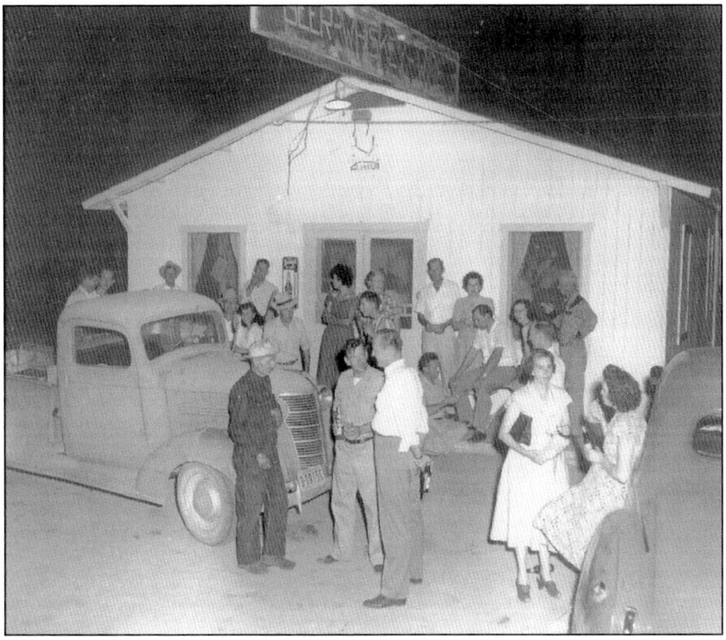

Creating the Bartlett and Horseshoe Dams provided needed jobs, flood control, and was a boon for Cave Creek. Cave Creek's oldest business, Harold's Cave Creek Corral, was built in 1936 during the heyday of the Bartlett Dam construction. From 1929 to 1950, decreasing supplies of water, overgrazing, and federal regulations made raising cattle less profitable, and former cattle ranges became dude ranches. (Courtesy of the Cave Creek Museum.)

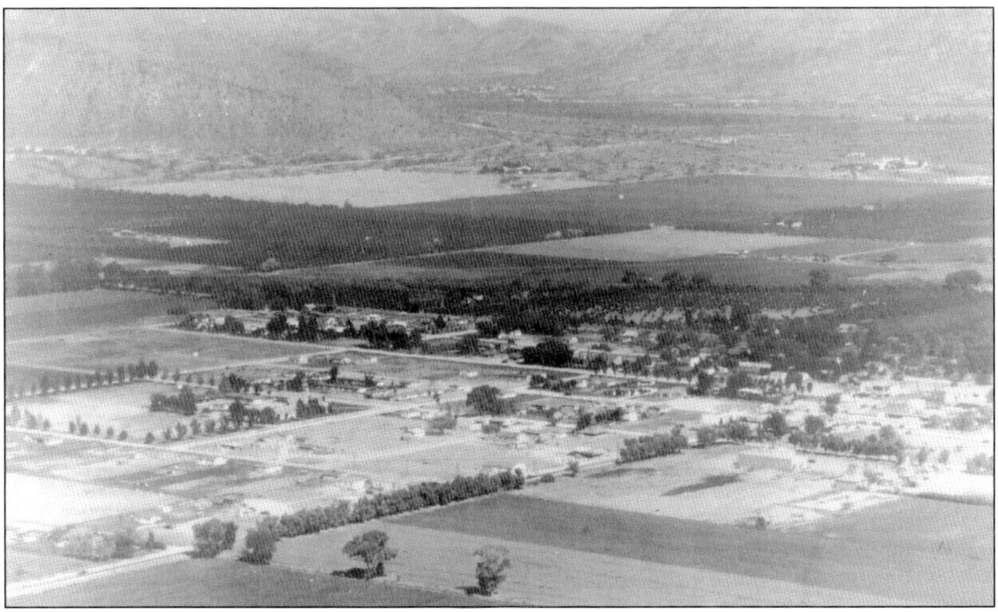

By the 1930s, the number of Scottsdale farms and plowed fields had increased dramatically. In the early 1930s, John B. Curry and three other homesteaders used hand tools to make a dirt track connecting their homesteads to Cave Creek Road. The dirt track eventually became known as Pinnacle Peak Road. Curry erected a shack and a sign on the southeast corner of today's Scottsdale and Pinnacle Peak Roads, naming it Curry's Corner. (Courtesy of the Scottsdale Public Library.)

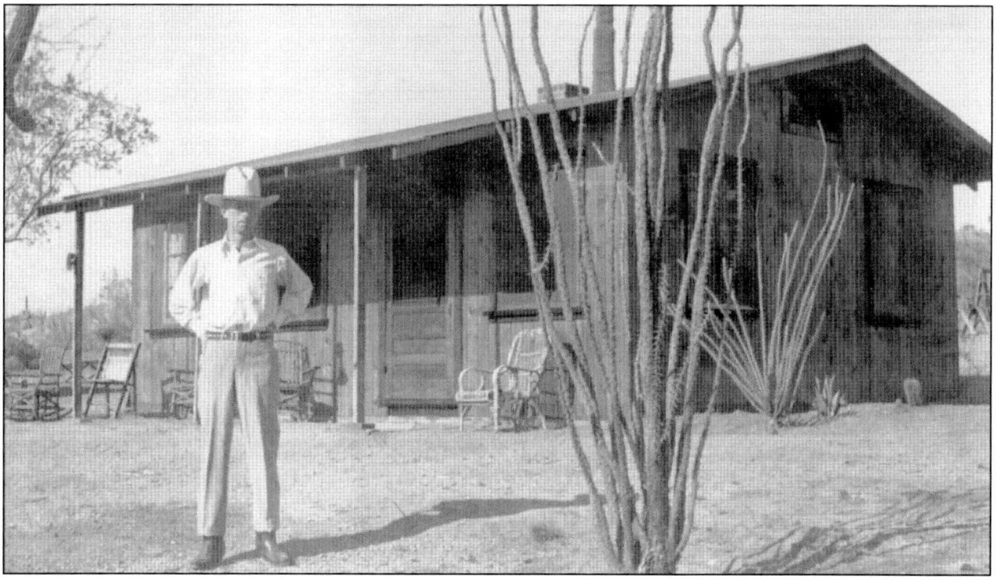

Kenyon Turner Palmer stands near his homestead on the western slopes of Pinnacle Peak. In 1933, Palmer, a World War I veteran, obtained 640 acres of land by paying a small fee and filing a homestead application. He was required to live on the land for seven months, improve it, and pay for improvements. On weekdays, Palmer drove 60 miles round-trip to his Phoenix law practice. (Courtesy of Gerry Jones.)

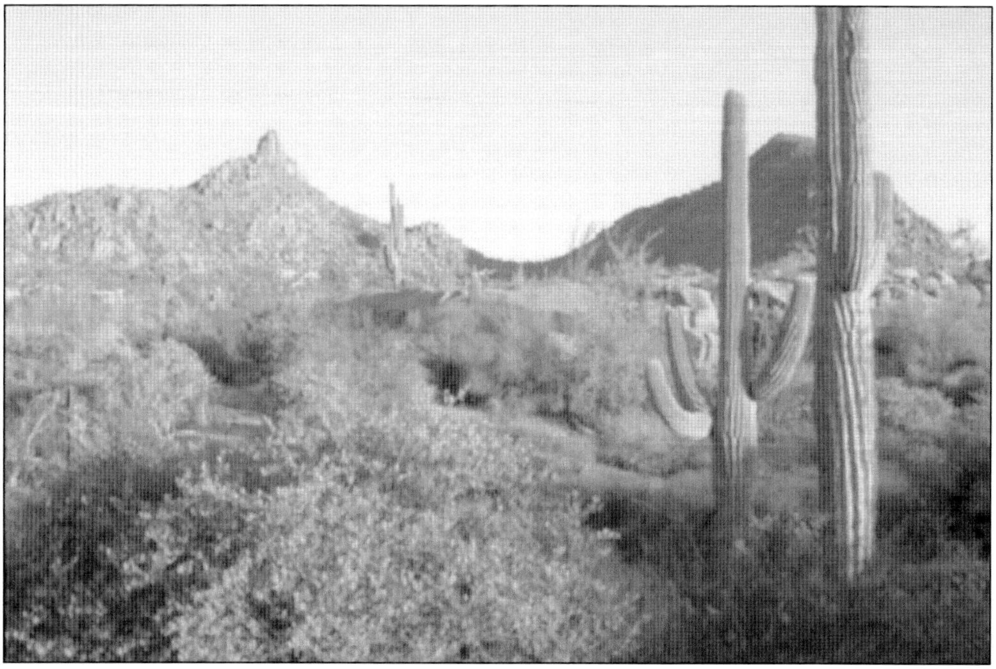

To initially access his land and transport supplies, Palmer had to cut a trail from Pinnacle Peak Road, which was just a dirt track at that time. It was a five-mile drive to the nearest neighbor. There was no electricity, telephone, or water infrastructure. The family members enjoyed clear views to the south, east, and west that included Pinnacle Peak and Red Face Mountain, but they could not see human habitation in any direction. (Courtesy of *The Peak*.)

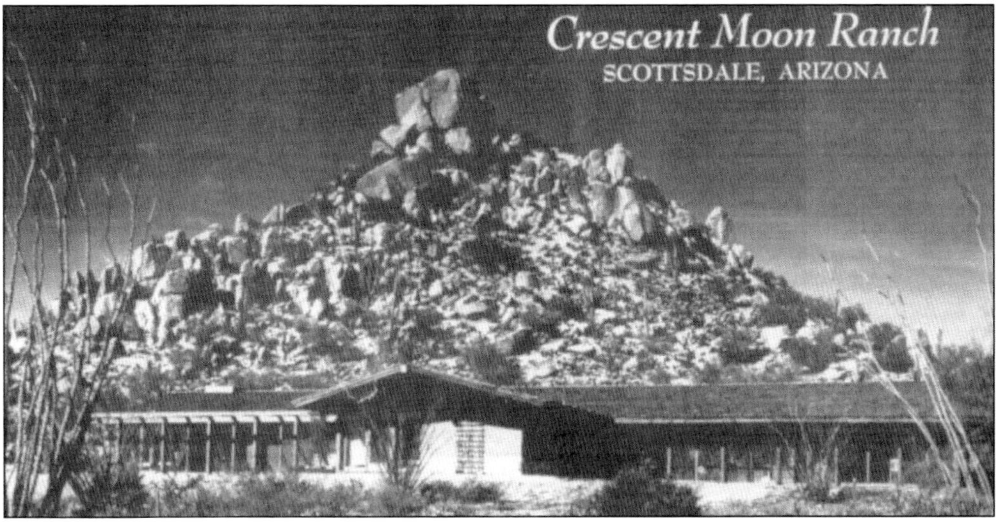

The Crescent Moon Ranch was located on the land now occupied by the Four Seasons Resort at Troon North. The 127-acre ranch was owned by the family of Lois Kellogg from Battle Creek, Michigan. Built in the 1930s, the house had approximately 4,500 square feet of living space. Its guest cottages were rented to seasonal visitors. Lois married three times; her third husband was a local wrangler. (Courtesy of Marv Dickson.)

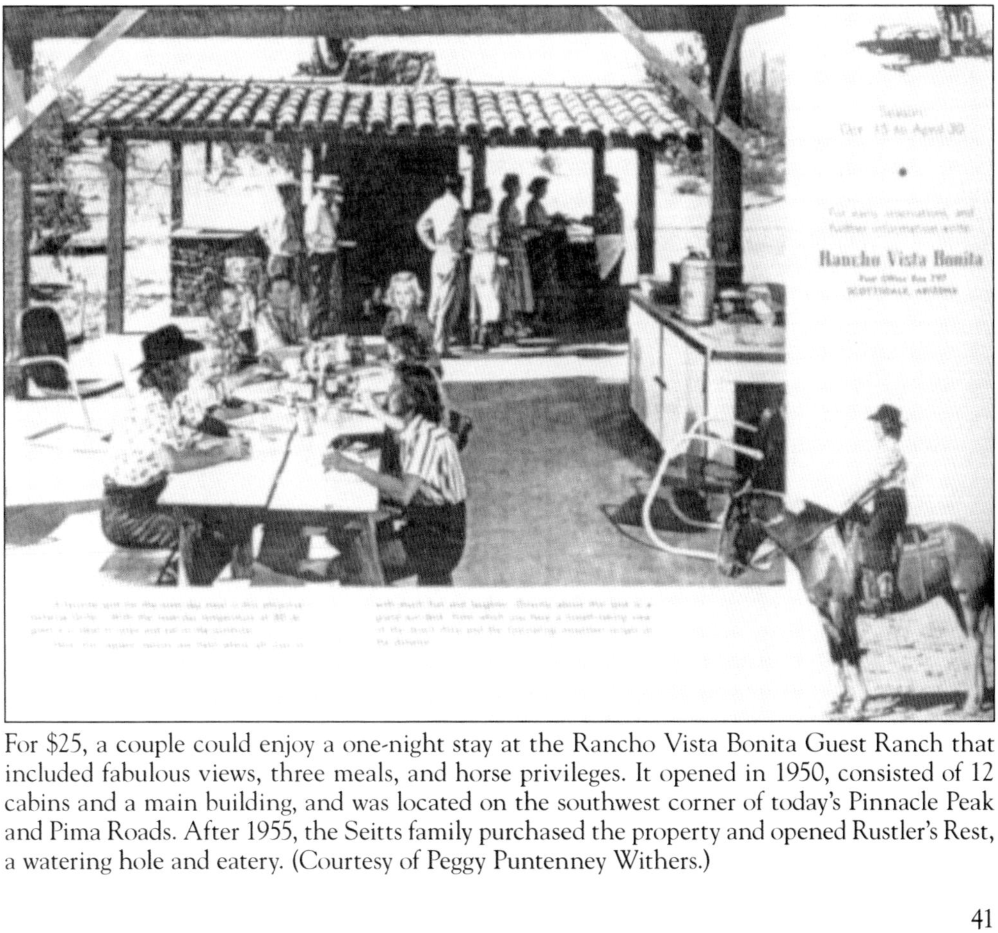

For $25, a couple could enjoy a one-night stay at the Rancho Vista Bonita Guest Ranch that included fabulous views, three meals, and horse privileges. It opened in 1950, consisted of 12 cabins and a main building, and was located on the southwest corner of today's Pinnacle Peak and Pima Roads. After 1955, the Seitts family purchased the property and opened Rustler's Rest, a watering hole and eatery. (Courtesy of Peggy Puntenney Withers.)

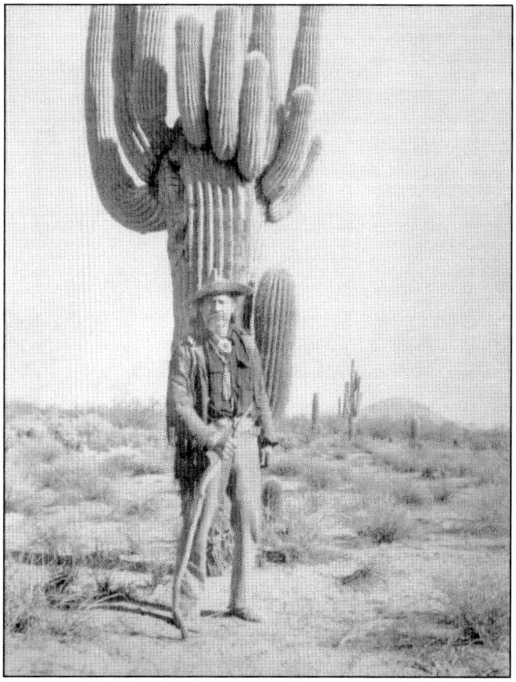

In 1950, after leaving his Scottsdale location, trader Don Pablo established Don Pablo's House of Relics on the remote northeast corner of Scottsdale and Pinnacle Peak Roads, both dirt tracks at that time. On the southeast corner was a small grocery store, opened by John B. Curry in the mid-1940s after the military extended Scottsdale Road northward from Thunderbird Airfield to Curry's Corner to improve access to crash sites. (Courtesy of the Scottsdale Historical Society.)

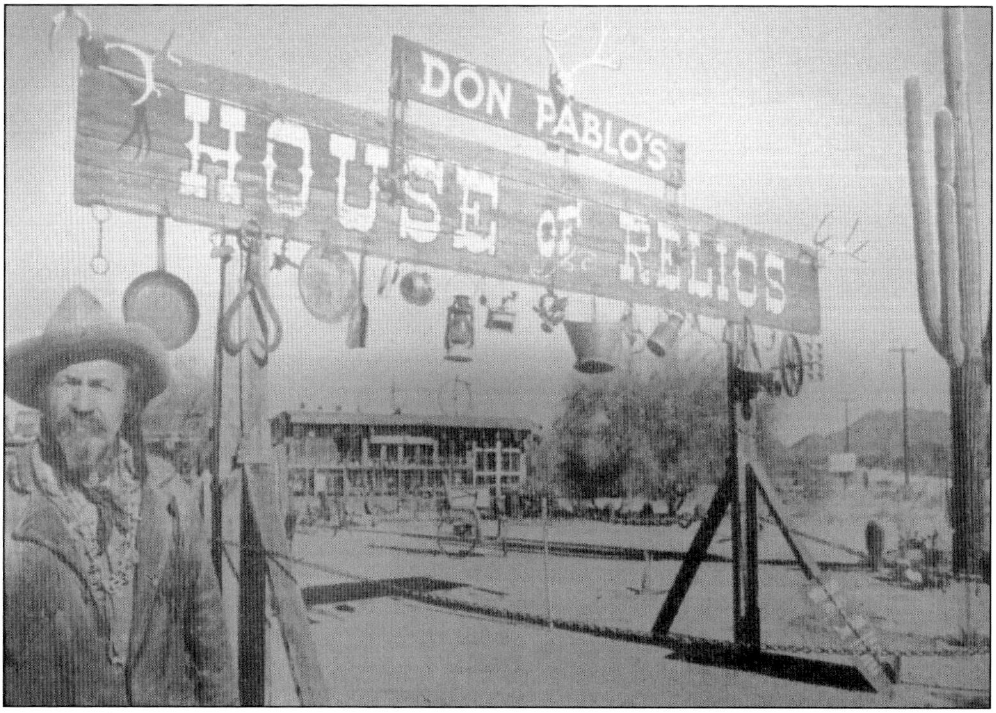

Protected by two pet timber wolves, Don Pablo lived in a one-room, dirt-floored shack. He was surrounded by hogans filled with Indian jewelry, guns, pottery, cowboy paraphernalia, teapots, and other wonders. Outside were a gas pump and collections of used bicycles and harnesses. After his death, thousands of people attended two auctions of his collections, which generated more than $100,000 in sales. (Courtesy of *Days and Ways.*)

June Santos was hired by Don Pablo's bank as caretaker of his home and the House of Relics. She was reputed to be an excellent shot and would not hesitate to pull the trigger. Her dozen roaming dogs and tendency to fire warning shots when unauthorized visitors appeared discouraged people from stopping at Don Pablo's. After Pablo's belongings were sold, she moved on. (Courtesy of *The Peak*.)

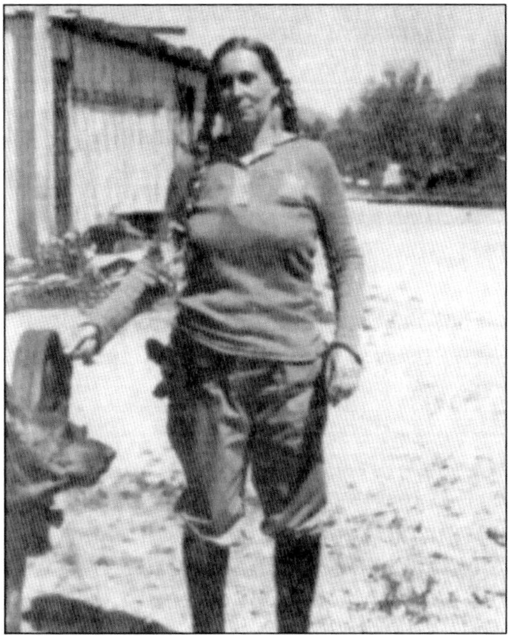

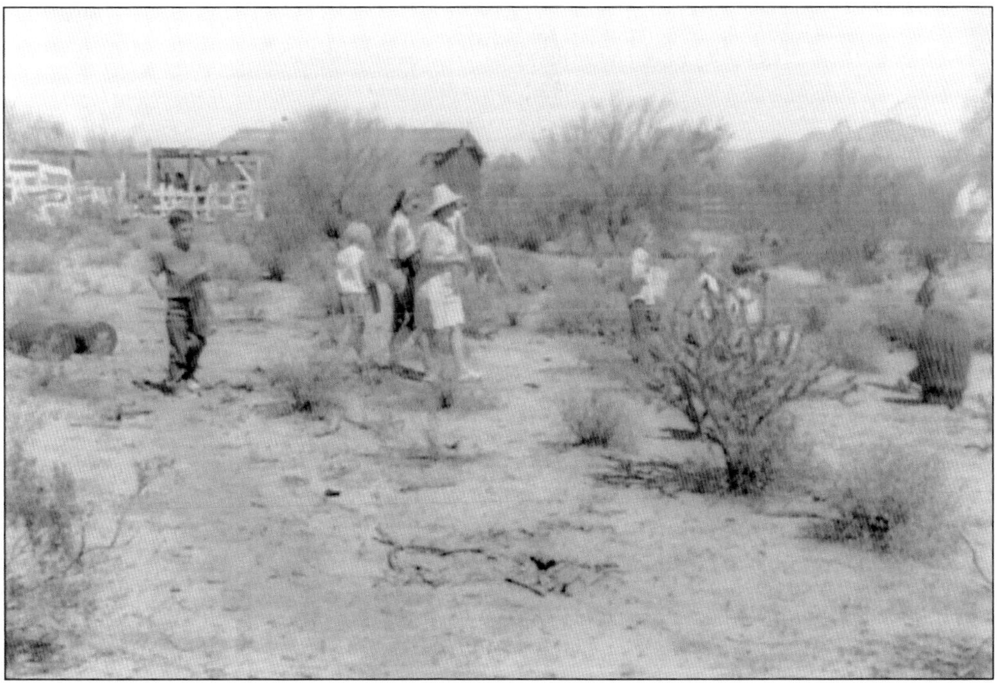

Leona Richardson leads guests on an Easter egg hunt at MacDonald's Ranch in 1970. In the 1950s, the Richardsons began the ranch, which was located on the southwest corner of Scottsdale and Jomax Roads, by leasing 31,000 acres of trust land east of Pima Road. In 1970, much of the land was sold to developers, and the family began offering children's entertainment and trail rides to Pinnacle Peak and elsewhere. (Courtesy of MacDonald's Ranch.)

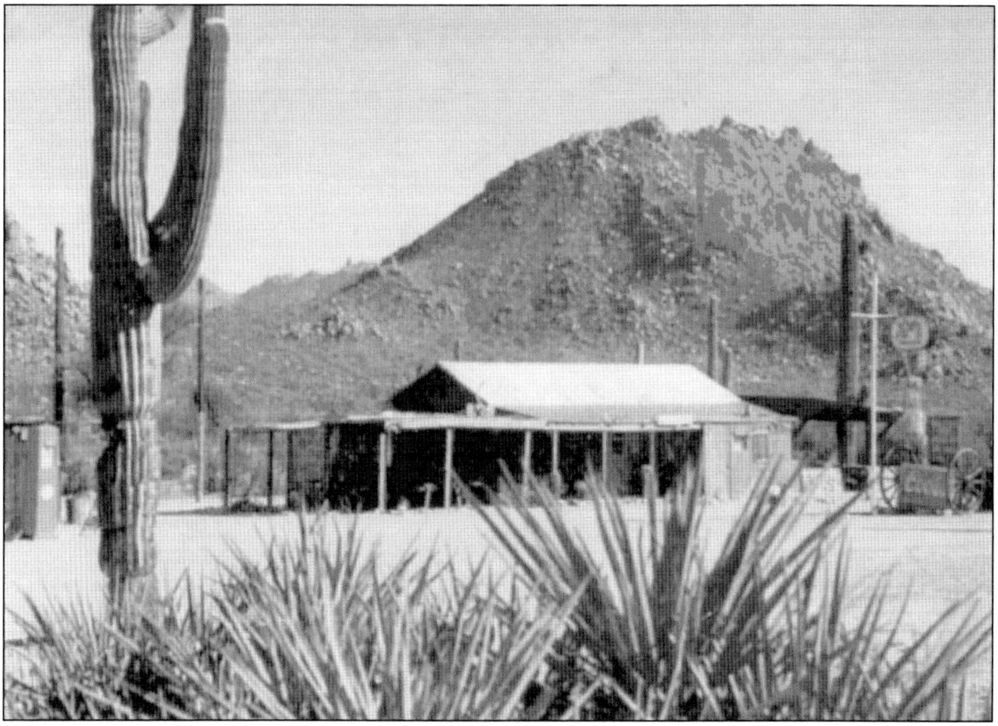

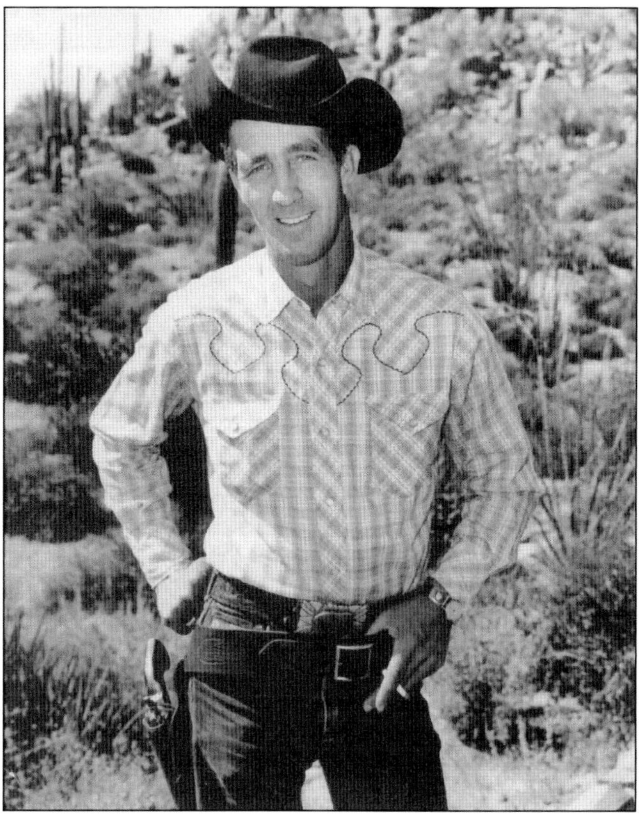

Pinnacle Peak Patio opened in 1957 as a small store on a dusty trail in the remote Pinnacle Peak area, today's Alma School Parkway. The trail was used by fisherman and others on their way to Bartlett Lake, Horseshoe Lake, and the Verde River. Some old-timers say that the track once served as a stagecoach route, but others disagree. (Courtesy of Marv Dickson.)

Bill DePew and his wife, Dottie, started Pinnacle Peak Patio. Called Black Bart, Bill was known to dress in black and stare at customers while sitting in a chair with his gun, just as sheriffs had done in the past. (Courtesy of Marv Dickson.)

The DePews moved their increasingly popular business, Pinnacle Peak Patio, across the road to the foot of Pinnacle Peak. The new place was tiny and could only seat 50 diners. During a renovation in the 1970s, a wall was removed and this 1958 advertisement was discovered. The DePews obtained the 10-acre parcel from Lois Kellogg (Maury), owner of the Crescent Moon Ranch. (Courtesy of Marv Dickson.)

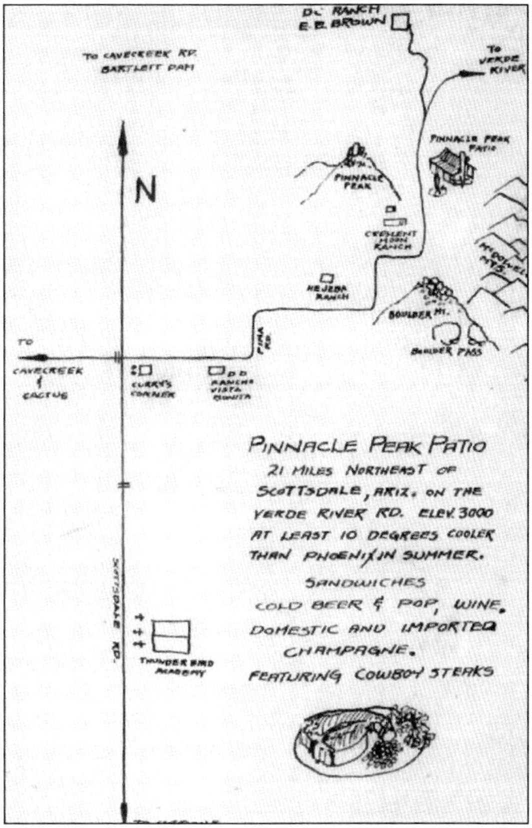

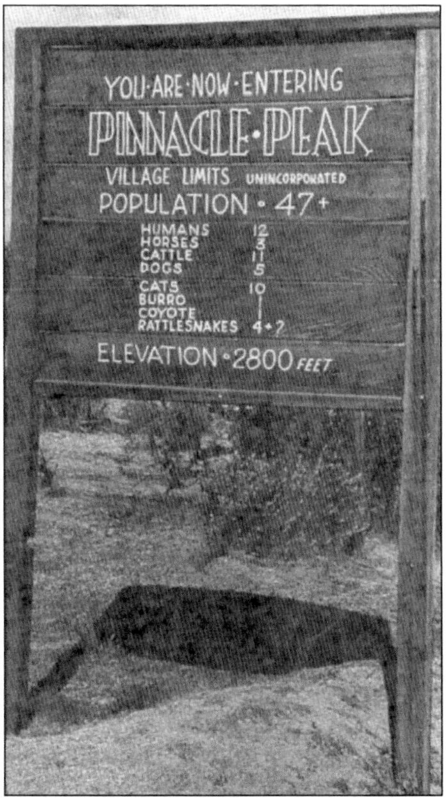

A December 1958 issue of *Days and Ways* highlighted the area's remoteness with this photograph and the caption, "Little is left to the imagination as they enter Pinnacle Peak, a refreshing stop on a dusty, desert road northeast of Phoenix. The sign is a model of a complete census." (Courtesy of *Days and Ways*.)

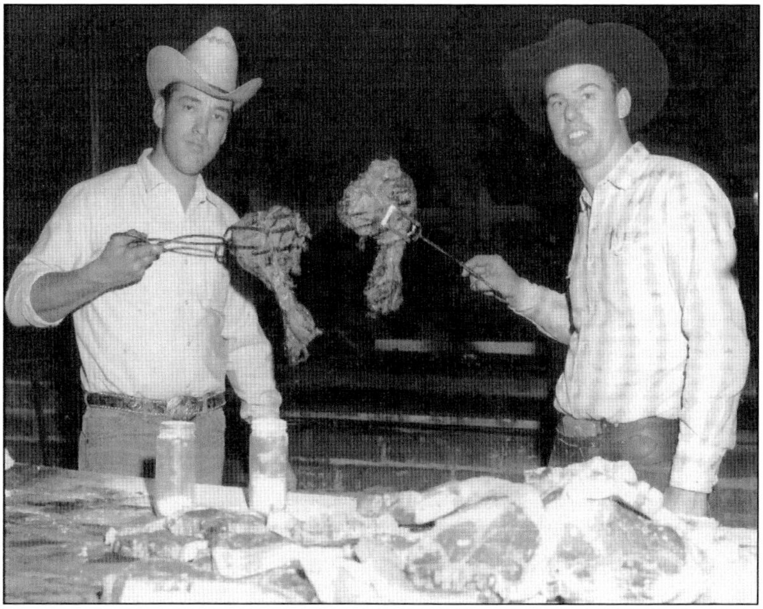

Initially, Pinnacle Peak Patio got the public's attention by serving only one dish, a 32-ounce porterhouse steak that was cooked using mesquite wood. Back in 1962, Bill Thurston (left) and Marv Dickson prepared the steaks at the restaurant. (Courtesy of Marv Dickson.)

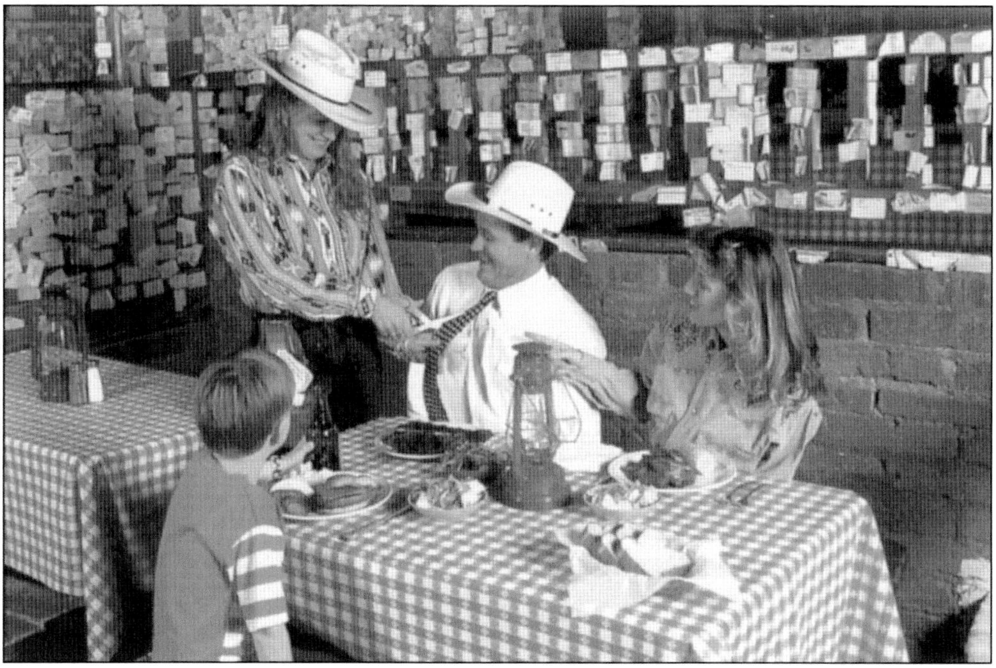

Pinnacle Peak Patio increased its fame by cutting off customer's neckties and then hanging them from the ceiling. At first, a knife was used to separate the tie from its owner; later scissors became the tool of choice. The back of this 1970s postcard states, "WARNING TO CITY SLICKERS: Scissor-wielding waitresses will cut off any neckties worn into this steak house." (Courtesy of Marv Dickson.)

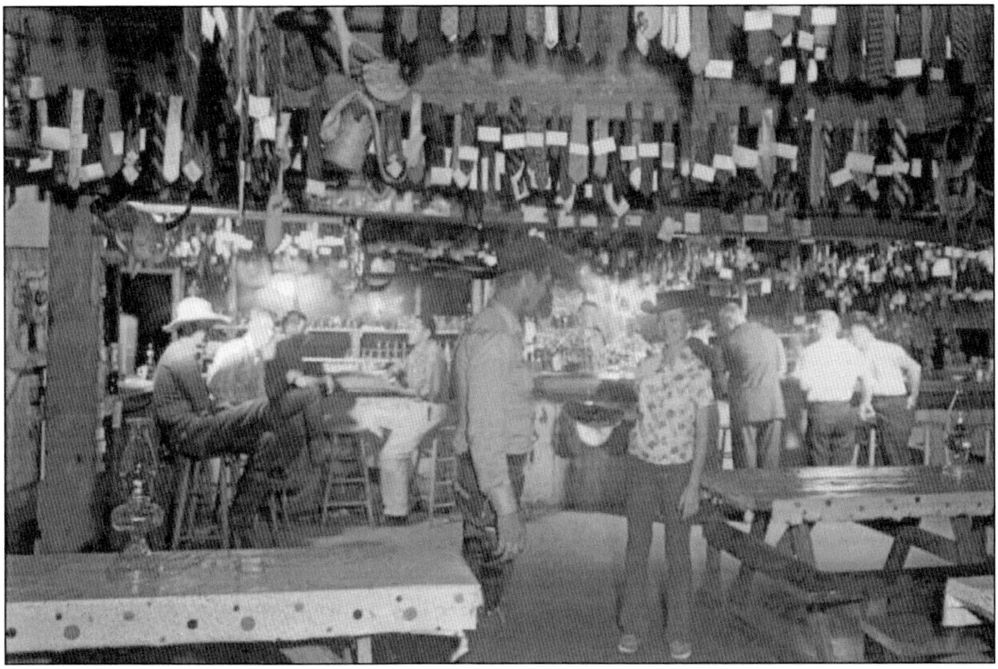

A newspaper advertisement from 1969 advised guests to "check their guns at the bar." Up until the 1980s, all the cooks and managers carried loaded guns to "handle" people who walked out without paying their bills. The guests did not seem to care; they assumed it was part of the western flavor. This 1960s photograph of the dining room shows neckties hanging from the ceiling. (Courtesy of Marv Dickson.)

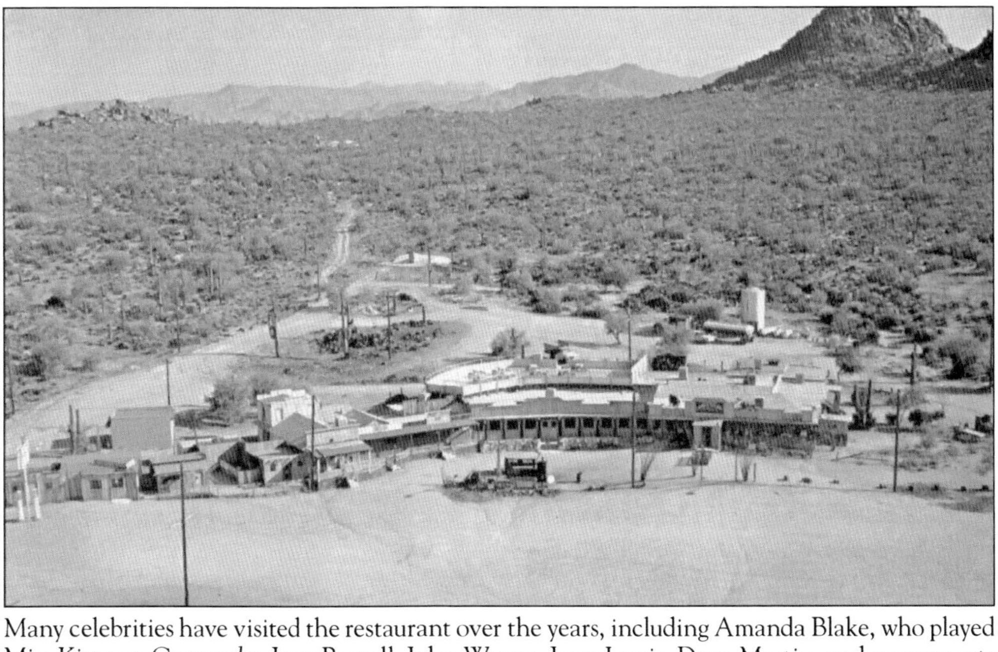

Many celebrities have visited the restaurant over the years, including Amanda Blake, who played Miss Kitty on *Gunsmoke*, Jane Russell, John Wayne, Jerry Lewis, Dean Martin, and many sports figures. This 1970s postcard shows the front of Pinnacle Peak Patio. Pinnacle Peak is in the background. (Courtesy of Marv Dickson.)

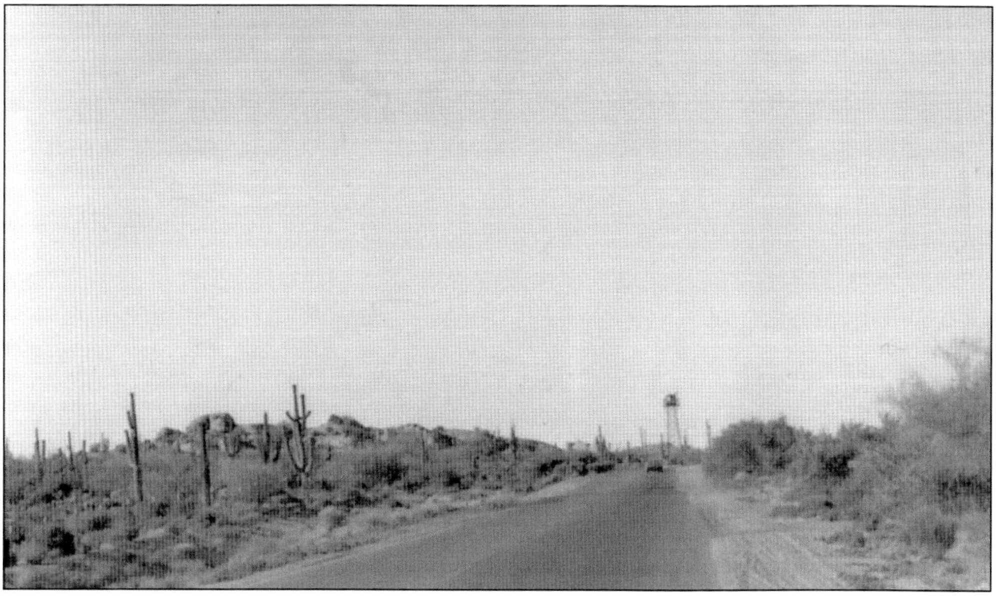

In the late 1950s, Alma School Parkway was usually a quiet, lonely road. George R. Cavalliere, who owned Reata Pass Steakhouse, made sure that the blinking light on the tower was switched on every night so that it could be seen all the way to Scottsdale. The power company installed the light so ranchers knew electricity was available. (Courtesy of Joyce Eller.)

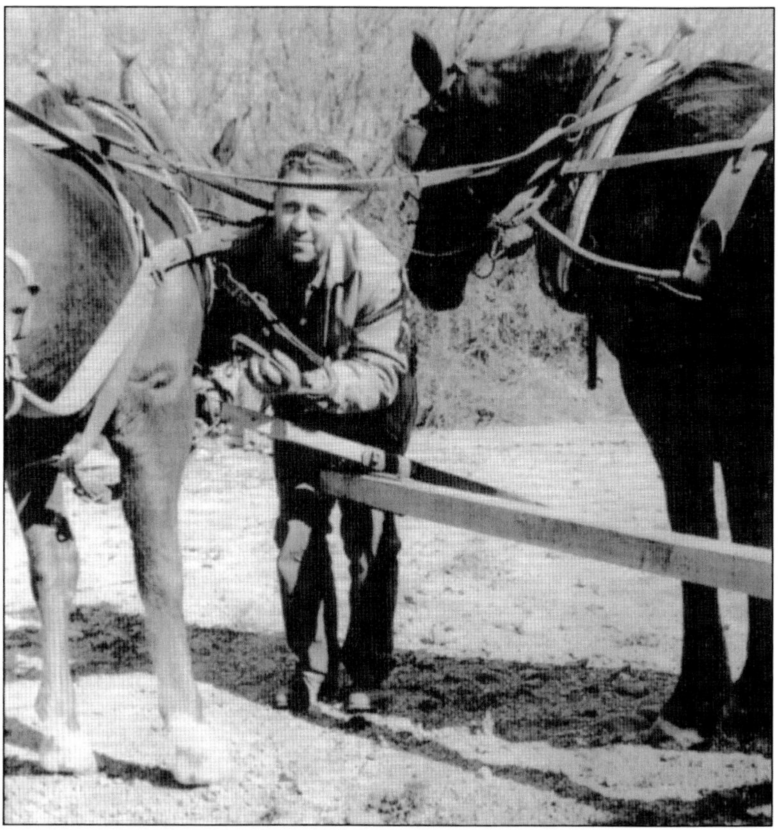

George R. Cavalliere was known as "Doc." He was the son of George Sidney Cavalliere, who had done the dredge work on the Arizona Canal before settling in Scottsdale. In his early years, Doc had a small ranch on the Verde River. He bought cattle from Mexico, fattened them in the desert, and sold them. Later, he learned the blacksmith trade from his father. (Courtesy of Joyce Eller.)

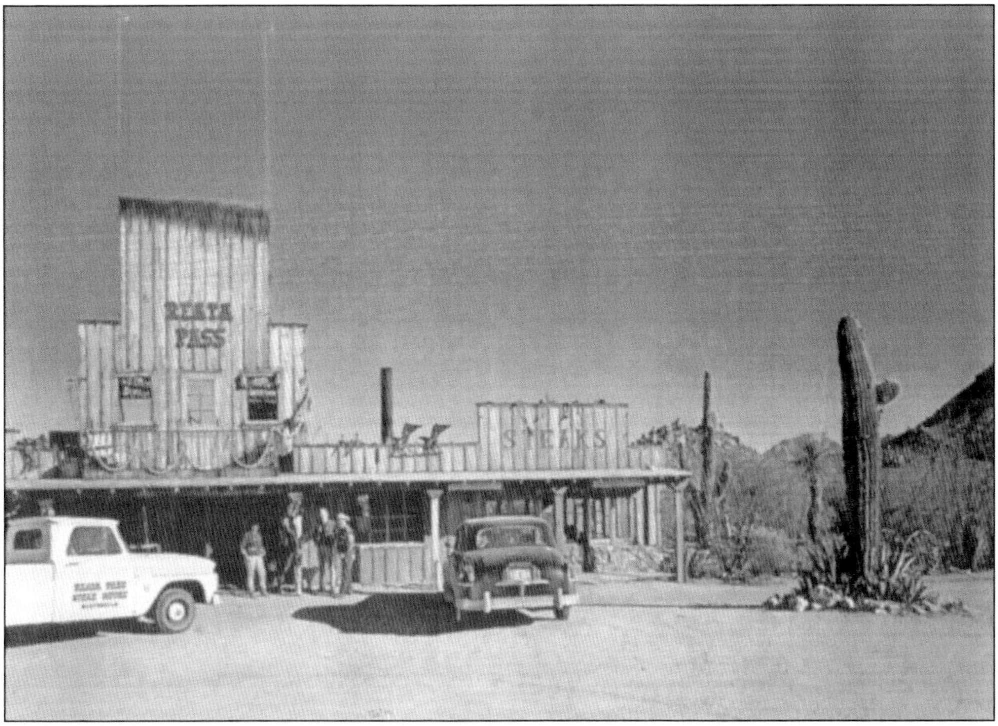

Reata Pass Steakhouse was built in the original location of Pinnacle Peak Patio. Over the years, Reata Pass was used as a backdrop for several western movies and early segments of *Bonanza*. (Courtesy of Joyce Eller.)

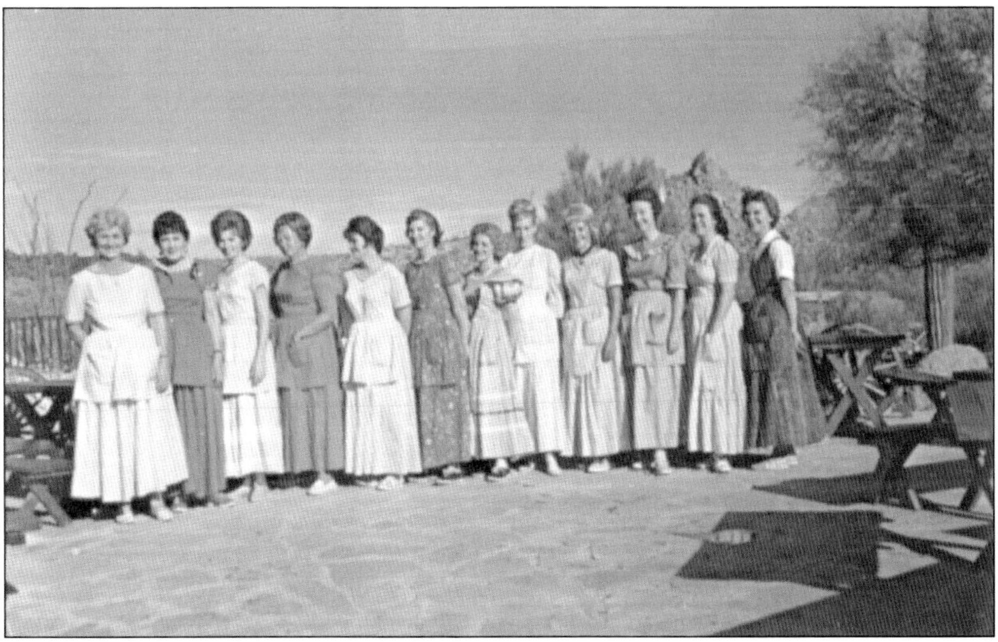

This postcard from the 1960s shows Reata Pass Steakhouse waitresses dressed in Old West–style attire. In the 1950s, Reata's waitresses made their own Western dresses. All 12 waitresses were needed to serve customers. (Courtesy of Joyce Eller.)

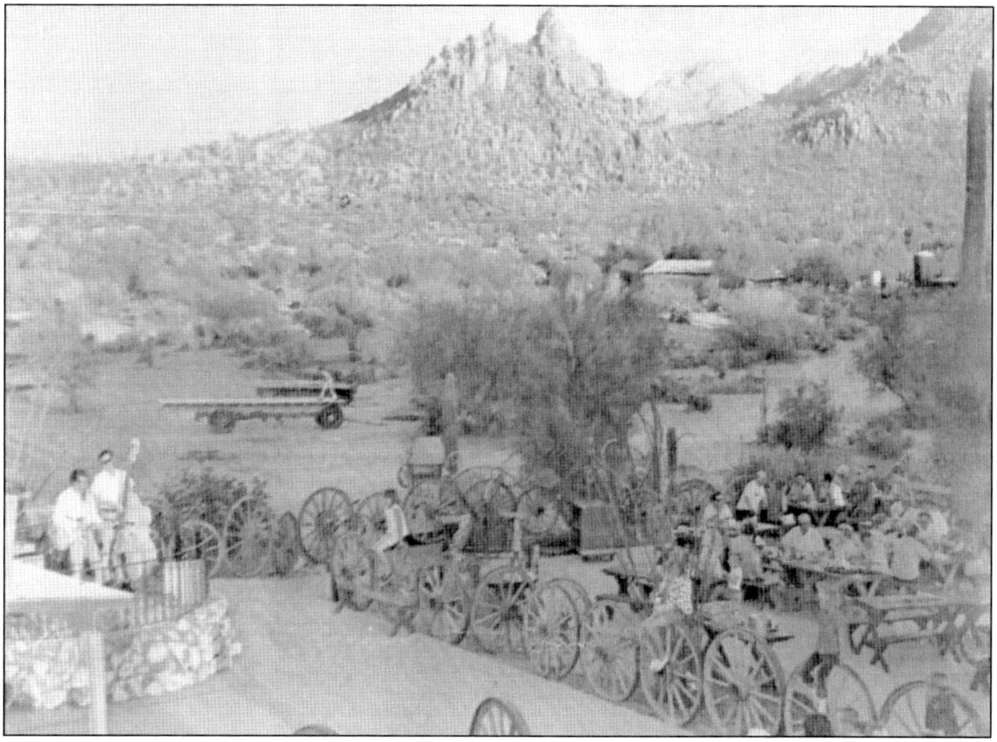

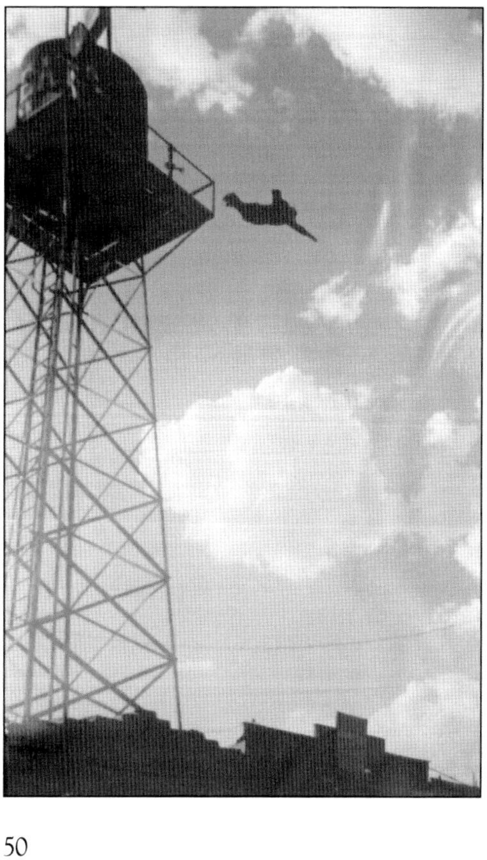

This Reata Steakhouse postcard from the 1960s shows customers enjoying the dining area behind the restaurant. At the time, the peak in the background was called Rattlesnake Mountain. Today, it is called Troon Mountain. The Cook Shack, located west of the steakhouse on Alma School Parkway, was originally the site of Hope's Hogan, an antique shop owned by Hope Bennett. The wife of Leon Bills worked with Hope. (Courtesy of Joyce Eller.)

In 1975, the Two Cowboys event was held at Reata Pass. Sparky Spangler, a Hollywood stuntman, jumped off the tower across the street from the restaurant. Spangler, also known as "the original fall guy" and "the falling star," used a large pile of cardboard boxes to cushion his successful landing. (Courtesy of Joyce Eller.)

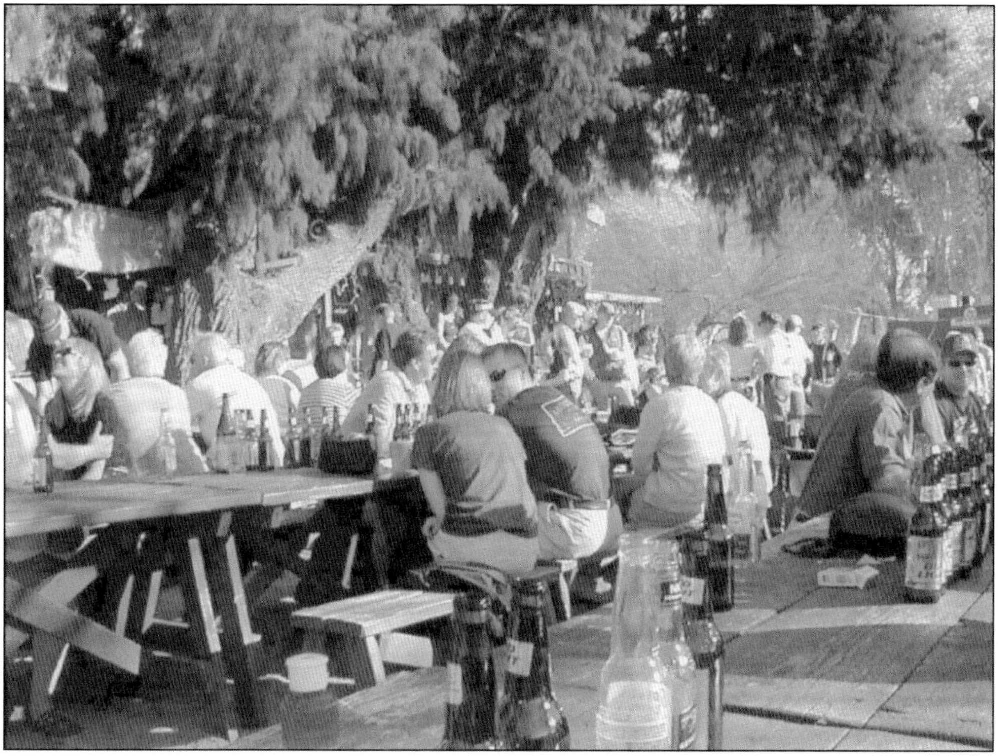

A few years after opening Reata Pass Steakhouse, George R. Cavalliere opened the family's sister cowboy bar, Greasewood Flat, next door amidst the tamarisk trees in a vacant ranch bunkhouse. A dirt road led from today's Alma School Parkway to Greasewood Flat. (Courtesy of *The Peak*.)

The folks at Greasewood Flat have always prided themselves on not having a telephone or promoting the business. The restaurant's popularity has grown by word of mouth, with first-time visitors returning and bringing their friends. Up until the 1990s, there was a jukebox in the bar. On most evenings and weekend afternoons, a country-and-western singer provided entertainment. (Courtesy of *The Peak*.)

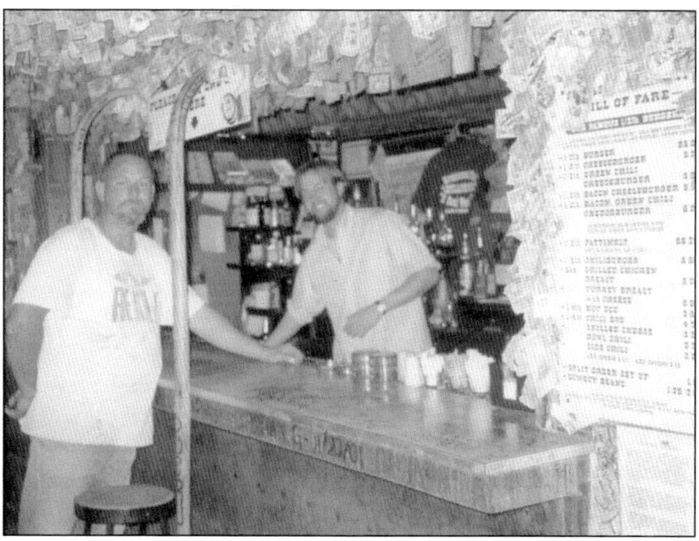

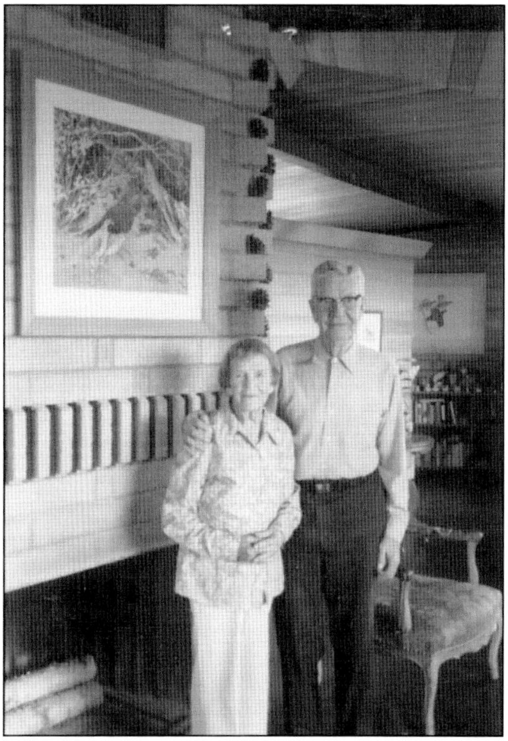

Anne and Walter Bohl stand in their home in the 1960s. Walter, an artist, depicted wildlife from his 30-acre property on the western slopes of Pinnacle Peak. Eleanor Roosevelt was a customer. His work was featured in *Esquire*, *Arizona Highways*, and other magazines. He was commissioned to create a design for the 1943–1944 Migratory Bird Hunting and Conservation Stamp. Three of Walter's etchings are in the Smithsonian American Art Museum. (Courtesy of Liz Stapleton Ogden.)

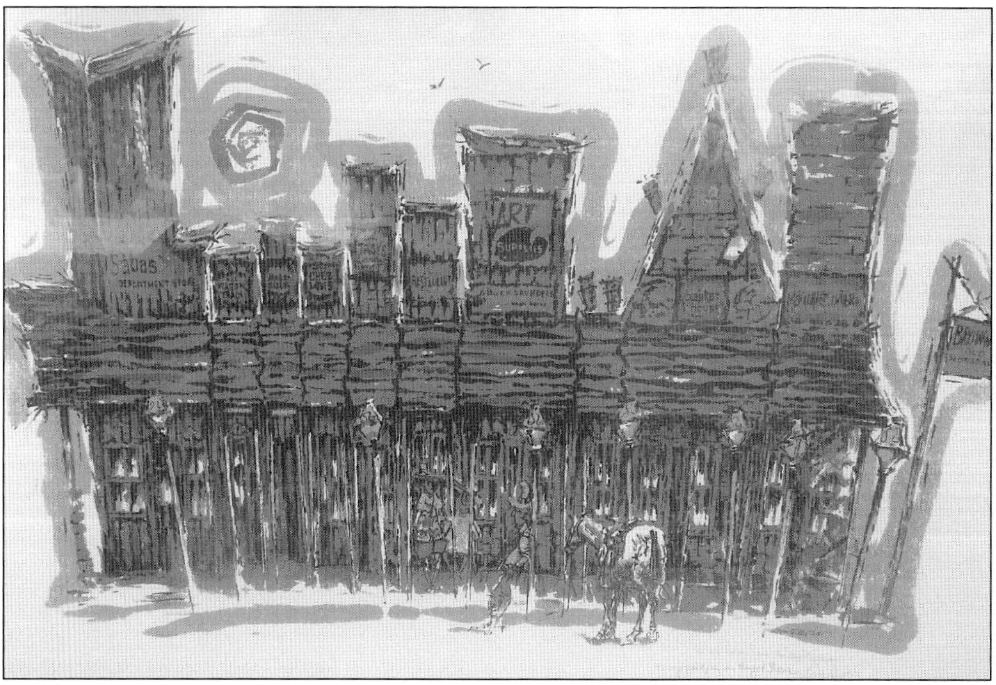

This painting by artist Leon Bills is of downtown Scottsdale in the 1960s. Bills moved to Scottsdale in 1963 because of his son's asthma. While his adobe home near Pinnacle Peak was being built, he lived at Crescent Moon Ranch. It rained, and most of his future home melted because the faulty mortar had not hardened. They had to start over. (Courtesy of Joyce Eller.)

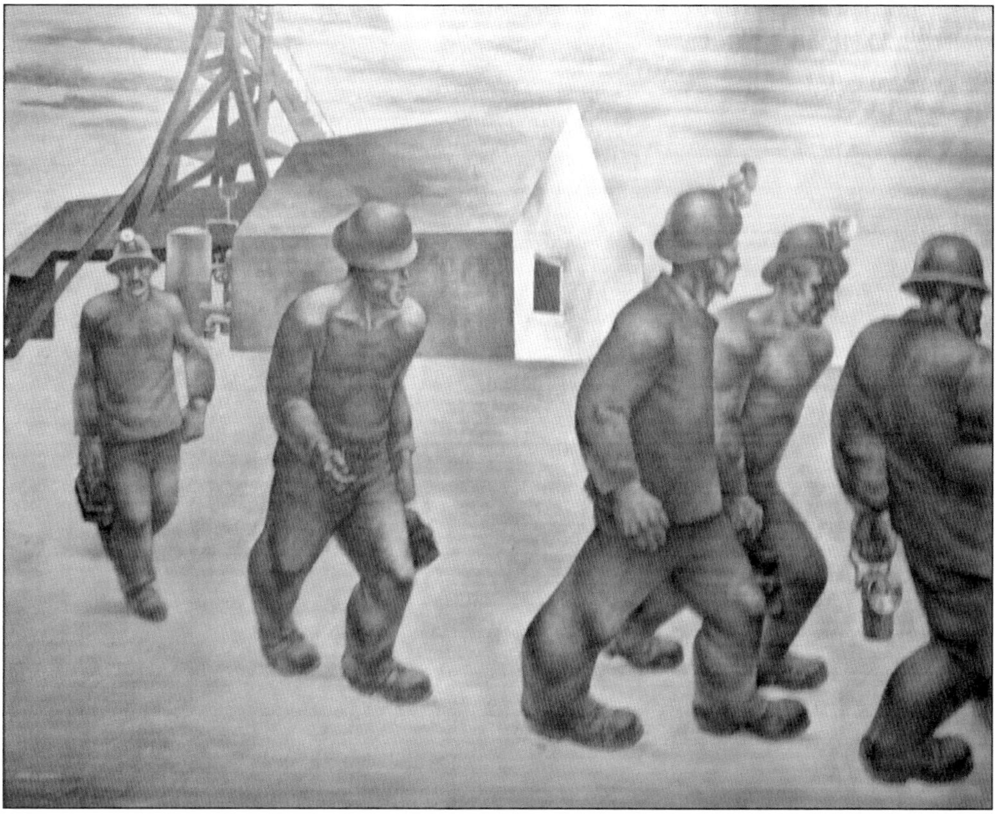

Afternoon at the Little Daisy was painted in 1934 by Lew Davis. Davis and his wife, Mathilde, lived on 40 acres on the western foothills of Pinnacle Peak. They hosted Sunday salons, and neighbors had the opportunity to meet international travelers, prominent valley artists, politicians, and businessmen. In the 1950s, the couple sponsored the first Metropolitan Museum traveling exhibition ever shown in Arizona. (Courtesy of Liz Stapleton Ogden.)

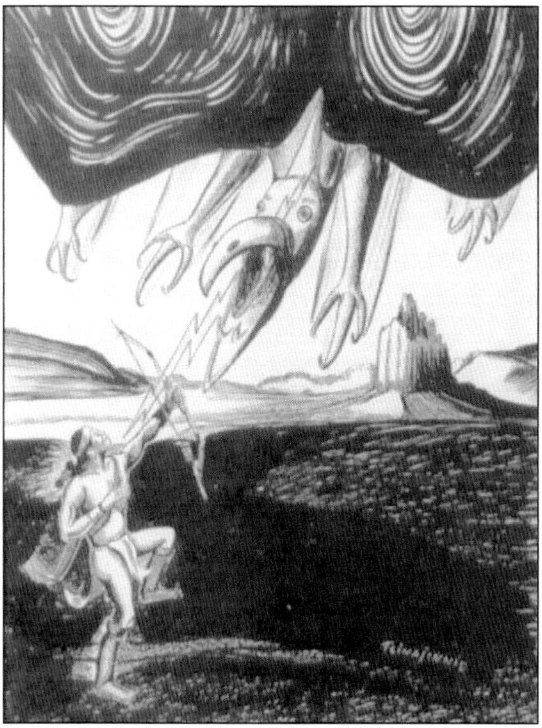

Monster Slayer Killing Monster Bird was drawn by Andrew Tsihnahjinnie. Recognized as one of the finest of 20th-century Navajo artists, he had a studio near the southwestern base of Pinnacle Peak in the late 1950s and 1960s. His art is part of the collections at the Heard Museum. The governor designated him as a Living Treasure of Arizona in 1991. (Courtesy of Kiva Gallery.)

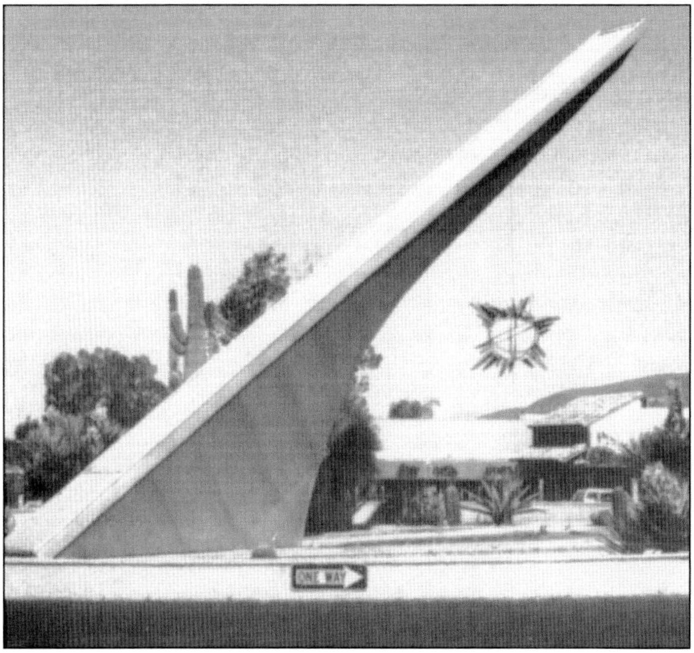

Failing to find water in the Pinnacle Peak area where he owned 2,000 acres, Kenyon Turner Palmer and his partner Tom Darlington established one of Arizona's first planned communities, Carefree. The community and its trademark sundial sat at the corner of Scottsdale and Cave Creek Roads. Palmer and Darlington sought to preserve the area's natural beauty and considered existing rock formations and terrain when plotting homesites and roads. Lots went on sale in 1959. (Courtesy of *The Peak*.)

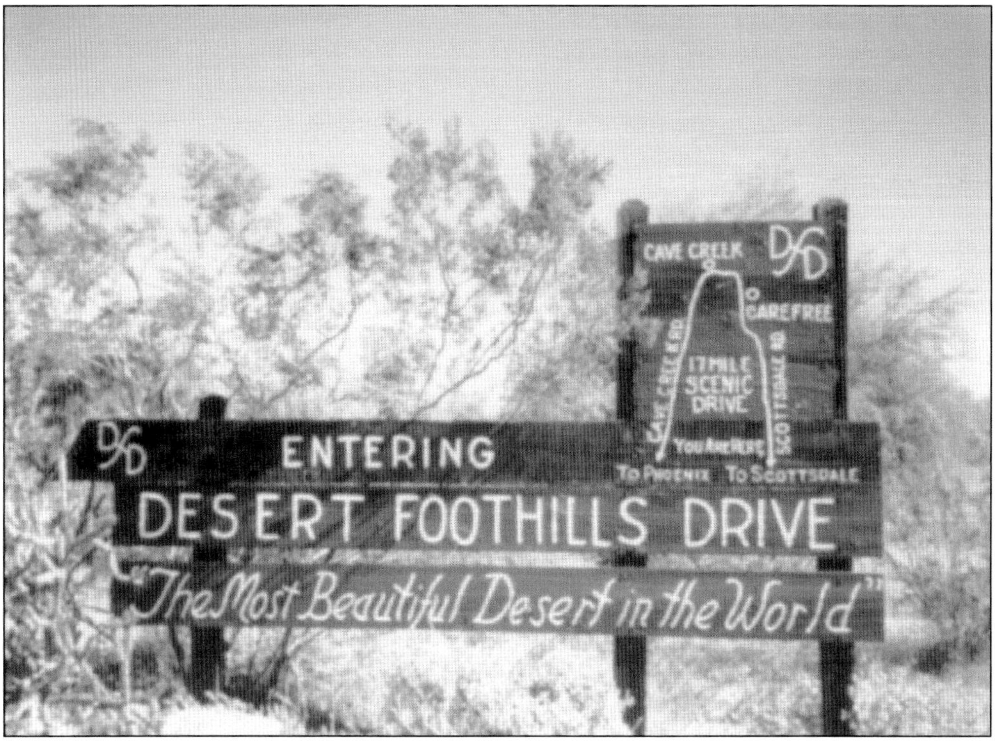

In 1963, area residents created the Desert Foothills Scenic Drive to preserve desert vegetation and views along the northern reaches of Scottsdale and Cave Creek Roads. Redwood plant identification signs were posted, and Maricopa County established scenic setbacks and small parks. Maricopa County hoped the drive would inspire other communities to preserve their natural habitats. (Courtesy of FSD.)

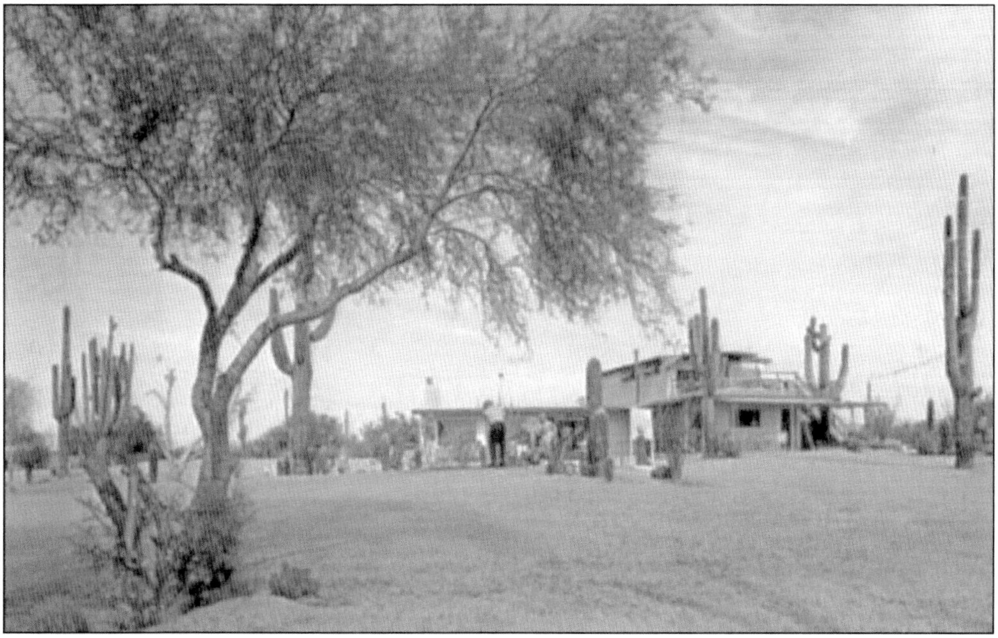

In the 1950s, retired executive Fitzgerald Durham created the nine-hole, par-three Ironwood Golf Course near today's Jomax and Scottsdale Roads. North Scottsdale's first course had no turf. Instead, it used fine sand that was kept in place by silicon oil for the greens and could be played all day for just $1. Scottsdale mayor Herb Drinkwater and the Scottsdale Jaycees held rip-roaring parties at the course. (Courtesy of *The Peak*.)

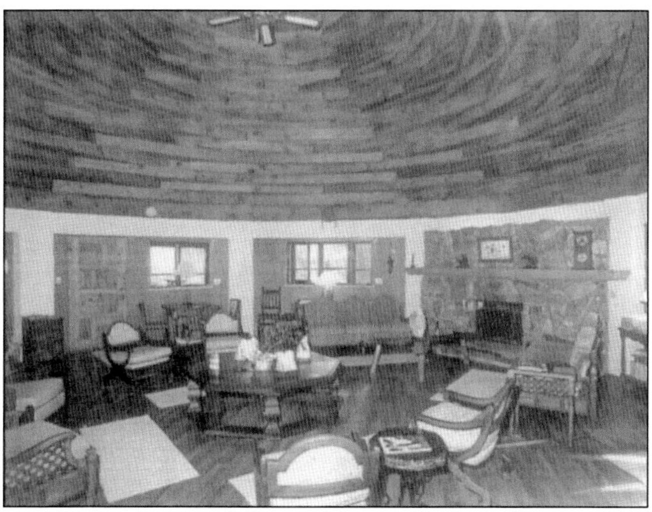

In 1967, Jane Rau and her husband, Leonard, purchased 20 acres off Dynamite Boulevard just west of Pima Road and built a hogan-shaped house. Their living room, pictured here, was the site of many community meetings during the 1970s and 1980s. Prior to the area's annexation into Scottsdale, Rau founded County Residents Against Scottsdale Harassment (CRASH). She later cofounded the McDowell Sonoran Land Trust. (Courtesy of Jane Rau.)

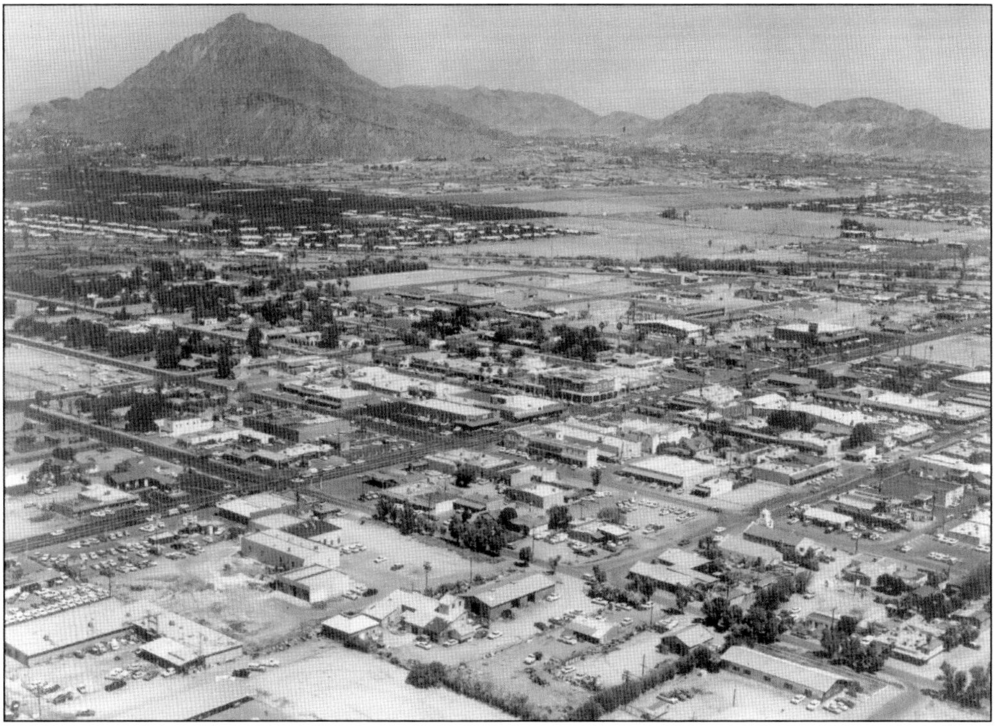

The City of Scottsdale was growing. At incorporation on June 25, 1951, its 2,032 residents were living in the downtown area, which was less than one square mile in size. By 1963, more than five square miles had been annexed, and the town had grown to approximately 43,000 residents. This photograph taken in 1957 or 1958 shows downtown Scottsdale with Camelback Mountain in the upper left corner. (Courtesy of the Scottsdale Public Library.)

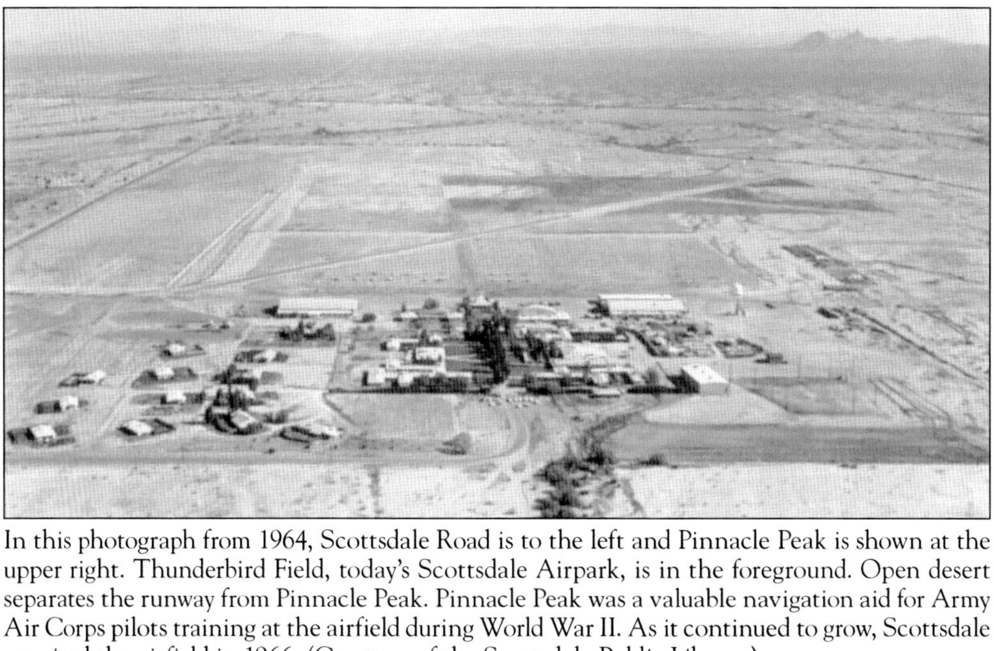

In this photograph from 1964, Scottsdale Road is to the left and Pinnacle Peak is shown at the upper right. Thunderbird Field, today's Scottsdale Airpark, is in the foreground. Open desert separates the runway from Pinnacle Peak. Pinnacle Peak was a valuable navigation aid for Army Air Corps pilots training at the airfield during World War II. As it continued to grow, Scottsdale acquired the airfield in 1966. (Courtesy of the Scottsdale Public Library.)

Four

Water Accelerates Development around Pinnacle Peak

For thousands of years, humans had lived near Pinnacle Peak, yet in 1969, saguaro still outnumbered people. The limited supply of water restricted development. Ironically, it took water to find water.

In 1969, when Jerry and Florence Nelson began drilling a well on the 160 acres they had purchased on the remote northwest corner of Pinnacle Peak and Pima Roads, they needed water to cool their drill bits. Homesteaders who collected rain sold some of the water to the Nelsons for $50 per barrel.

The day after the drill hit water, one of Jerry Nelson's foremen requested $50 to buy water. Nelson asked why he needed to buy water when they had discovered millions of gallons of it. The foreman, himself a local settler, advised Nelson to do three things: keep buying water every day, keep the discovery a secret, and start buying all the land he could. Nelson listened and acquired enough land to build Pinnacle Peak Village and Pinnacle Peak Country Club.

Once the Nelsons struck it wet, the rush was on in more ways than one. From 1974 to 1989, Nelson developed Pinnacle Peak Plaza, Pinnacle Peak Country Club (which had nine subdivisions), Troon Village, and Troon North. From 1982 to 1984, the City of Scottsdale annexed 95 square miles, including the Pinnacle Peak area. During the mid-1980s, Scottsdale approved other master-planned communities, including Desert Highlands, Estancia, and Legend Trails. In the 1990s, the Grayhawk, Terravita, Winfield, and Whisper Rock planned communities were approved.

The rapid development brought new conveniences. Paved roads took the place of dirt routes. New water and telephone services eliminated the need to carry water and to drive several miles to make a phone call. A new post office brought mail service. A general store and later a retail center made it easier to buy groceries and household items. Development also brought road construction and the installation of other infrastructure, which created challenges for residents. Conservation organizations sprang up to protect the desert, encourage sensitive planning, and work with developers and the City of Scottsdale to develop ordinances to protect the environment.

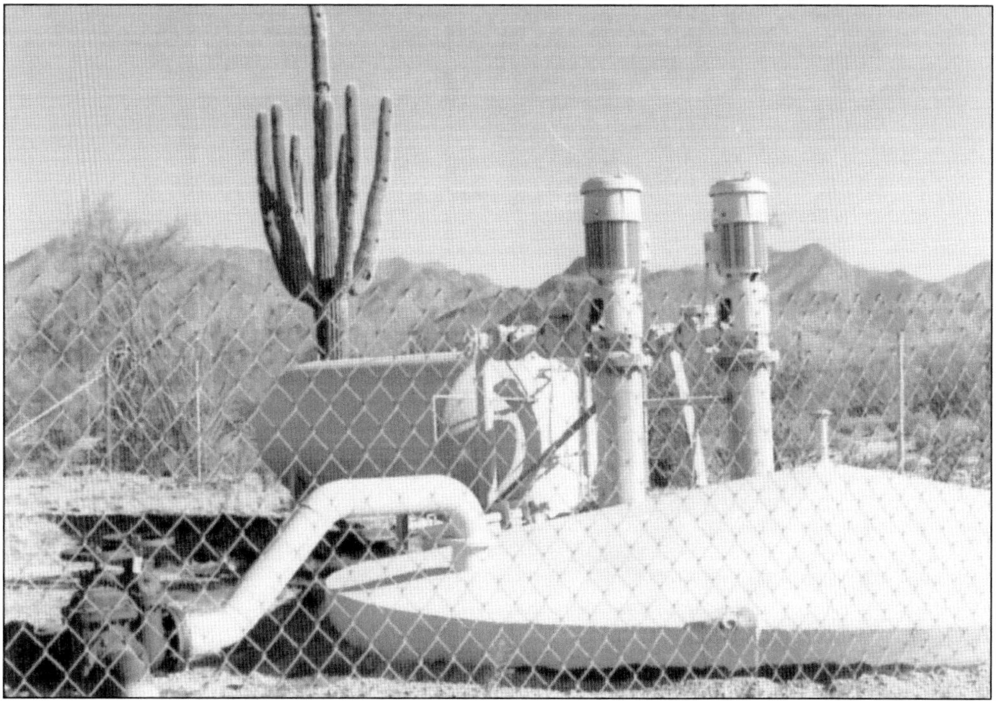

In 1969, Jerry and Florence Nelson drilled into a large aquifer at the intersection of Pinnacle Peak and Pima Roads. Camping on their land for weeks, they watched the drill churn up bone-dry sand and gravel before it hit water at 560 feet, 110 feet deeper than estimated. The well in the photograph provided water for Nelson's first master-planned development, Pinnacle Peak Village. (Courtesy of Pinnacle Paradise, Inc.)

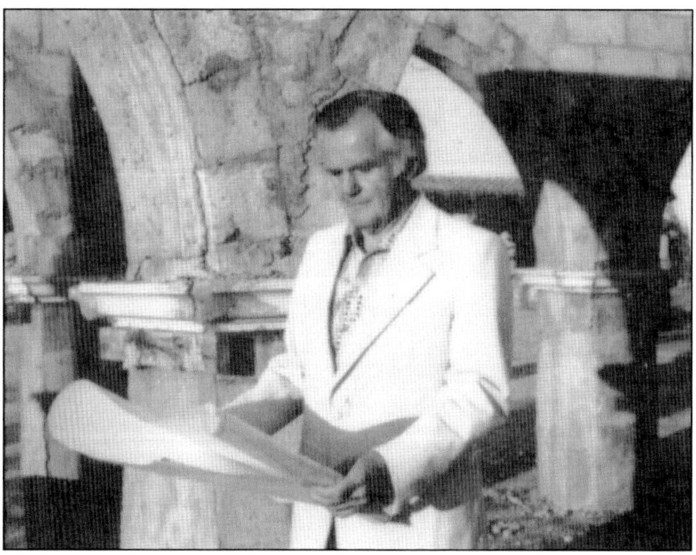

Jerry Nelson reviews blueprints during the construction of Pinnacle Peak Plaza, also known as Plaza de Alamos. Located on the southwest corner of Pinnacle Peak and Pima Roads, it was at the site previously home to Rancho Vista Bonita Guest Ranch, which was torn down in 1974 to make room for this development. Nelson purchased the 160-acre parcel for $1,100 an acre. (Courtesy of Pinnacle Paradise, Inc.)

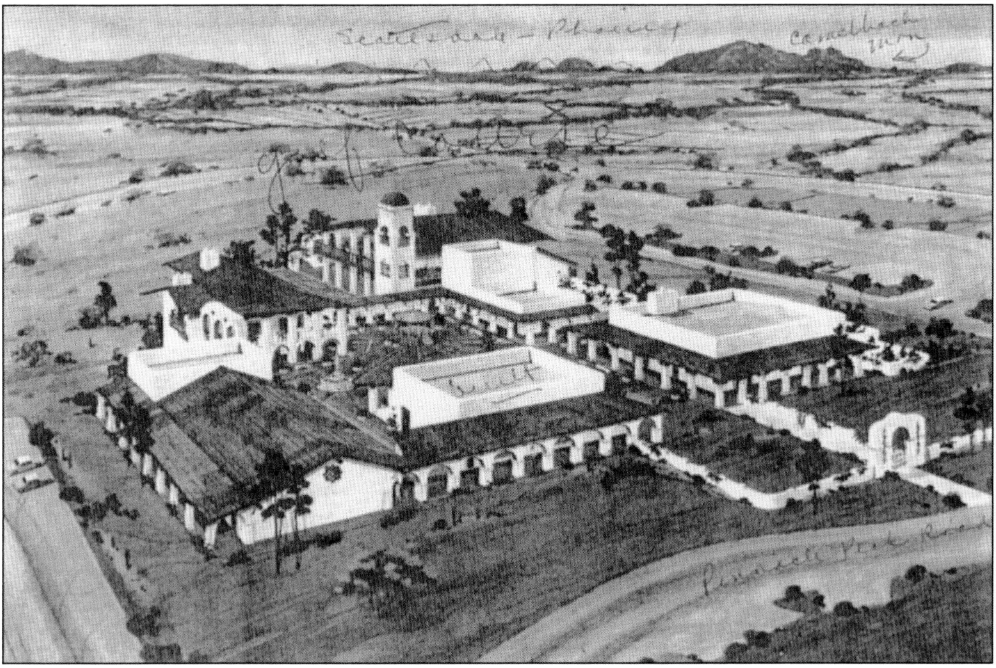

This illustration was part of a marketing brochure developed by Jerry Nelson's company, Pinnacle Paradise, Inc., for the Pinnacle Peak Village project. Note the vacant desert surrounding the plaza and the salesman's note indicating the location of Camelback Mountain. Plans for the plaza included a general store, post office, gas station, and shops. (Courtesy of the Pinnacle Peak Country Club.)

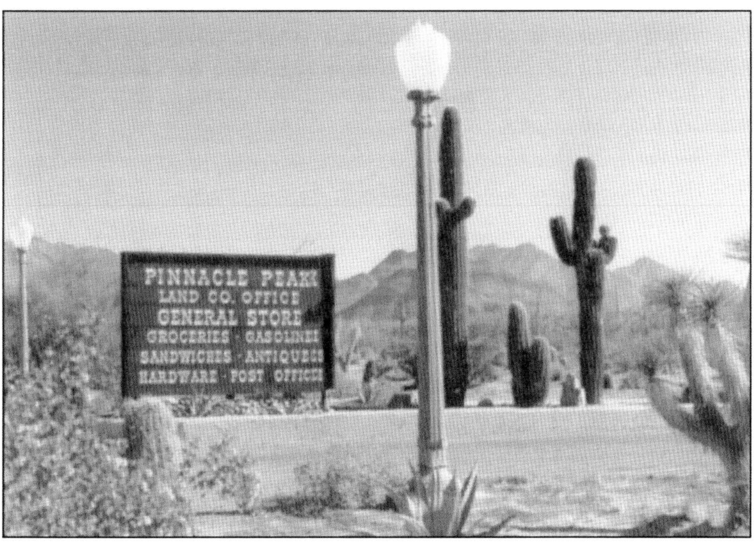

An important part of Nelson's Pinnacle Peak Plaza was the general store that opened in 1975. Located on the northwest corner of Pinnacle Peak and Pima Roads, Pinnacle Peak Paradise was the first neighborhood to be built as part of the Pinnacle Peak Village master plan. (Courtesy of Pinnacle Paradise, Inc.)

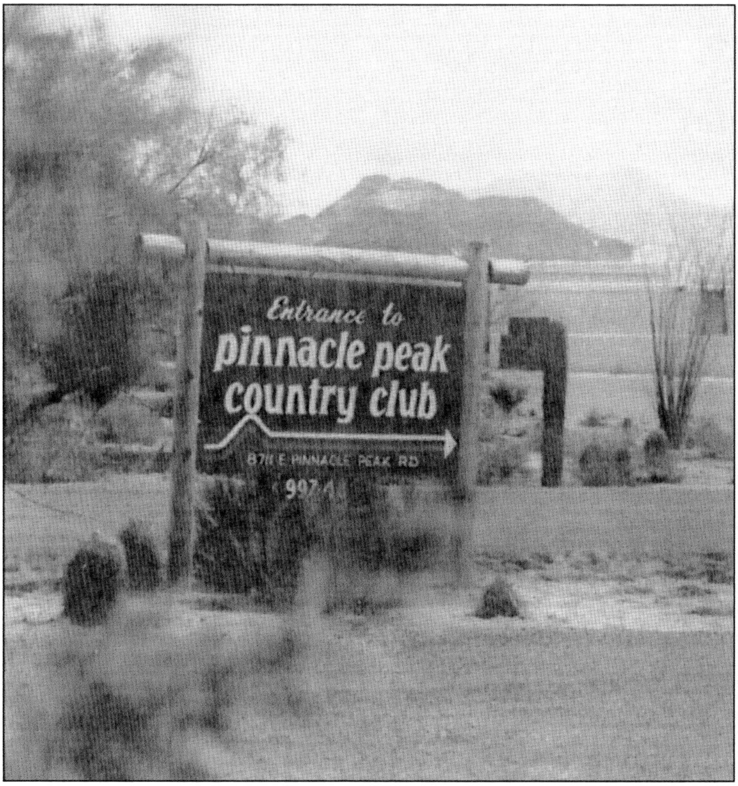

In 1976, Nelson's company opened Pinnacle Peak Country Club for private membership. Adjacent to Pinnacle Peak Plaza, it featured an 18-hole golf course surrounded by luxury homesites. Within five years, all the homesites were purchased. By 1980, Nelson had opened nine more subdivisions. (Courtesy of the Pinnacle Peak Country Club.)

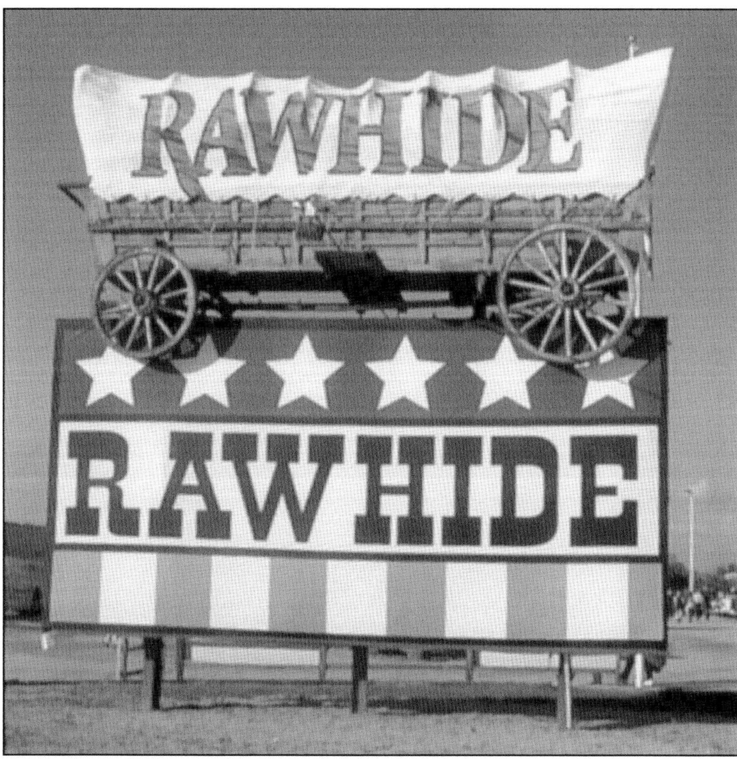

The owner of Rawhide, Jim Paul, wanted to build an attraction that looked like an 1880s western village. He purchased 160 acres on the southeast corner of Scottsdale and Pinnacle Peak Roads, known as Curry's Corners, after John B. Curry, who had owned a small grocery store there prior to the 1950s. On opening day in 1971, Rawhide had 25,000 visitors. By 1996, Rawhide was visited by more than 960,000 people annually. (Courtesy of *The Peak*.)

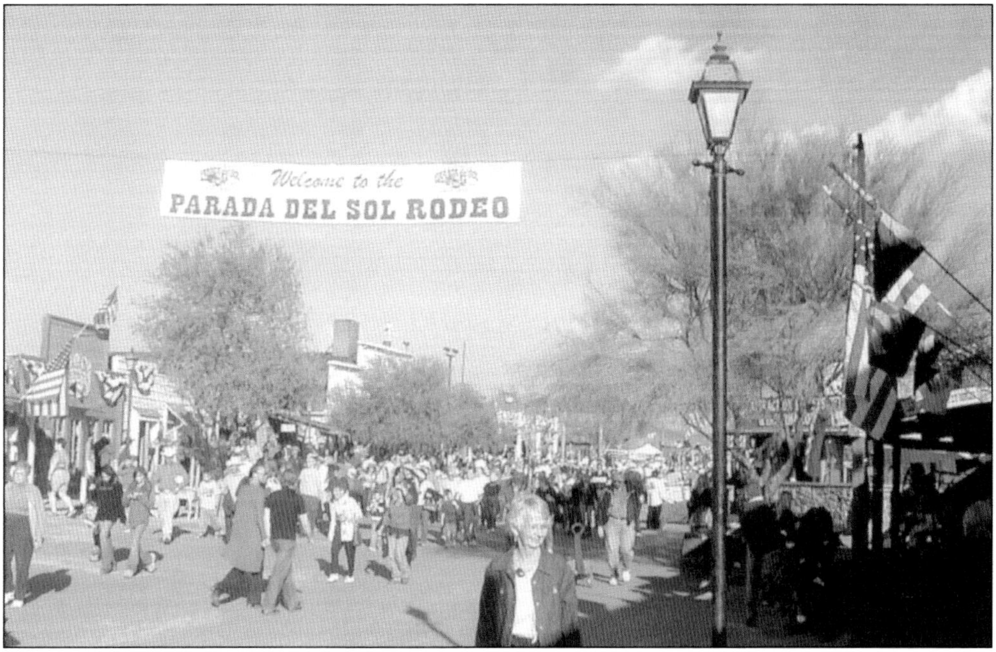

This photograph from 2005 shows Rawhide's Main Street as it becomes crowded with people leaving the Parada del Sol Rodeo. The street featured Golden Belle's Steakhouse and Saloon, a general store, a sheriff's office, a western clothing store, a museum, the office of the *Rawhide Sentinel*, and more. Just off Main Street were a gold mine and a railroad station where visitors could go for a desert train ride. (Courtesy of *The Peak*.)

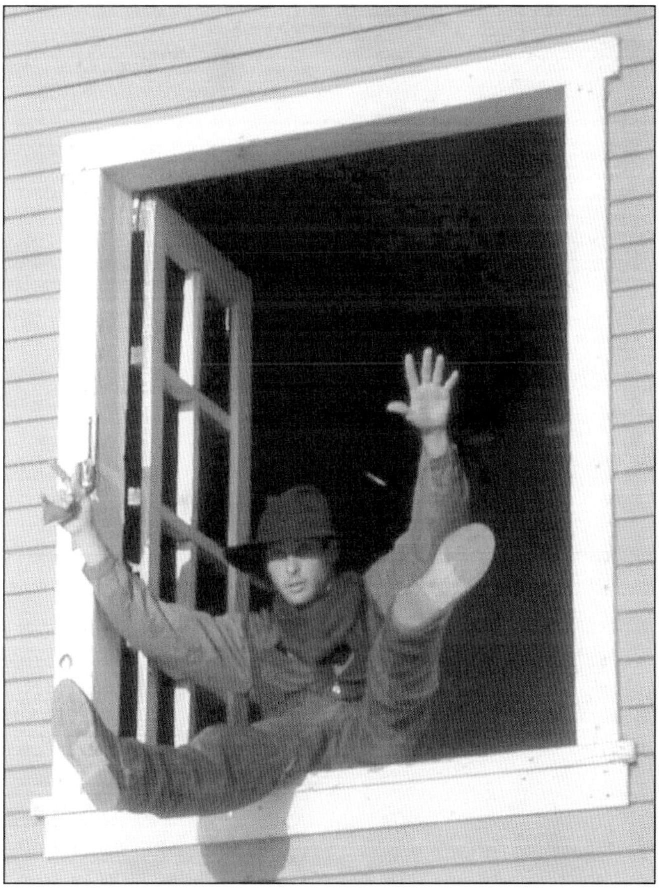

It was not unusual for staged arguments and gunfights to break out along Rawhide's Main Street. Skilled actors and professional stunt men provided lively entertainment for visitors. (Courtesy of *The Peak*.)

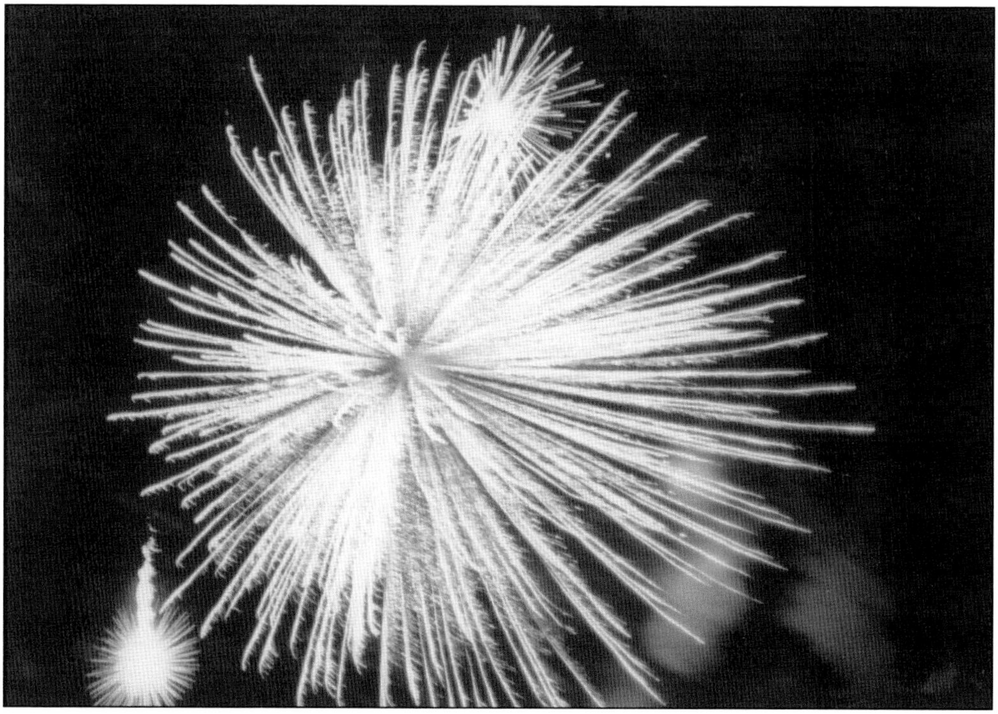

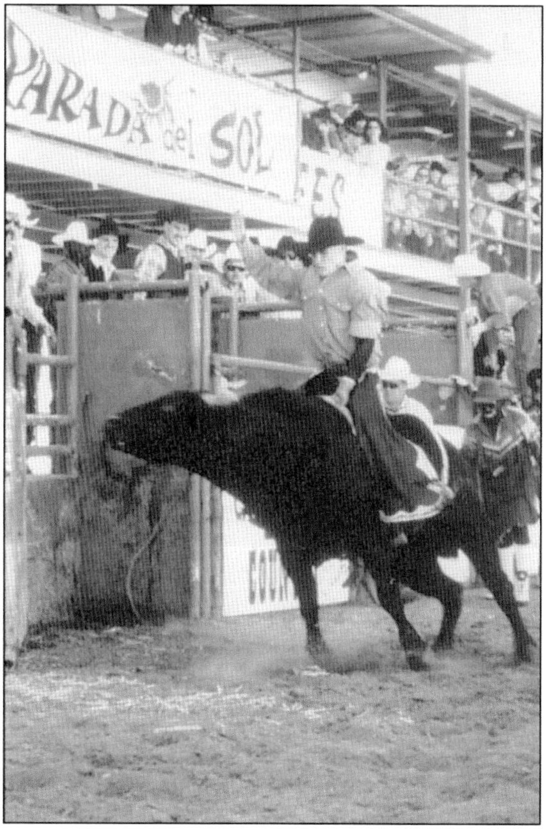

Fireworks were part of the fun at Rawhide during Scottsdale's Parada del Sol Rodeo. During the 1990s, Rawhide usually held a fireworks show on Saturday evenings when the weather was warm. The bursting rockets and colorful explosions lit the night sky over Rawhide. (Courtesy of the Scottsdale Public Library.)

In July 1975, Rawhide was annexed by the City of Scottsdale. A rodeo competitor is shown riding a bull at the Scottsdale Jaycees' annual Parada del Sol Rodeo. Between 1984 and 2005, the rodeo was held at Rawhide, with the exception of 2001 when the rodeo was held at WestWorld. Rawhide closed its North Scottsdale location in 2005. (Courtesy of the Scottsdale Public Library.)

In 1977, Ralph and Nancy Knight founded the Greater Pinnacle Peak Homeowners Association (GPPHA). At the time, there were only about 100 people living in the Pinnacle Peak area. The Knights shared a passion for the desert and its wildlife. They knew that development was coming and wanted it to occur in a planned and orderly way that protected the quality of life for residents. (Courtesy of *The Peak*.)

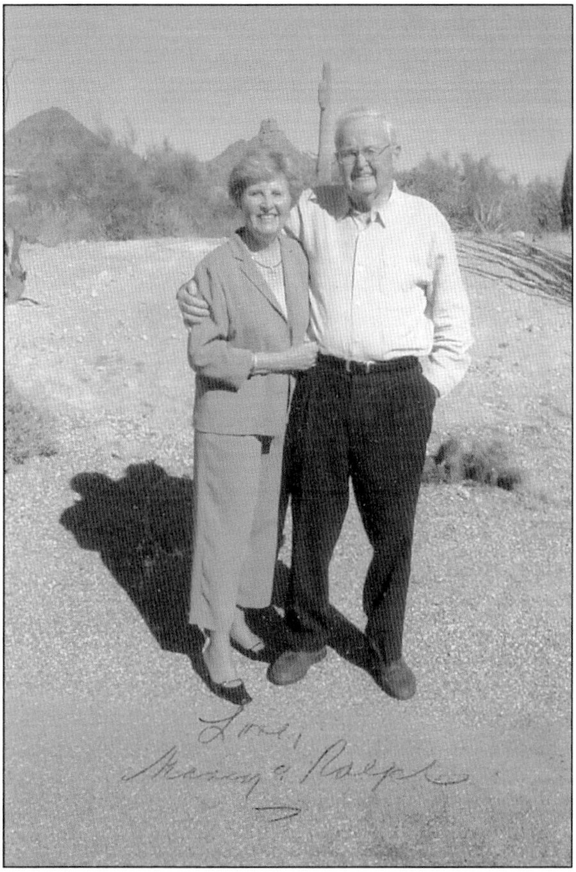

From 1982 to 1984 under the leadership of Mayor Herb Drinkwater, the City of Scottsdale annexed 95 square miles, including Pinnacle Peak. Drinkwater, who later became a resident of the Pinnacle Peak area, worked to enhance communication and understanding between the older downtown section of Scottsdale and its remote northern neighborhoods. This photograph shows Drinkwater riding in the 1996 Parada del Sol Parade. (Courtesy of the Scottsdale Public Library.)

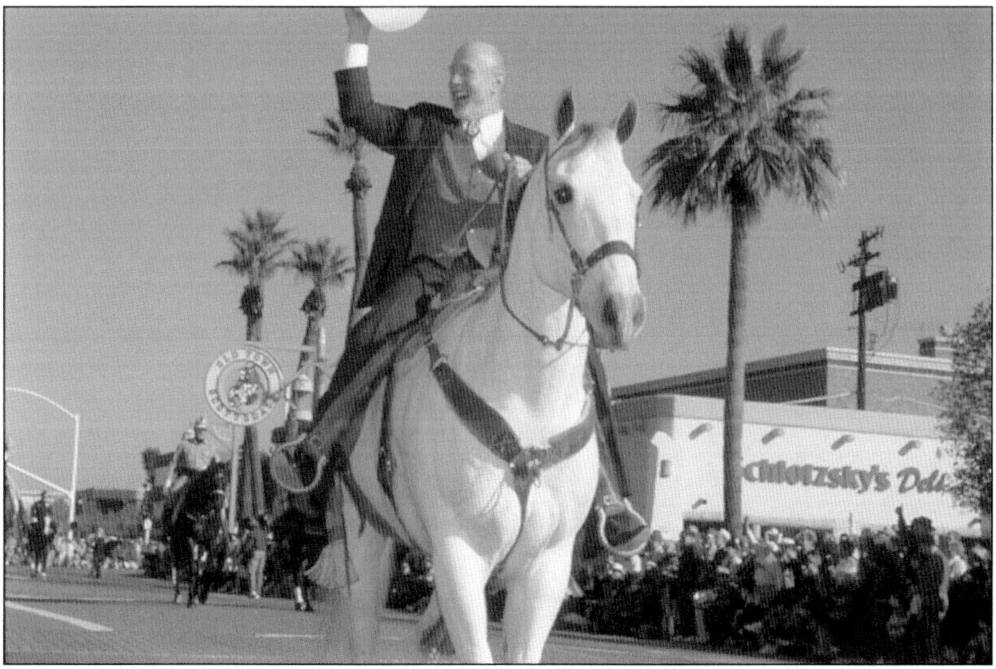

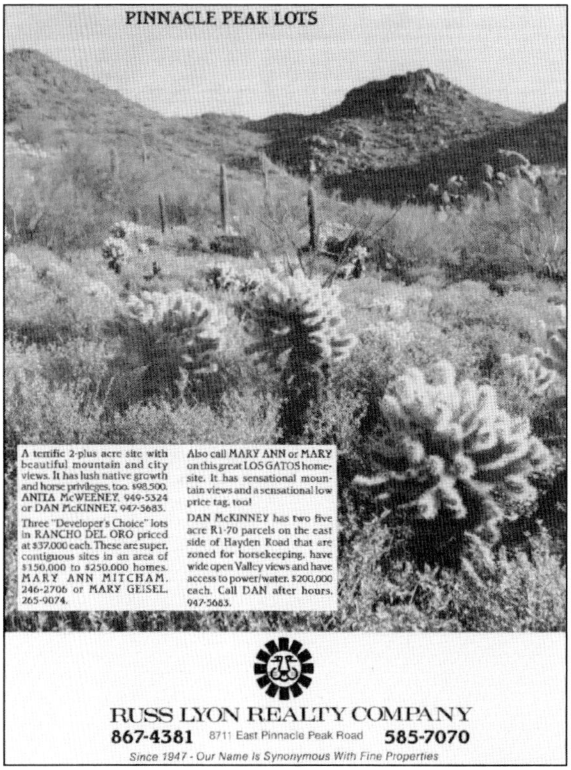

The annexation of the Pinnacle Peak area by Scottsdale increased the demand for property. This advertisement is from the April 1983 issue of *A Peek at the Peak*, which the GPPHA began publishing a few months earlier. (Courtesy of *The Peak*.)

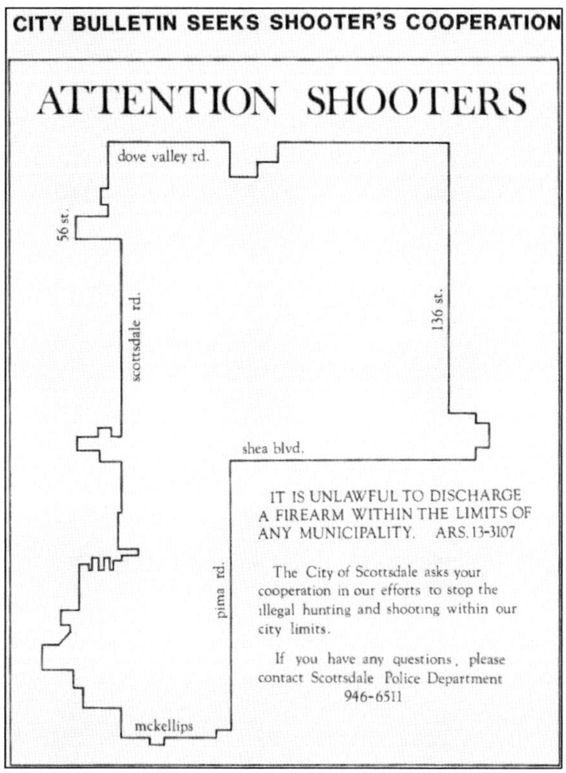

For decades, the remote, undeveloped Pinnacle Peak area had been a popular location for hunting and target practice. Some gun owners were annoyed by Scottsdale's regulations to protect residents and tourists. To assist the city in publicizing the regulations, this notice was published in the May 1984 issue of *A Peek at the Peak*. (Courtesy of *The Peak*.)

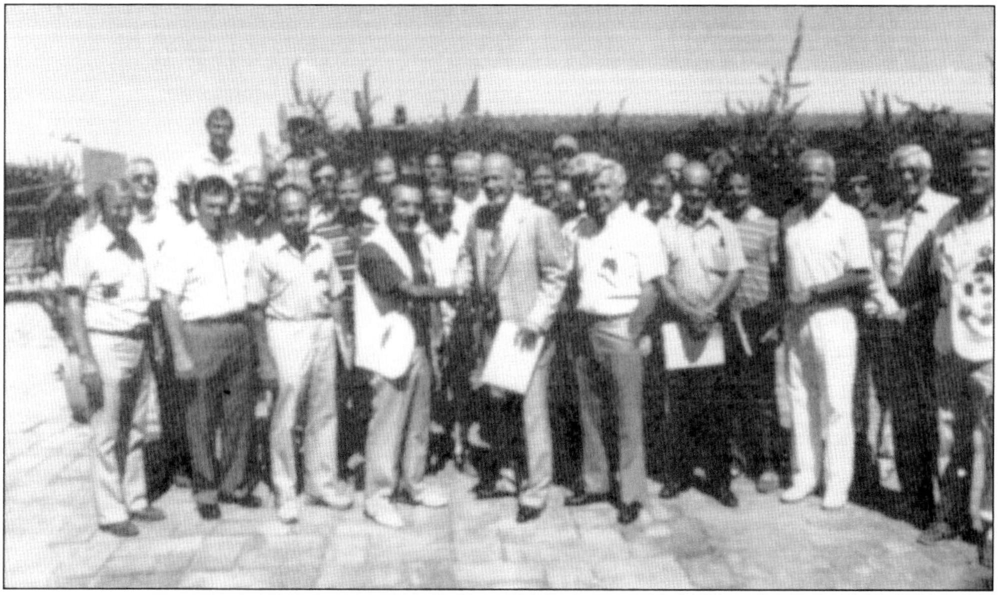

In October 1984, the Pinnacle Peak Lions Club held the three-day Festival of the Nations celebration at Pinnacle Peak Plaza. Mayor Drinkwater spoke, a 1985 Cadillac was raffled off, and guests enjoyed entertainment, ethnic food, and pony rides. In this club photograph from the September 1984 issue of *A Peek at the Peak*, Drinkwater is shown standing in the first row, fifth from left. (Courtesy of *The Peak*.)

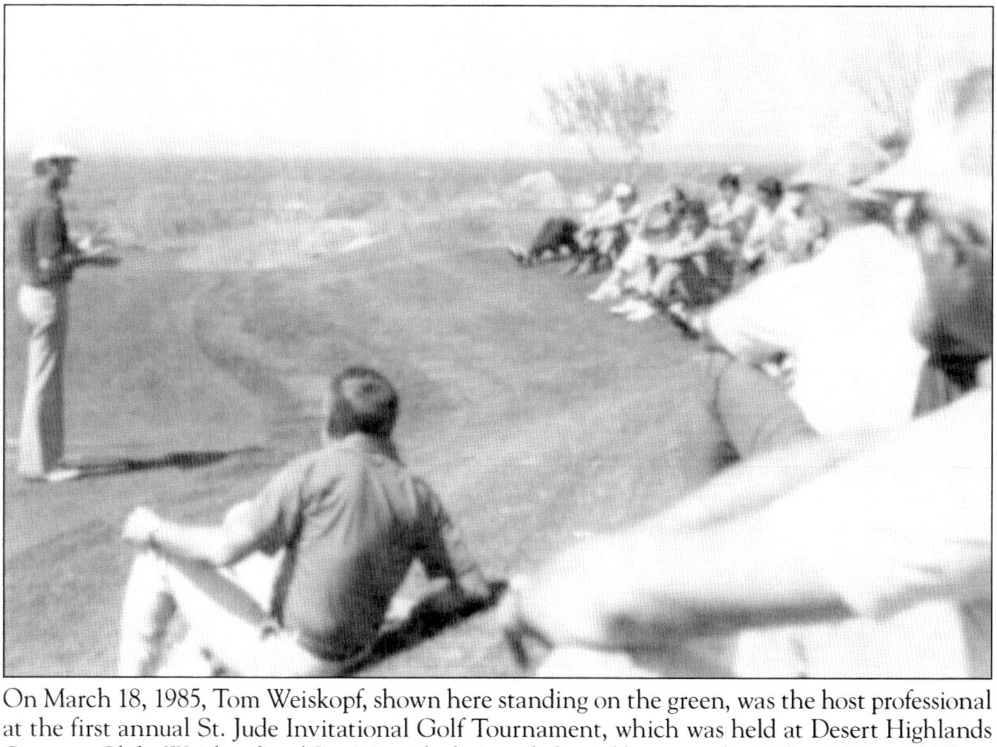

On March 18, 1985, Tom Weiskopf, shown here standing on the green, was the host professional at the first annual St. Jude Invitational Golf Tournament, which was held at Desert Highlands Country Club. Weiskopf and Jay Morrish designed the golf courses for Nelson's Troon Village and Troon North communities. (Courtesy of *The Peak*.)

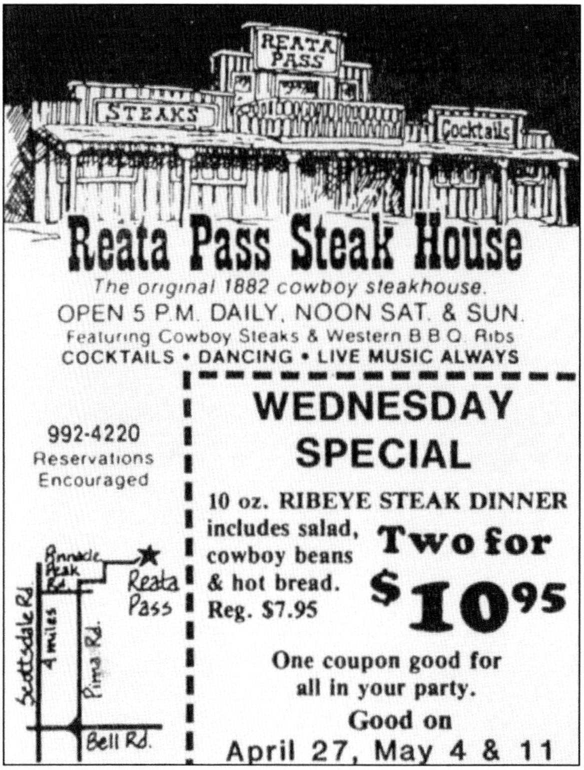

Advertisements in the GPPHA monthly *A Peek at the Peak* reflect the changes that were taking place in the community. It was the only publication serving the area. Liz Stapleton Ogden, the founder and first editor of *The Peak*, produced the inaugural issue in February 1983. The first advertisement was placed by Reata Pass Steakhouse in the March 1983 issue. (Courtesy of *The Peak*.)

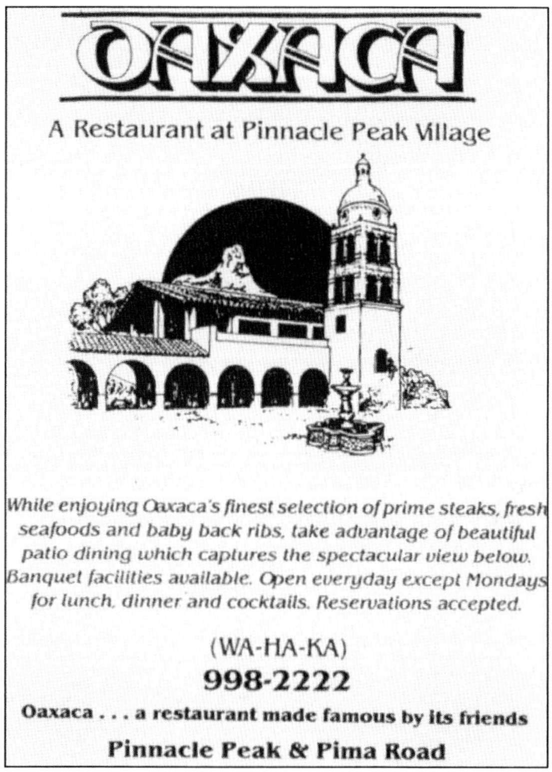

This advertisement appeared in the January 1984 issue of *A Peek at the Peak*. Oaxaca, a favorite restaurant for local residents, was on the second floor of Pinnacle Peak Plaza. Patrons dined on the outside balcony in the evening to enjoy the outstanding views to the south and the southwest. From the balcony, they could see miles of open desert and the night lights of distant downtown Scottsdale and Phoenix. (Courtesy of *The Peak*.)

The Citadel, located on the northeast corner of Pinnacle Peak and Pima Roads, had just opened when it ran this advertisement in the March 1986 issue of *A Peek at the Peak*. (Courtesy of *The Peak*.)

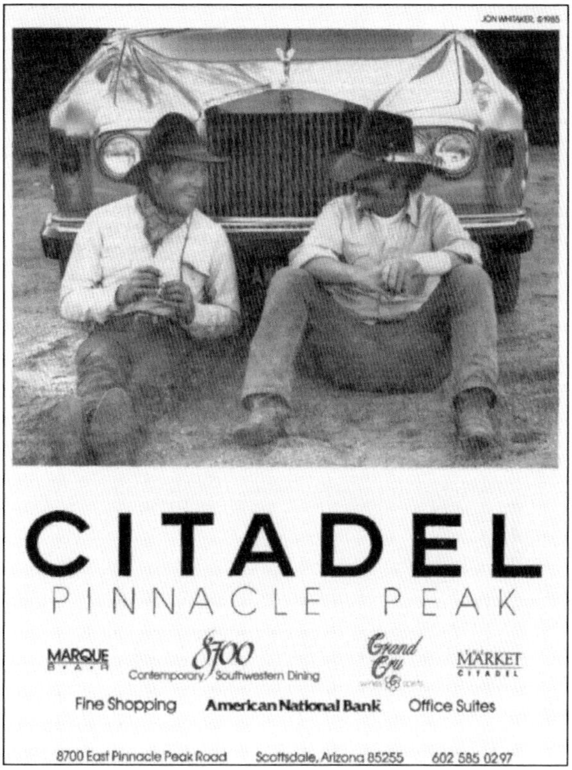

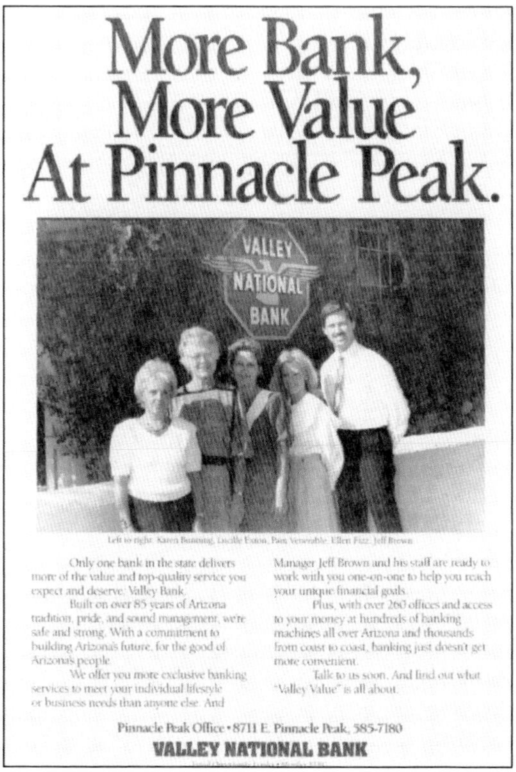

Valley National Bank was Arizona's largest bank when it opened a branch office at Pinnacle Peak Plaza. This advertisement appeared in the December 1986 issue of *A Peek at the Peak*. Ironically, before he discovered water, Jerry Nelson had applied for a loan from the bank in Phoenix to buy Pinnacle Peak land. He was told there would be no development in the area before 2000. (Courtesy of *The Peak*.)

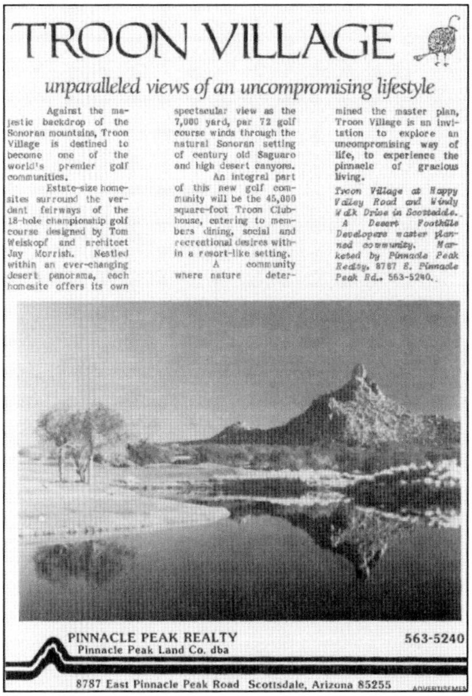

In 1985, Jerry Nelson began building Troon Village, a 2,655-acre community anchored by Troon Golf and Country Club. It cost Nelson's company $1 million to remove the cacti from the course's site and replant them after construction. Nelson incurred additional expenses when his crew discovered an ancient Hohokam settlement on the land he was developing. The construction project was temporarily halted, and the archeological site was excavated and studied. This advertisement is from the February 1986 issue of *A Peek at the Peak*. (Courtesy of *The Peak*.)

When Pinnacle Peak residents had visitors from out of town, they would often take them to Rawhide to enjoy the sights on Main Street and perhaps a meal at the Golden Belle Restaurant. This advertisement was published in the February 1986 issue of *A Peek at the Peak*. (Courtesy of *The Peak*.)

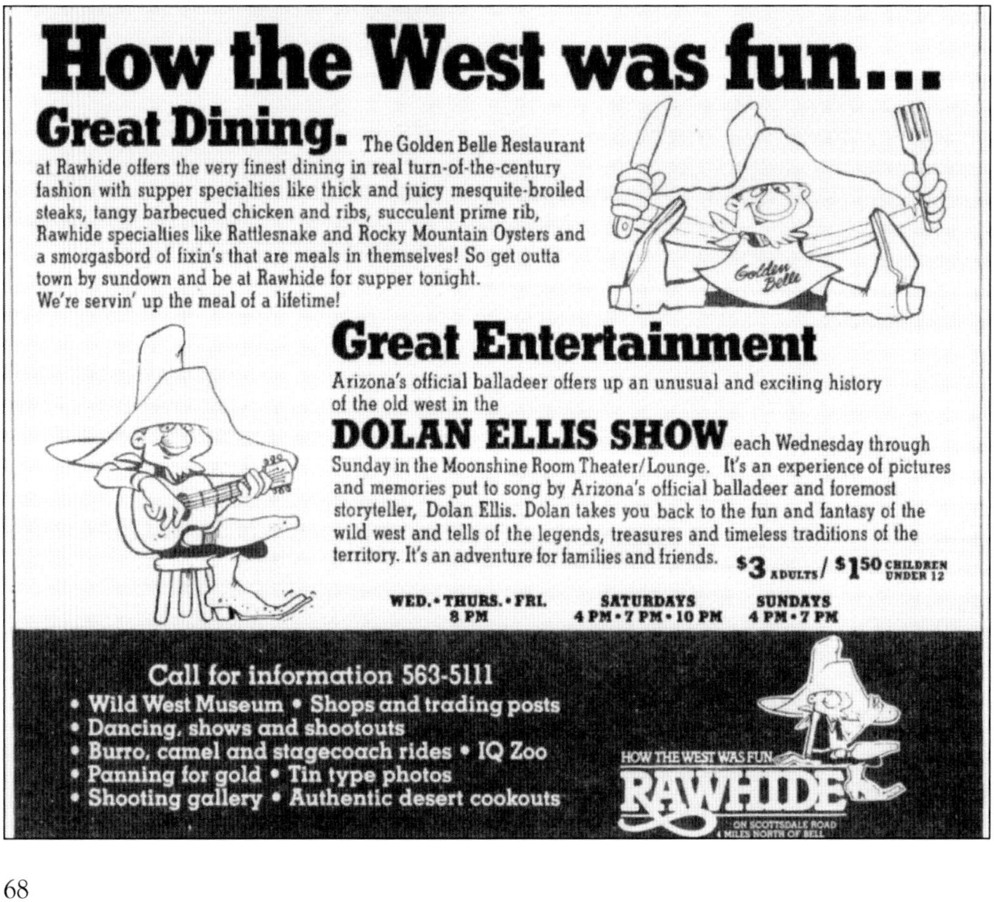

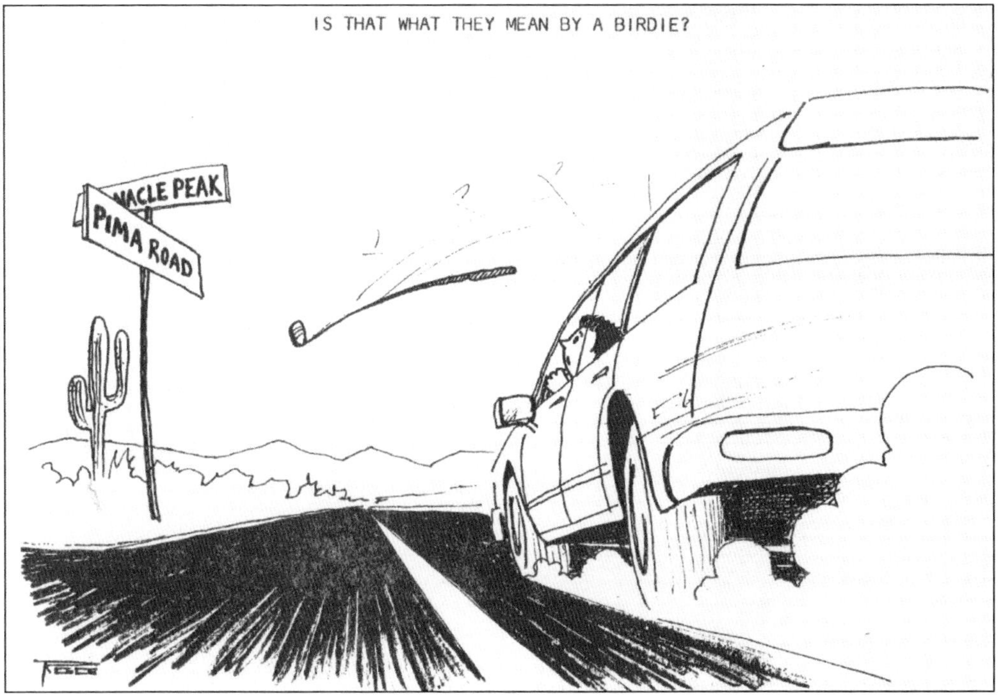

This cartoon appears in the May 1987 issue of *A Peek at the Peak*. The number of golf courses in the Pinnacle Peak area was increasing and included those at Pinnacle Peak Country Club, Desert Highlands, and Troon Village. Evidently, this birdie was from someone playing at Pinnacle Peak Country Club, which is located on land near the intersection of Pima and Pinnacle Peak Roads. (Courtesy of *The Peak*.)

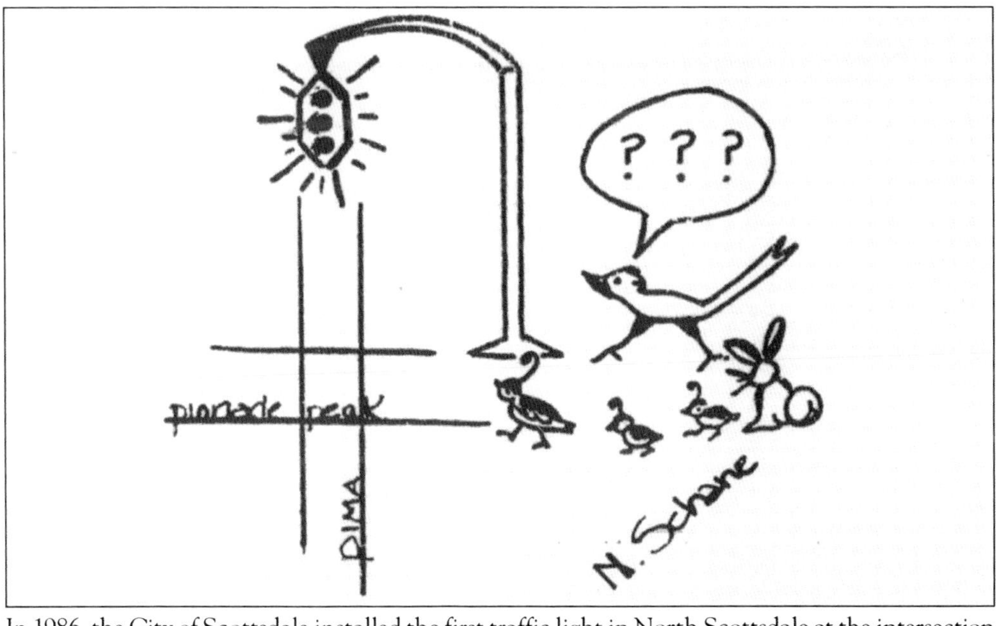

In 1986, the City of Scottsdale installed the first traffic light in North Scottsdale at the intersection of Pinnacle Peak and Pima Roads. This cartoon, published in the June 1986 issue of *A Peek at the Peak*, notes the event. (Courtesy of *The Peak*.)

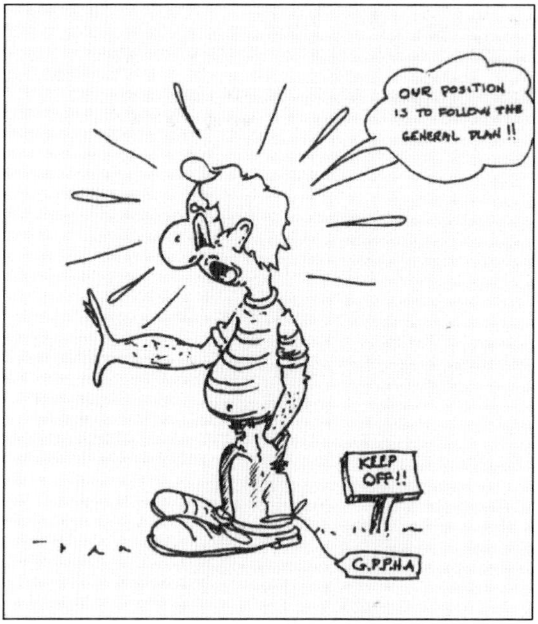

Under the leadership of the GPPHA, Pinnacle Peak residents were actively engaged in the development of the Pinnacle Peak area. GPPHA members attended City of Scottsdale planning meetings at city hall, and developers presented their plans to board members for feedback. Development plans and commentaries, including this March 1989 cartoon, were published in *A Peek at the Peak*. (Courtesy of *The Peak*.)

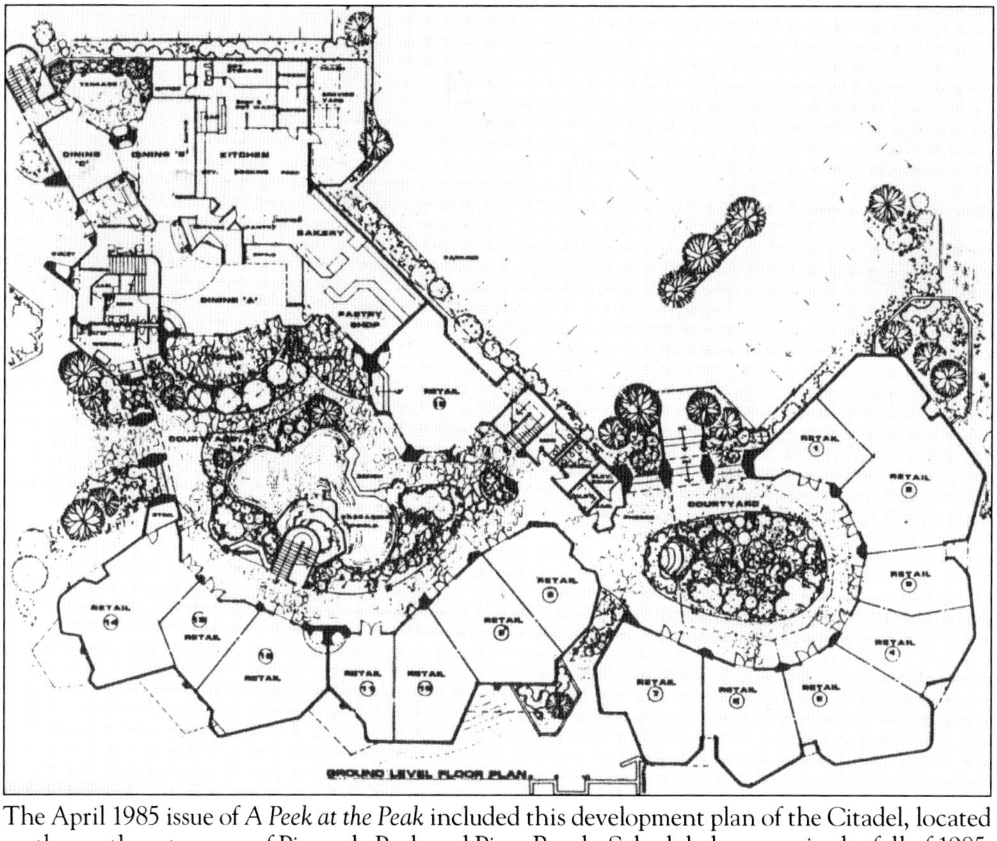

The April 1985 issue of *A Peek at the Peak* included this development plan of the Citadel, located on the northwest corner of Pinnacle Peak and Pima Roads. Scheduled to open in the fall of 1985, the Citadel was designed by Scottsdale's Vernon Swaback and Associates. Plans included a bank, restaurant, and a variety of shops. (Courtesy of *The Peak*.)

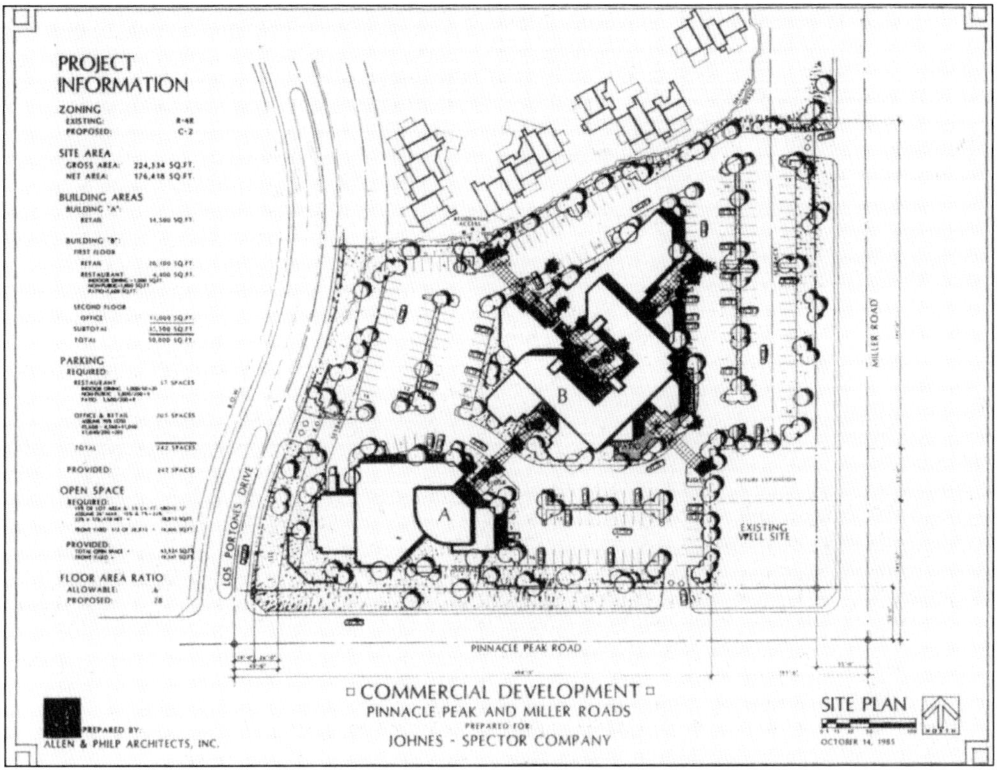

On January 27, 1986, at the annual meeting of the GPPHA at the Pinnacle Peak Country Club, Al Spector, president of Johnes & Spector Development Corporation, described the company's plans for a 40,000-to-50,000-square-foot retail center on the corner of Pinnacle Peak and Miller Roads. The plans included patio homes, townhouses, and small single-family homes on the adjacent land. (Courtesy of *The Peak*.)

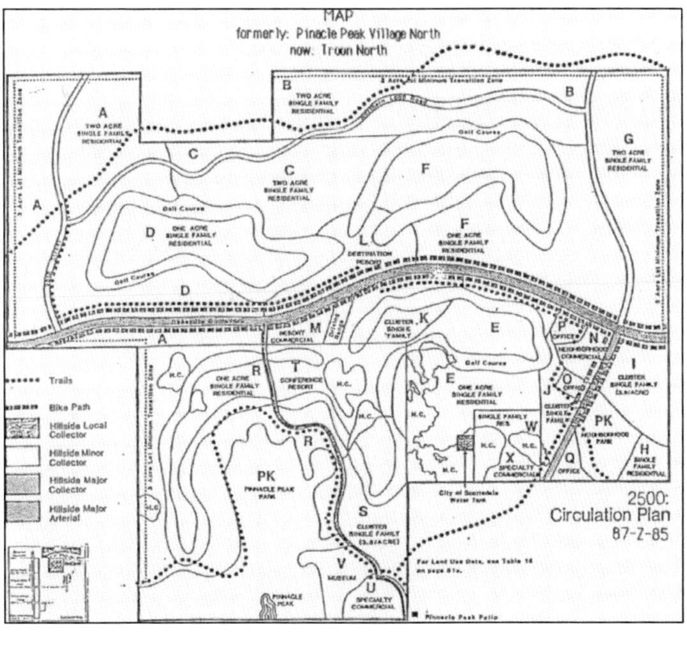

In 1989, Nelson broke ground for Troon North, straddling Dynamite Boulevard between Pima Road and Alma School Parkway. The plan for Troon North included parks, schools, two golf courses, a resort, and several types of living quarters. The plan shown here was published in the August 1989 issue of *A Peek at the Peak*. (Courtesy of *The Peak*.)

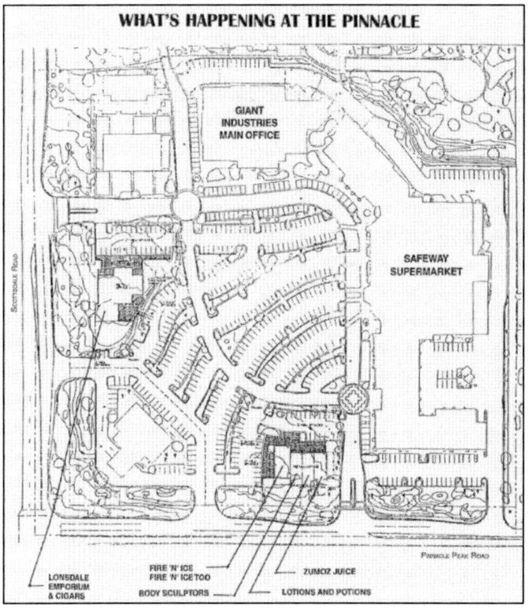

The February 1996 issue of *A Peek at the Peak* provided information about the upcoming completion of two new retail buildings in the Pinnacle of Scottsdale Shopping Center, which is located at Pinnacle Peak and Scottsdale Roads. The shopping center's core was developed in 1991 on the parcel occupied in the 1950s by Don Pablo's House of Relics. (Courtesy of *The Peak*.)

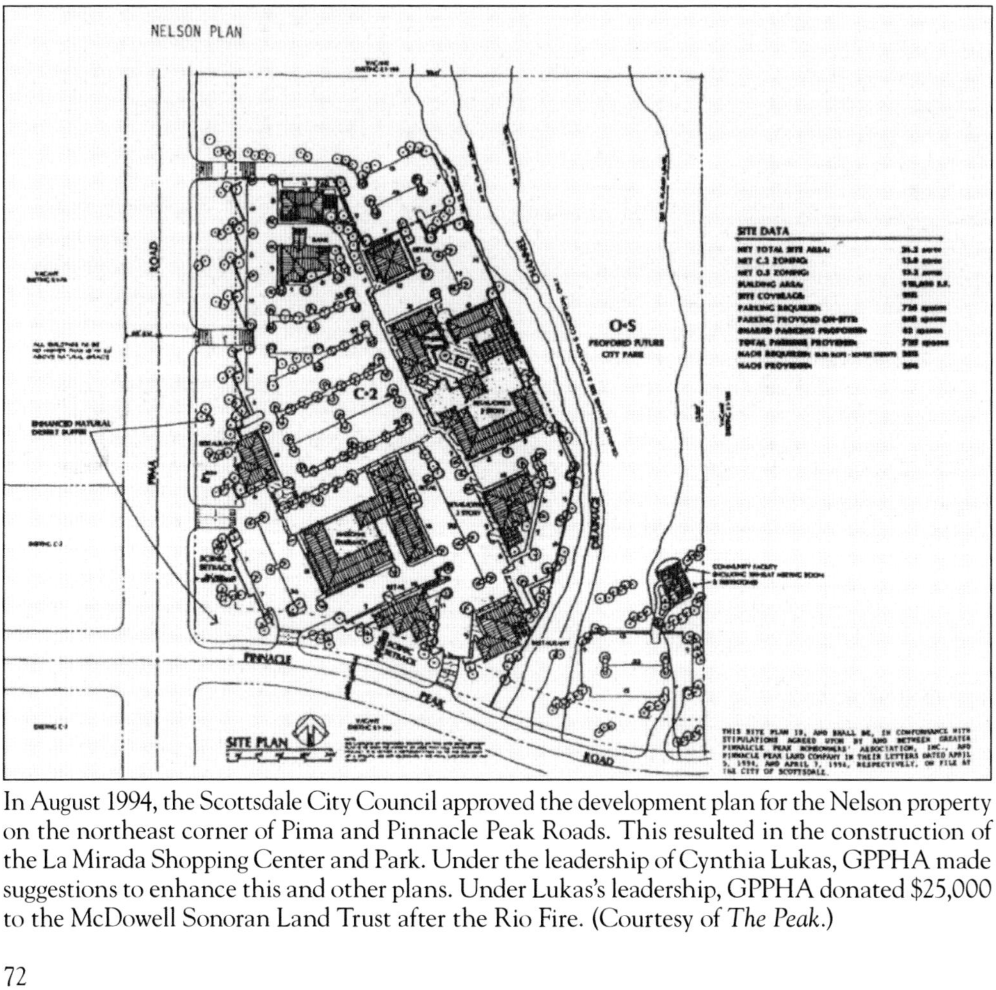

In August 1994, the Scottsdale City Council approved the development plan for the Nelson property on the northeast corner of Pima and Pinnacle Peak Roads. This resulted in the construction of the La Mirada Shopping Center and Park. Under the leadership of Cynthia Lukas, GPPHA made suggestions to enhance this and other plans. Under Lukas's leadership, GPPHA donated $25,000 to the McDowell Sonoran Land Trust after the Rio Fire. (Courtesy of *The Peak*.)

In the 1970s, Florence Nelson began visiting schools and presenting information about desert survival and stewardship. In the 1980s, her program began operating from the Desert Center, located in Pinnacle Peak Plaza. Busloads of elementary school children arrived, were given a presentation on the desert, and then visited four stations that offered information on rocks, animals, Native Americans, and plants. (Courtesy of *The Peak*.)

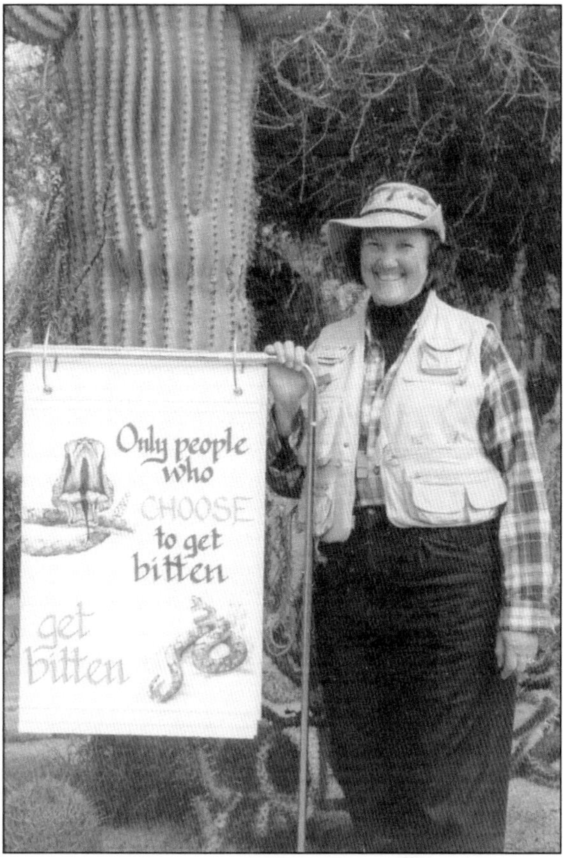

The October 1997 issue of *A Peek at the Peak* published this photograph with the caption, "Florence Nelson, Director (far left), Donna Ropp, Volunteer Coordinator (fifth from left), and Sue Livingston, Operations Manager (ninth from left), gather with volunteers at the Desert Center. Photo by Becky Cooke." After La Mirada opened, the program began using the park's facilities. (Courtesy of *The Peak*.)

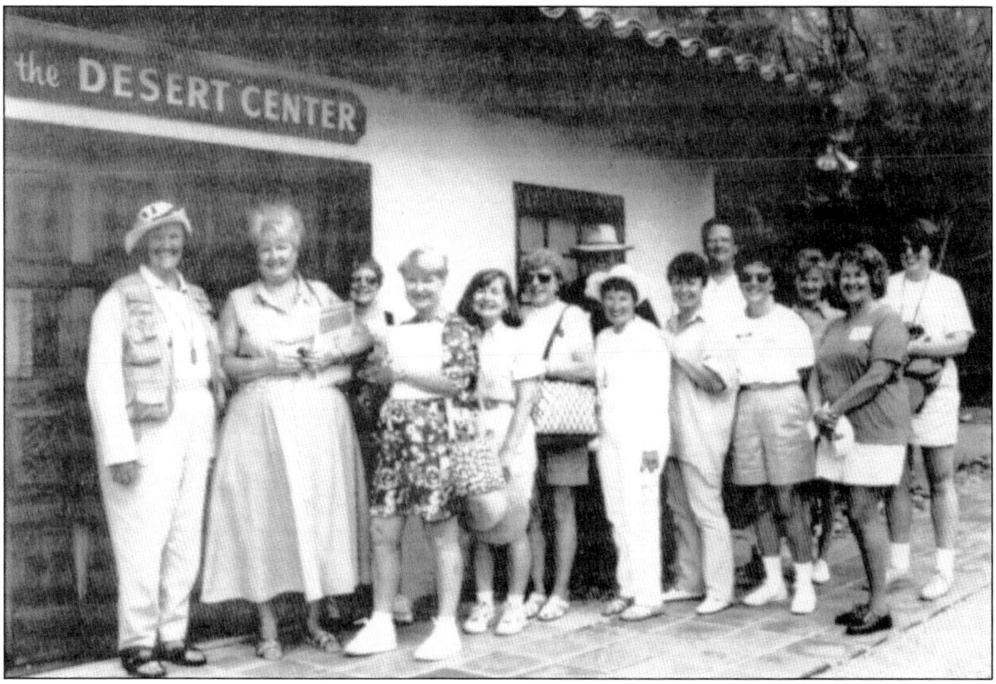

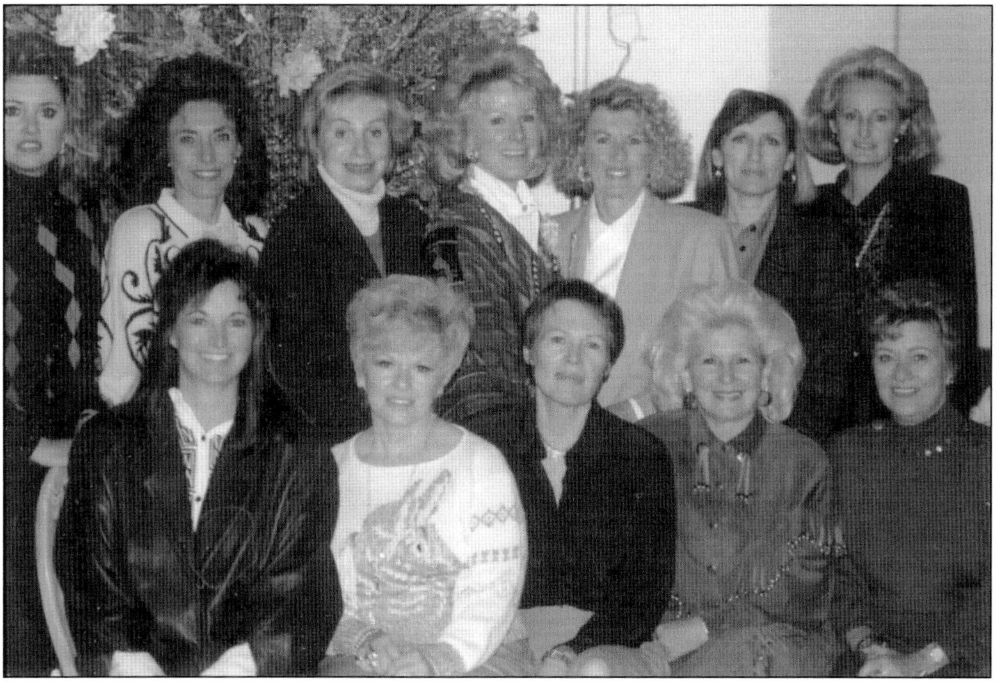

In 1991, the Creative Women of Pinnacle Peak (CWPP) held its first meeting. Attending the meeting are, from left to right, (first row) Mona Schooley, Darlene Johnson, Sherry Stuart, Polly Reed, and Beverly Holquist; (second row) Roni Dalton, Penny Bradley, Marcia Harrison, Sheila Walsch, Betty Lee, Nancy Brinton, and Joan Tuttle. The women were all residents of North Scottsdale. (Courtesy of CWPP.)

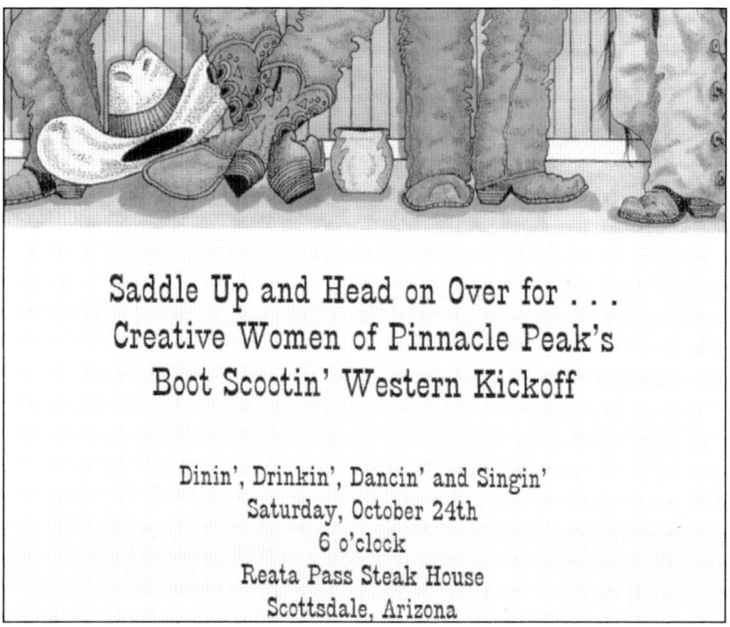

The 1991 spring edition of *Scottsdale Magazine* reported, "Education, charity, fellowship, and support were the motives that sparked the first meeting of the CWPP. The organization's members are residents of North Scottsdale." The group planned to hold a monthly meeting and an annual fundraiser. This promotional piece was created for one of the group's first fundraisers. (Courtesy of CWPP.)

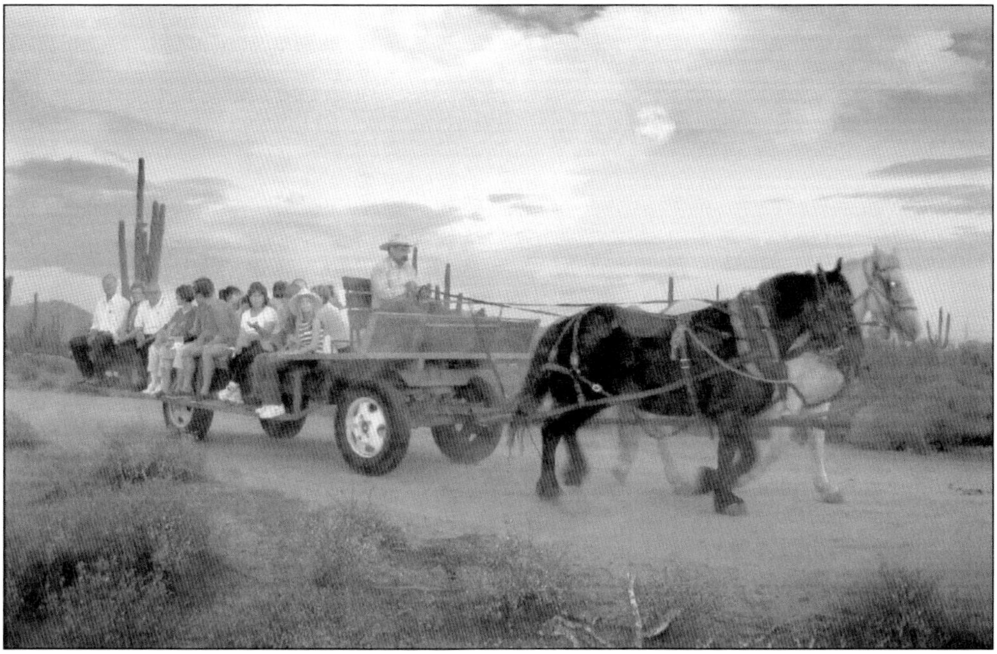

Guests at the Cookout at the Ranch IX event rode a wagon to the desert cookout site in October 2004. The inaugural cookout was held in June 1996 and organized by Friends of the Scenic Drive, the Scottsdale Pride Committee, Outback Steakhouse, MacDonald's Ranch, and Desert Foothills Cookouts to promote the Desert Foothills Scenic Drive and desert preservation. (Courtesy of Dennis Liddell.)

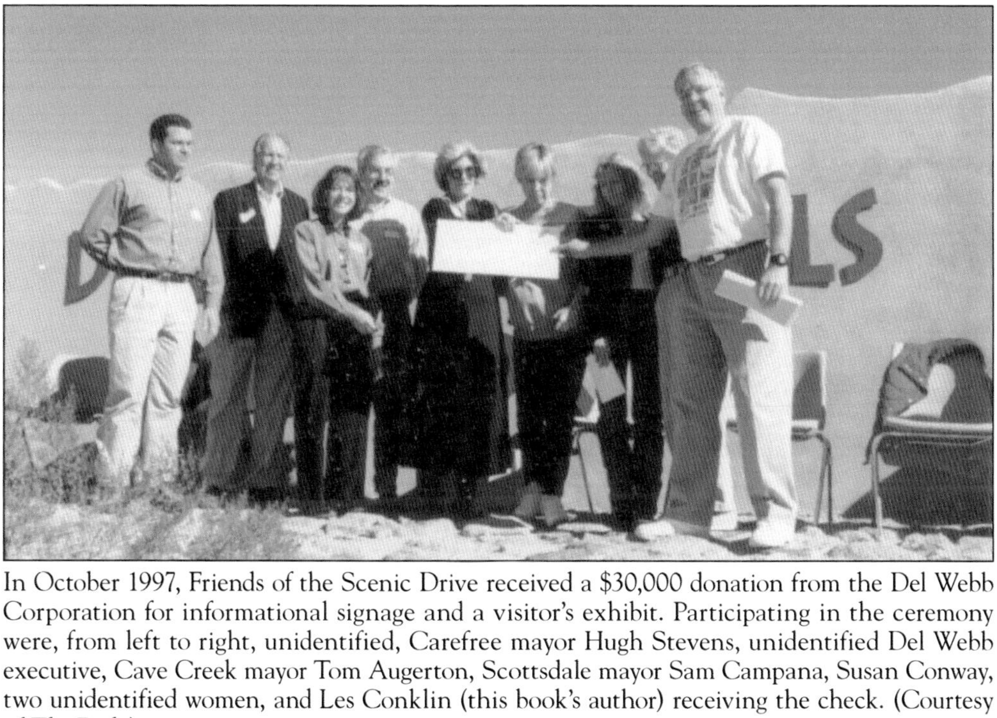

In October 1997, Friends of the Scenic Drive received a $30,000 donation from the Del Webb Corporation for informational signage and a visitor's exhibit. Participating in the ceremony were, from left to right, unidentified, Carefree mayor Hugh Stevens, unidentified Del Webb executive, Cave Creek mayor Tom Augerton, Scottsdale mayor Sam Campana, Susan Conway, two unidentified women, and Les Conklin (this book's author) receiving the check. (Courtesy of *The Peak*.)

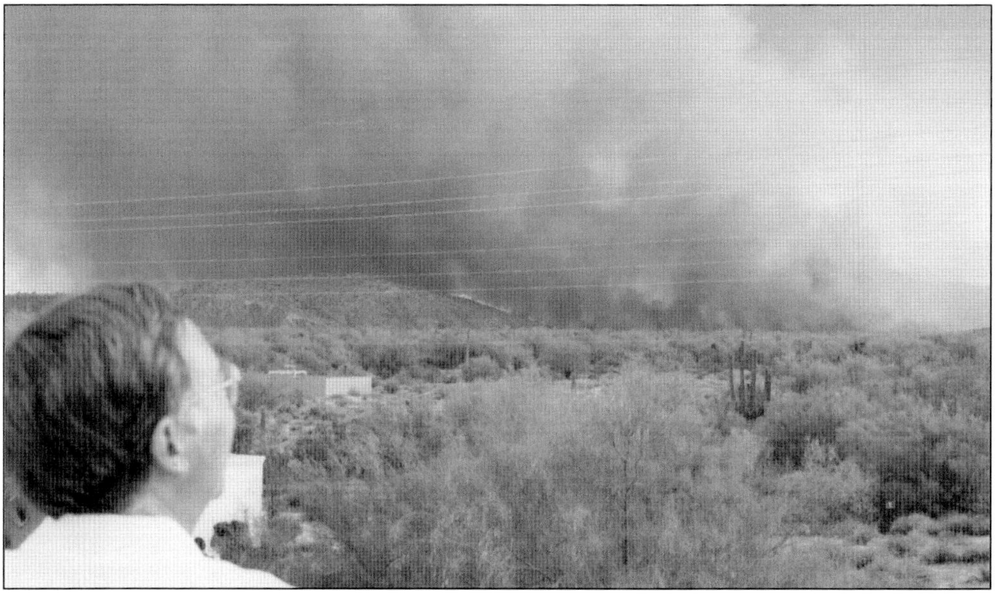

Late in the afternoon of July 7, 1995, a dry thunderstorm hit the Pinnacle Peak area. A bolt of lightning struck the desert less than two miles north of the mountain. This photograph was taken several miles west of the peak from the author's home. Approximately 45 minutes after the fire started, Pinnacle Peak is completely enveloped by smoke from the fire. (Courtesy of Les Conklin.)

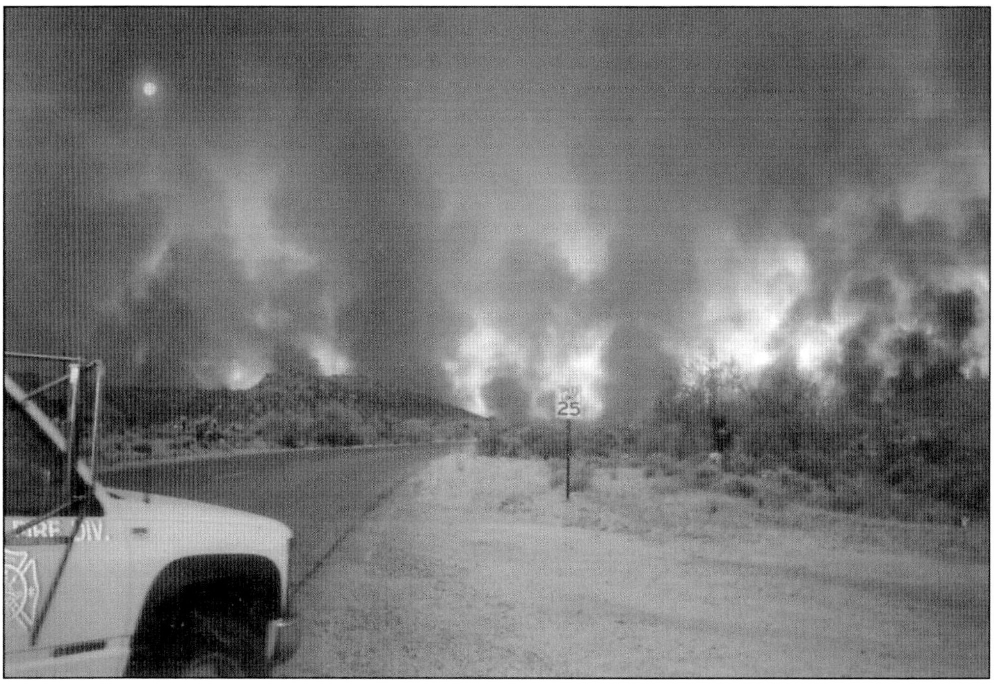

Dry grass was ignited by the lightning strike. No cattle had grazed the area for several years, and the tall, dry grass covered the desert like a blanket of kindling. Winds quickly carried the fire to the south and southeast. The quick actions of firefighters saved Greasewood Flat, Reata Pass Steakhouse, and homes in the Pinnacle Peak area. (Courtesy of the Scottsdale Historical Society.)

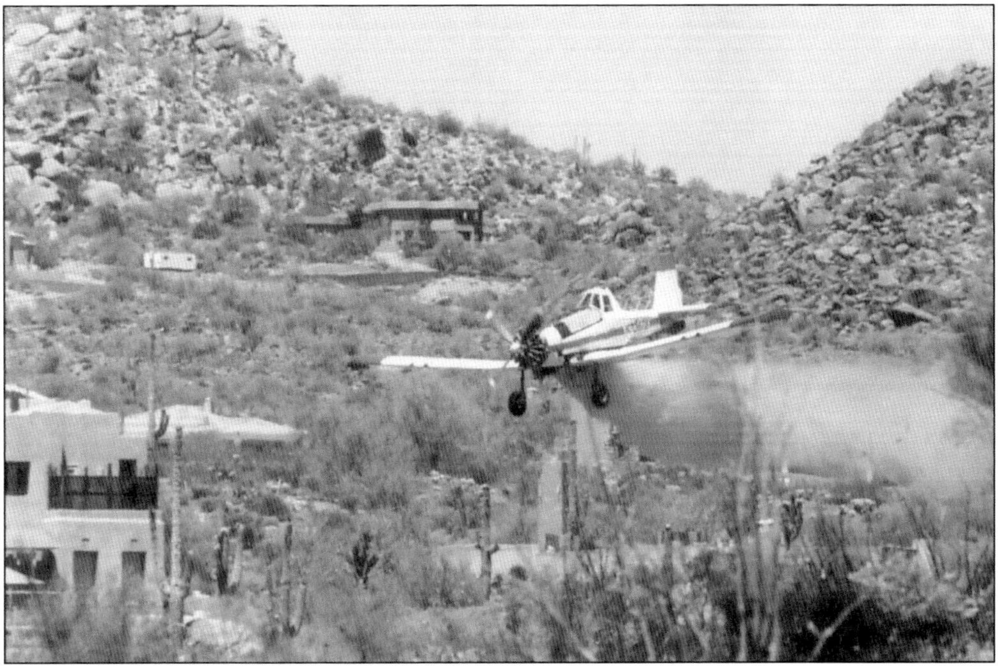

Helicopters, spotter and tanker planes, and more than 500 firefighters battled the blaze for three days. This plane is dropping flame retardant east of Pinnacle Peak to create a barrier between the fire and the homes. Residents watched from Pima Road as tankers made a successful effort to keep the fire from spreading to the west side of the McDowell Mountains. (Courtesy of the Scottsdale Historical Society.)

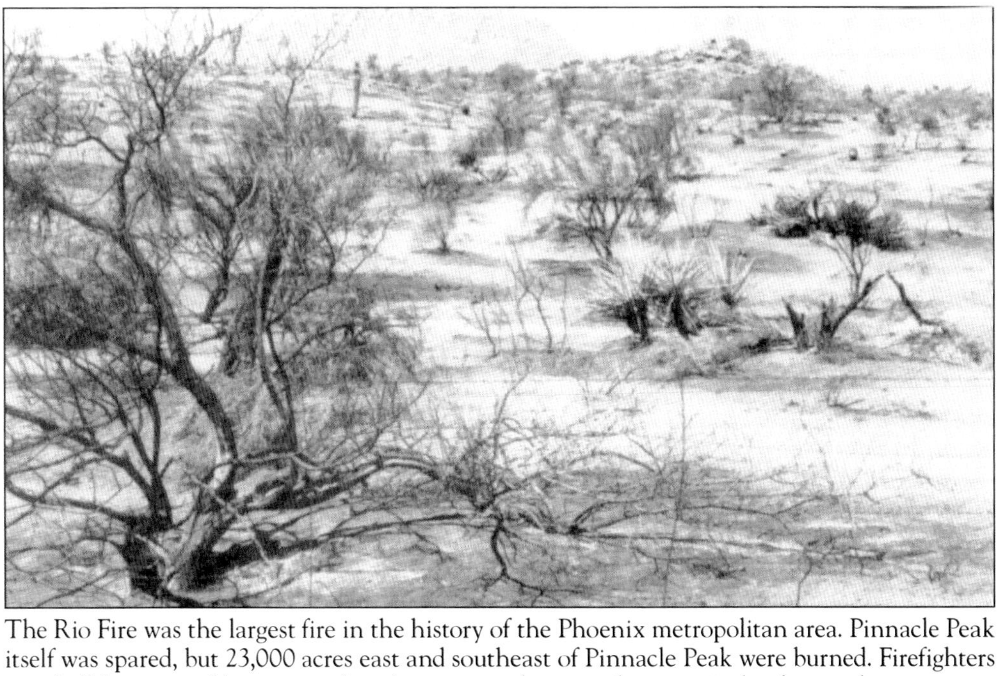

The Rio Fire was the largest fire in the history of the Phoenix metropolitan area. Pinnacle Peak itself was spared, but 23,000 acres east and southeast of Pinnacle Peak were burned. Firefighters saved all homes and businesses, but the pristine desert and mountain landscape that was once vibrant with birds and animals was charred and silent. (Courtesy of *The Peak*.)

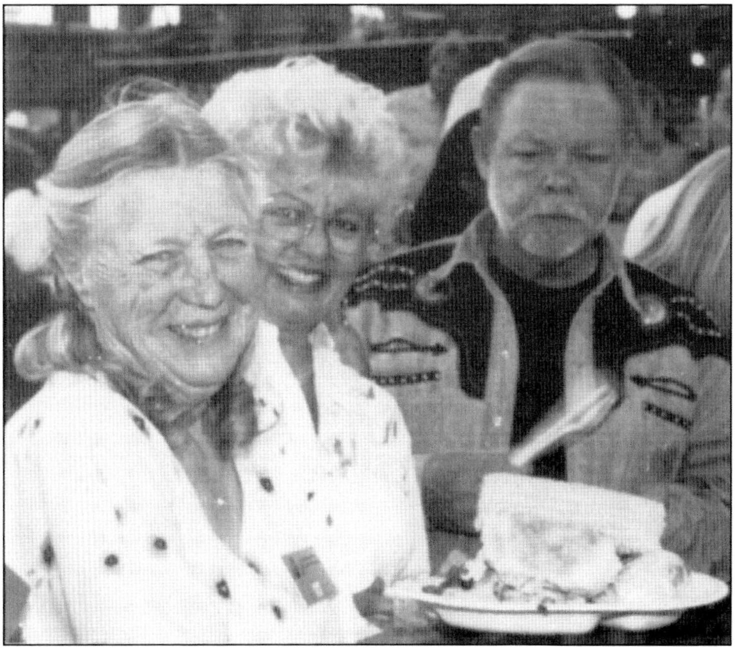

From left to right, Jane Rau, Barbara Copeland, and Bill Copeland are among the 1,100 residents attending the Rio Fire Fighters Appreciation Dinner at Reata Pass Steakhouse on September 24, 1995. Bob and Rachel Paradis, along with Don Schoenau and others from GPPHA and elsewhere, arranged the dinner. (Courtesy of *The Peak*.)

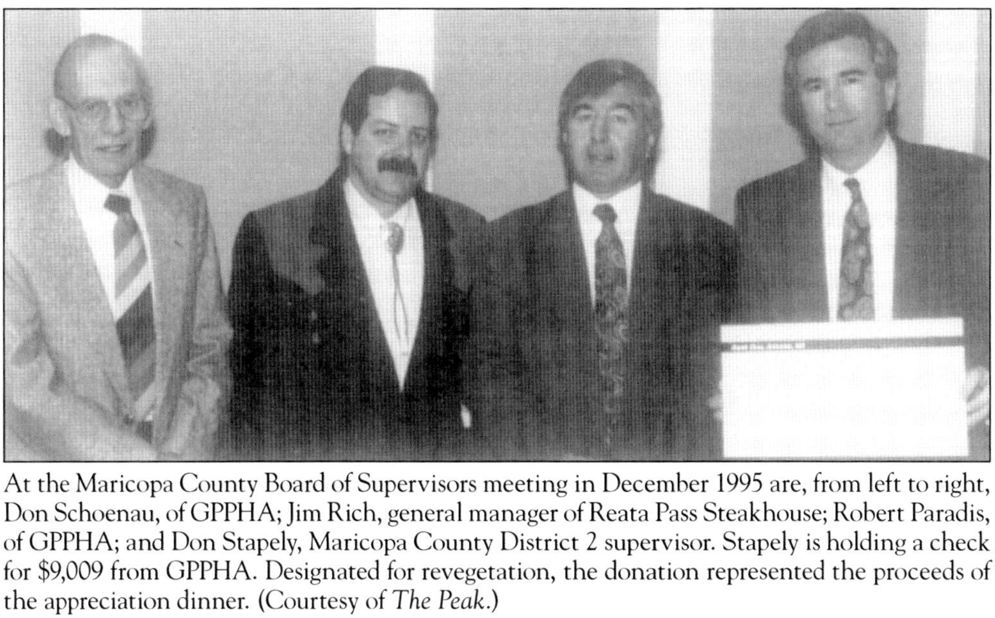

At the Maricopa County Board of Supervisors meeting in December 1995 are, from left to right, Don Schoenau, of GPPHA; Jim Rich, general manager of Reata Pass Steakhouse; Robert Paradis, of GPPHA; and Don Stapely, Maricopa County District 2 supervisor. Stapely is holding a check for $9,009 from GPPHA. Designated for revegetation, the donation represented the proceeds of the appreciation dinner. (Courtesy of *The Peak*.)

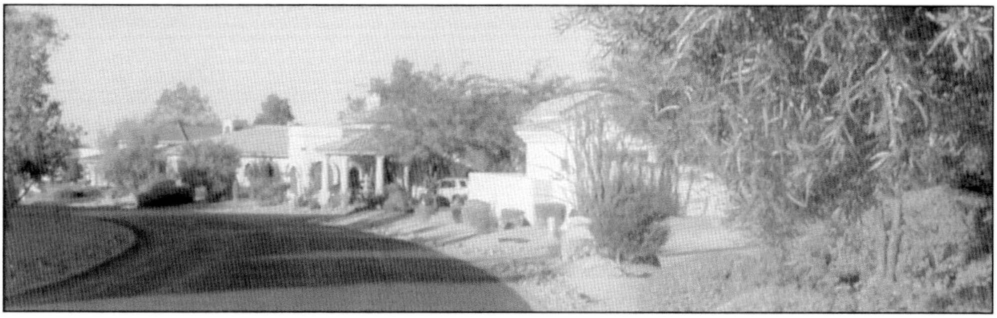

Developed in the late 1970s, Pinnacle Peak Country Club Estates was one of the first residential neighborhoods developed in the Pinnacle Peak area. This photograph, taken in 2000, provides evidence that the neighborhood has withstood the test of time. (Courtesy of *The Peak*.)

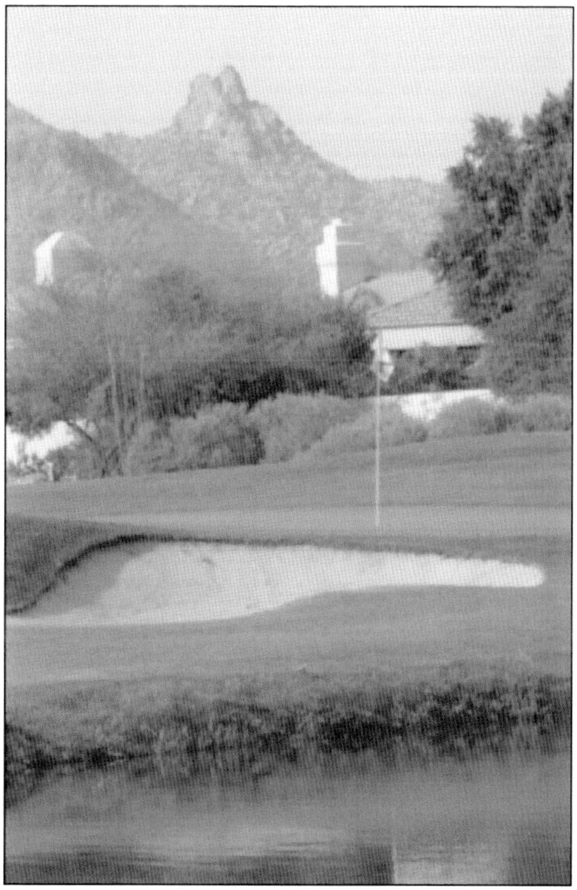

This photograph, taken in 2000, shows the 18th hole of the golf course at Pinnacle Peak Country Club Estates. (Courtesy of the Pinnacle Peak Country Club.)

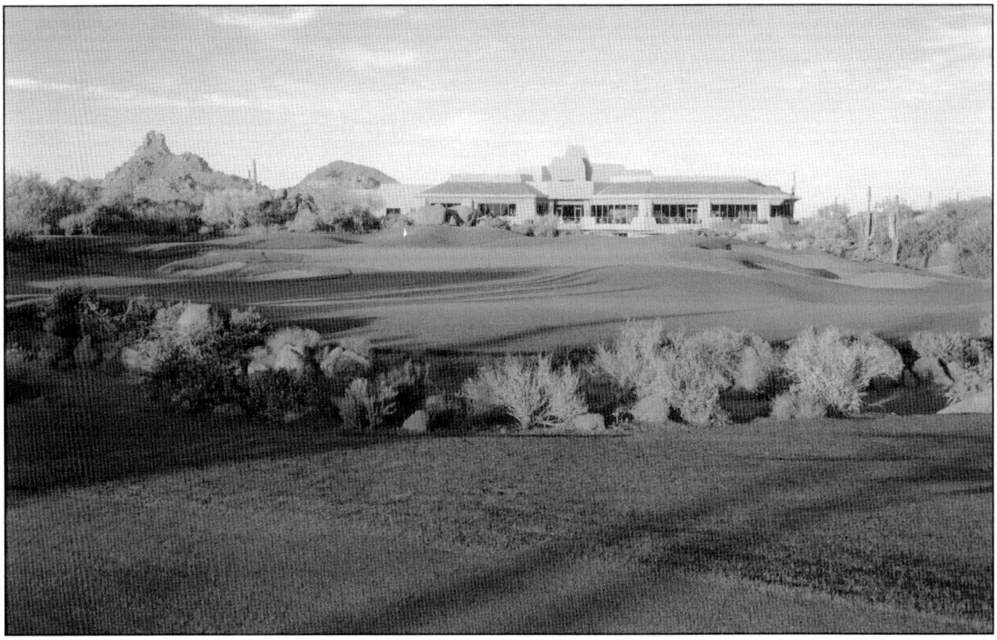

Development of Troon North began in 1989. The Troon North Golf Club opened in 1990 during the spring. The 35,000-square-foot clubhouse, pictured here, opened in 1991. Troon North Golf Club is part of a 1,800-acre master-planned resort and residential community. The community included plans for the Four Seasons Resort Scottsdale and the Pinnacle Peak Municipal Park. (Courtesy of the Troon North Golf Club.)

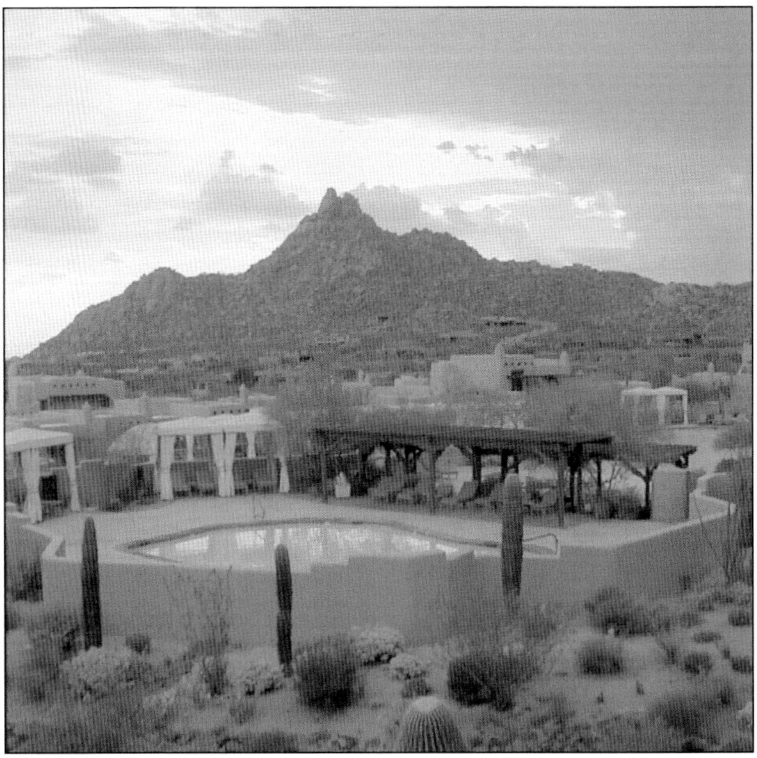

The Four Seasons Resort Scottsdale at Troon North is approximately one mile from Pinnacle Peak on the former site of the Crescent Moon Ranch. The 40-acre, 210-room resort opened in 1991. During its construction, all plants taller than three feet were removed, tagged, stored, and nurtured for over two years. Upon completion of the resort, the plants were replaced as close as possible to their original locations. (Courtesy of *The Peak*.)

Five

Pinnacle Peak Park Is Born

For many years, Pinnacle Peak, Pinnacle Peak Patio, Reata Pass Steakhouse, and Greasewood Flat had been favorite destinations for residents and tourists. As growth surged northward, calls for the creation of a park that included Pinnacle Peak increased. Creating a park, however, was no simple matter.

Pinnacle Peak and a majority of the surrounding land was Arizona State Trust Land, which was held by the state and managed for the benefit of the state's educational trust. From a practical standpoint, this usually meant that trust land must be sold and not given away, and if sold, the buyer would usually be the highest bidder. In urban areas, the highest bidders were often developers rather than local governments.

In 1982, a large area of land that included Pinnacle Peak was annexed into Scottsdale. Once the land was annexed, a series of steps choreographed by the State of Arizona, developers, the City of Scottsdale, and the surrounding community resulted in the opening of a City of Scottsdale municipal park that included Pinnacle Peak and the adjacent Red Face Mountain.

Pinnacle Peak Park opened on April 20, 2002. The same year, the City of Scottsdale received the Arizona Parks and Recreation Association's Natural Resources Award for creating the park. The award also cited the city's use of volunteers and fiscal responsibility. The citation states:

> Native granite boulders were used in the construction of the building walls and the retaining walls along the trail. The parking lot at the trailhead is composed of native, stabilized decomposed granite in order to reduce heat retention and to better blend into the surrounding desert. Much of the trailhead site was left undisturbed in accordance with Scottsdale's strict native plant and environmental ordinances. All landscaped areas were planted with species indigenous to the area, and the major wash corridor through the trailhead was left undisturbed.

PROTECT THE PEAK

GUEST EDITORIAL

by Mary Lou Torosian

Now that Scottsdale has adopted the Master Plan for the Northeast Section, it would seem this is an appropriate time for the City to purchase Pinnacle Peak.

The purchase will assure that Pinnacle Peak, with it's surrounding foothills, will remain in its natural state.

Since the state seems to be in a selling mood and the developers in a buying mood, quick action by the City would eliminate the possibility of this historic landmark being put on the auction block.

The desert is quickly disappearing as the lust for development and money grows. It would benefit all of us to encourage the City Fathers to act now.

The purchase of this natural, botanical wonderland with winding footpaths and equestrian trails would assure future generations the oportunity to enjoy the beautiful Sonoran desert and her majestic grandeur.

For many years, residents of the Pinnacle Peak area and government officials had discussed the need to preserve Pinnacle Peak. The October 1984 issue of *A Peek at the Peak* contained an editorial written by Mary Torosian, a member of the GPPHA. Torosian's editorial expressed feelings that were shared by many residents. (Courtesy of *The Peak*.)

THE PEAK MAY BE A PARK

On March 1st, Ralph and Nancy Knight met with Mr. Robert Lane, State Land Commissioner; Christin Laraway, Manager of Urban Planning, State Land Department; Larry Landry, Consultant; and Dudley Onderdonk and Larry Bussard of the City of Scottsdale Planning Department.

The State Land Department is eager to establish a City Park on the Pinnacle Peak site. It was suggested by Mr. Lane that the State Land Department would designate the Pinnacle Peak Site as a park on the plan being developed. The successful bidder at the State Land Auction would then be required to donate this park area to the City of Scottsdale. The developer would be able to transfer the density from this park site to the balance of the area purchased and planned.

It is important that we continue to obtain signatures on our petitions to present to the City and State at the Planning and Zoning sessions being held by both.

The March 1985 issue of *A Peek at the Peak* informed residents of an important meeting that had taken place between representatives of the GPPHA, the City of Scottsdale, and the state. At the meeting, state officials indicated a desire to work with Scottsdale to create a municipal park at Pinnacle Peak. (Courtesy of *The Peak*.)

In conjunction with the state and City of Scottsdale, Jerry Nelson's (pictured) company master-planned the state trust land that included Pinnacle Peak. In 1985, Nelson's Troon North plan was approved by the Scottsdale City Council. The plan included the preservation of Pinnacle Peak as a 185-acre City of Scottsdale Park. (Courtesy of the Estancia Club.)

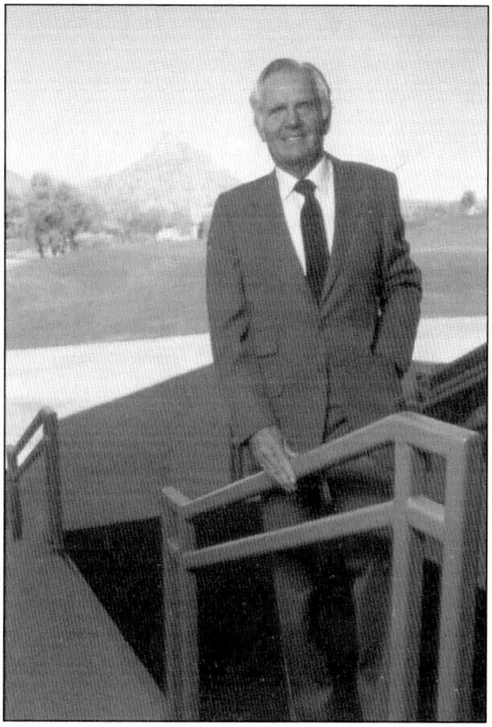

Nelson's Troon North plan included this 640-acre parcel south of Dynamite Boulevard. The development was to include hotel rooms, homes, shopping, golf, and a public park on Pinnacle Peak. In April 1989, Pinnacle Peak Partners purchased the parcel at a state land auction for just over $15.2 million. Jerry Nelson owned 20 percent of Pinnacle Peak Partners. (Courtesy of the Estancia Club.)

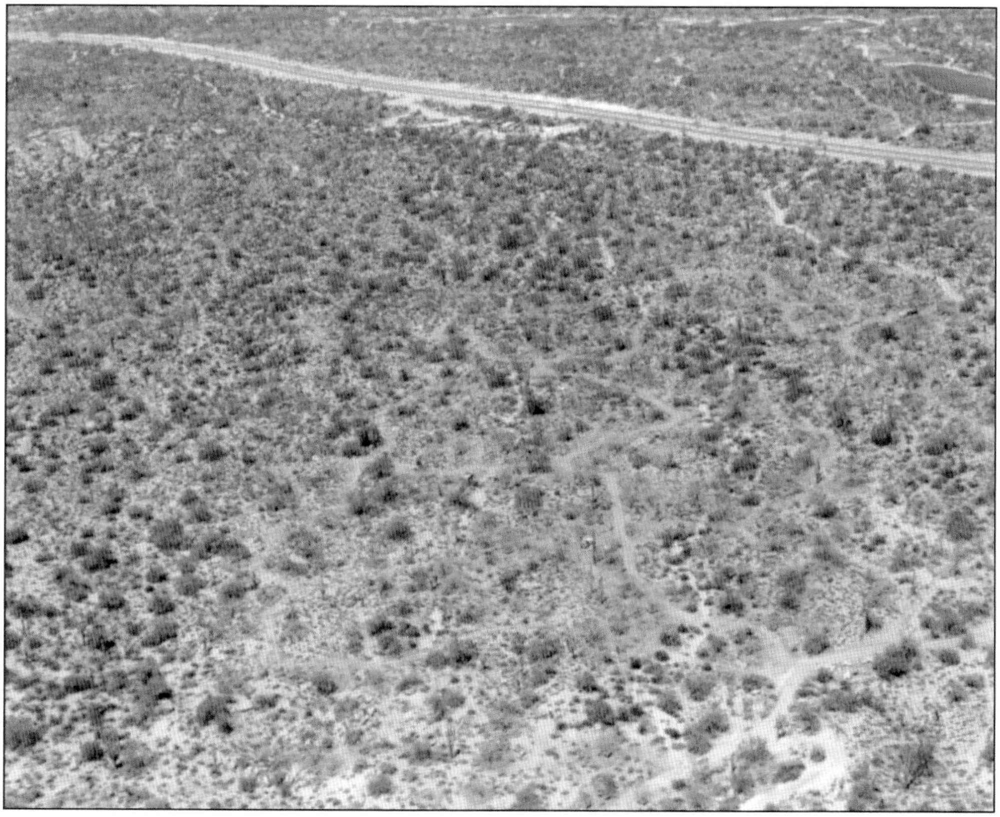

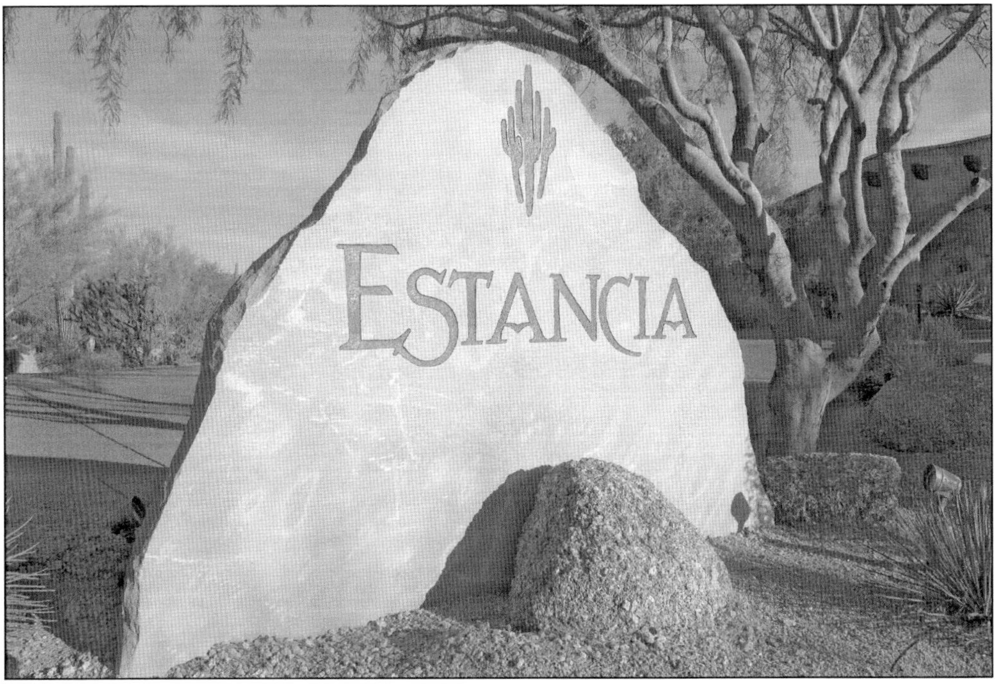

After a series of corporate and financial transactions, some of which involved negotiations with the State Land Department and City of Scottsdale, plans for the Estancia community evolved. In 1994, the site of future Pinnacle Peak Park was reduced from 185 to 150 acres. Because of this, Estancia's developer offered to pay for and develop the primary Pinnacle Peak trail. (Courtesy of the Estancia Club.)

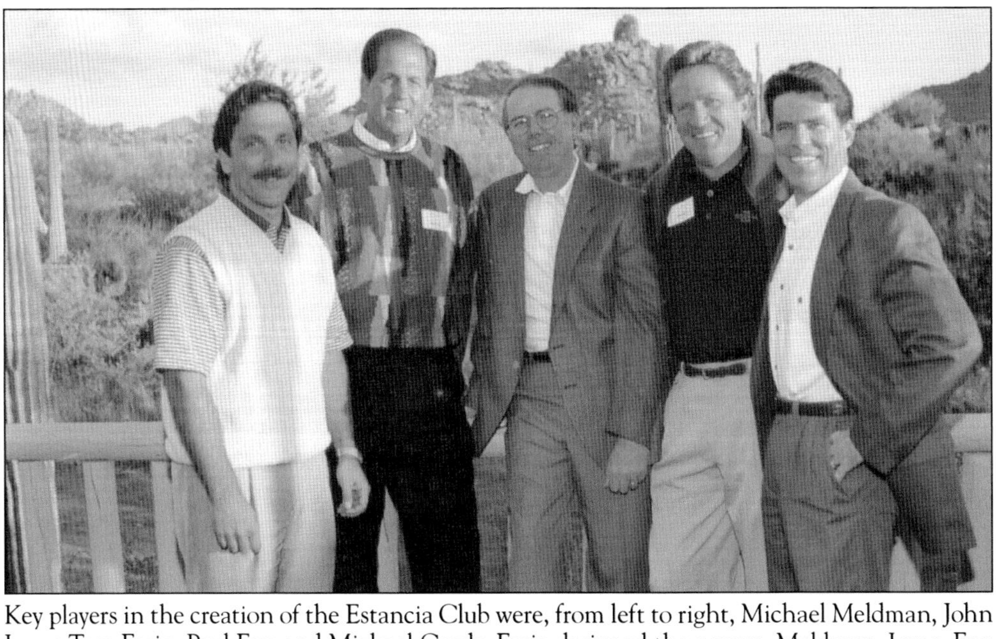

Key players in the creation of the Estancia Club were, from left to right, Michael Meldman, John Lang, Tom Fazio, Paul Fay, and Michael Grady. Fazio designed the course. Meldman, Lang, Fay, and Grady are considered founders of Estancia. Beginning in 1987, Lang was a constant force in the development of Estancia. (Courtesy of the Estancia Club.)

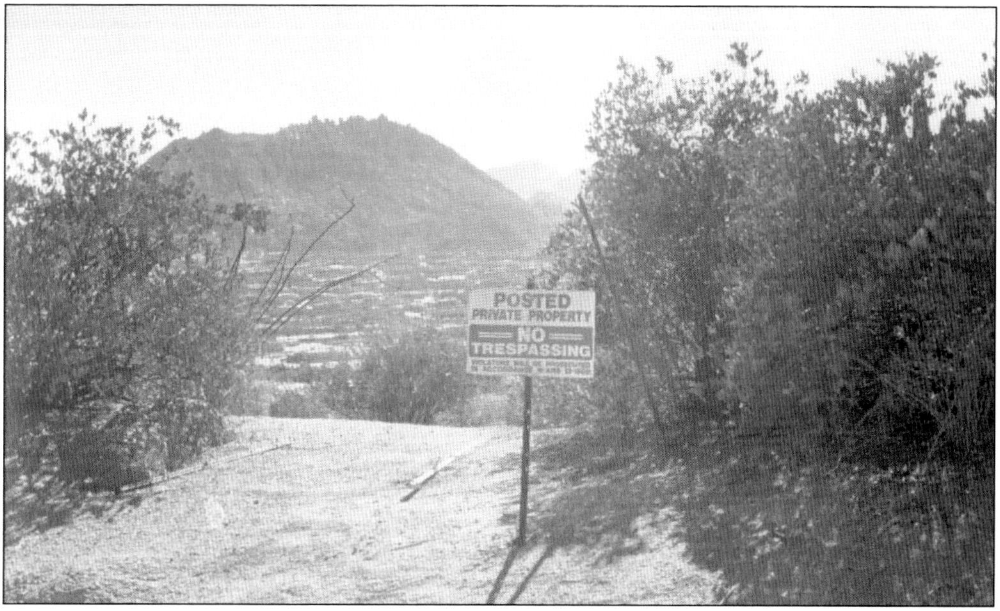

For many years, even though it was not a park or open public space, Pinnacle Peak and the surrounding area had been used for hiking, mountain biking, rock climbing, and horseback riding. During the construction of the park, which lasted from 1995 until 2002, the developer restricted access. This sign, photographed in 1997, informed visitors of the trail's closure. Residents had used the mountain as a place for recreation for many years and were frustrated by the restricted access. (Courtesy of Howard Myers.)

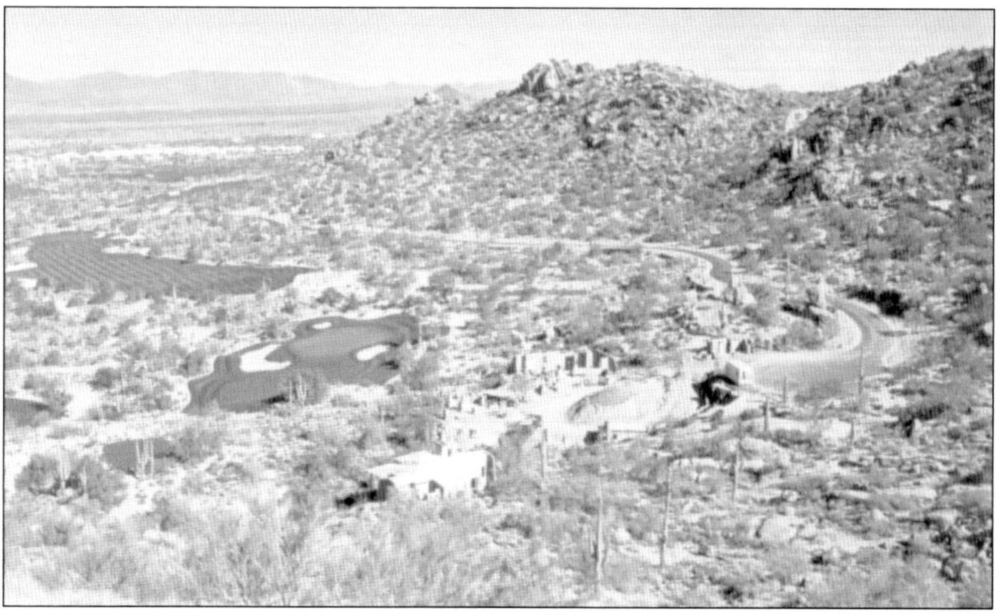

In accordance with Scottsdale's strict environmental laws and its desire to preserve the beauty of its property, Estancia painstakingly removed thousands of plants by hand and recorded where each plant, shrub, and cactus should be replanted. Some plants were not removed until the last minute to avoid damaging them. This photograph was taken in 1997 during the construction of Estancia. (Courtesy of Howard Myers.)

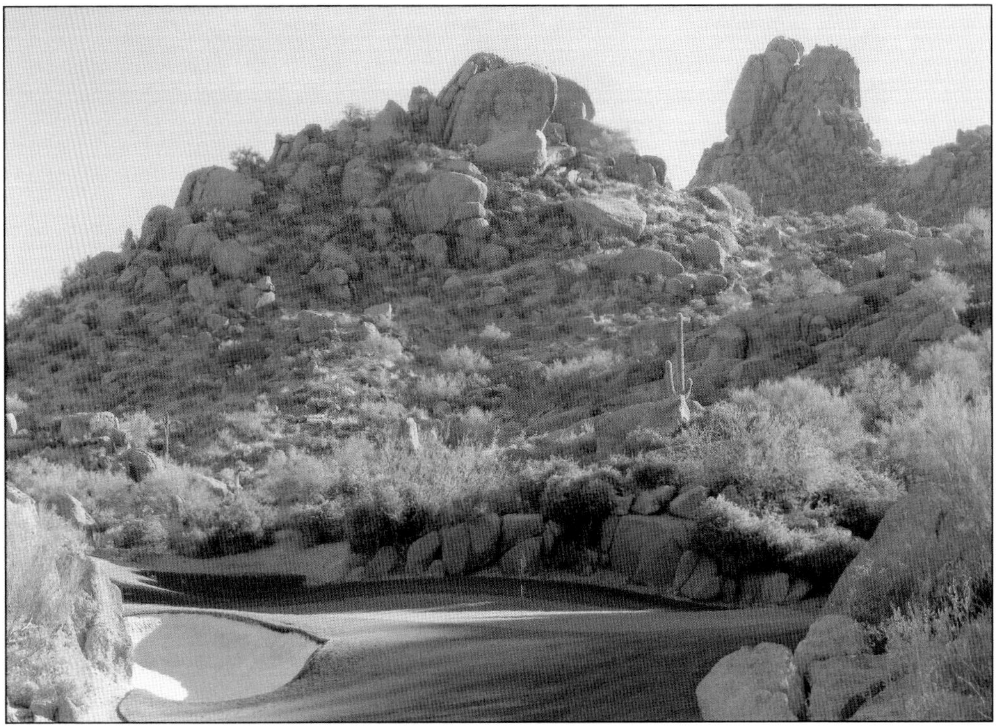

John Lang and his Estancia colleagues wooed Tom Fazio into designing the golf course. After visiting the site, Fazio was so enthusiastic about the project that he had all the drawings of the course completed before his contract was signed. After its opening in 1996, the course received several awards, including a designation from *Golf Magazine*'s as one of the Top 100 Courses in the World. (Courtesy of the Estancia Club.)

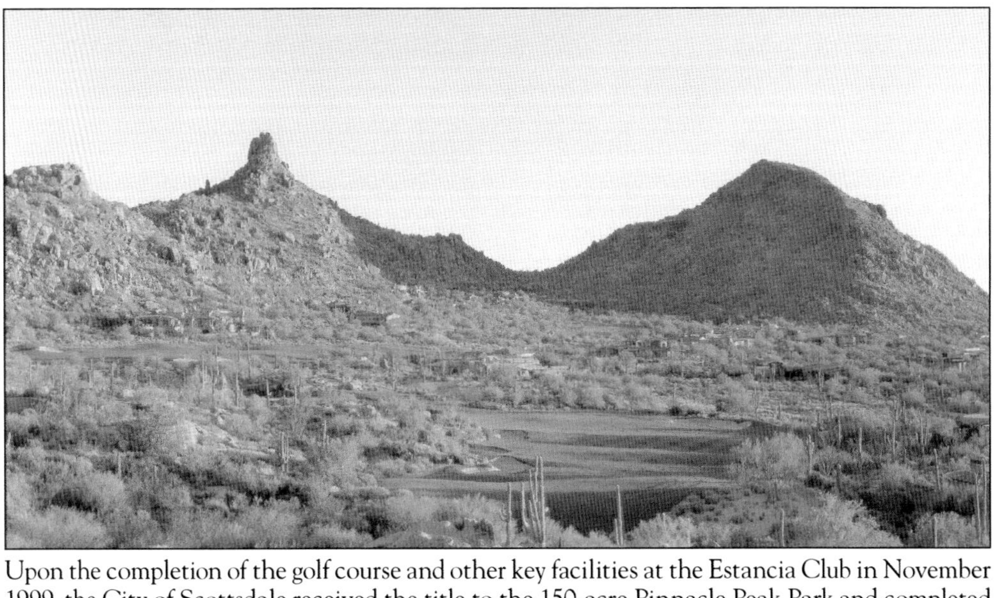

Upon the completion of the golf course and other key facilities at the Estancia Club in November 1999, the City of Scottsdale received the title to the 150-acre Pinnacle Peak Park and completed the main trail. The fantastic view of the park from Estancia's golf course includes Pinnacle Peak (left) and Red Face Mountain. (Courtesy of the Estancia Club.)

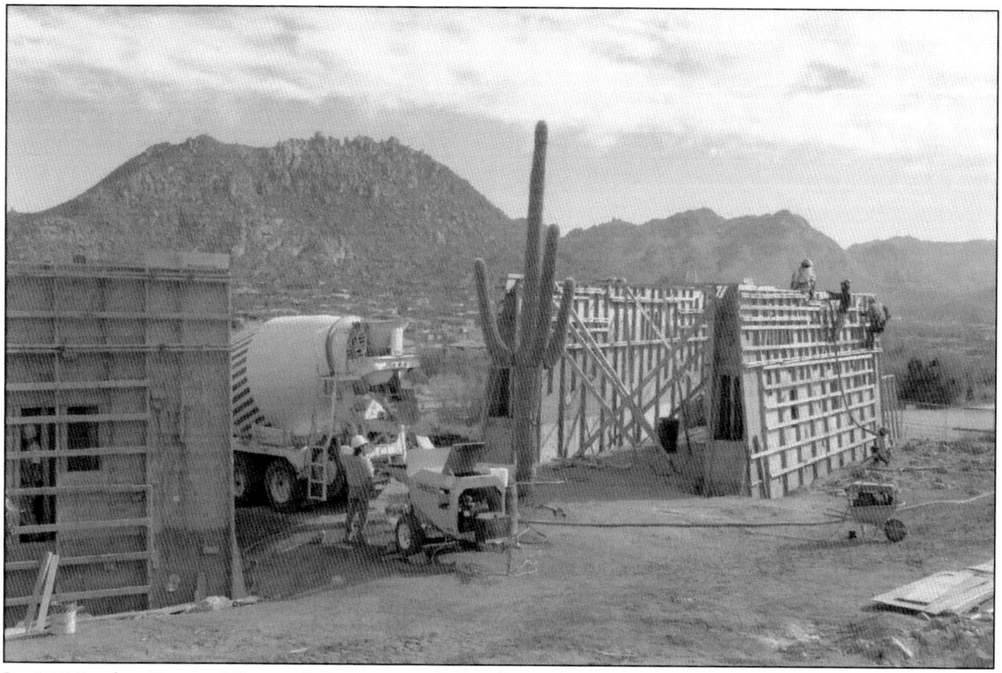

In 2000, the City of Scottsdale received the formal appraisal from the Arizona State Land Department for the cost of acquiring three acres for the trailhead area. After review and concurrence, the city began construction of the park headquarters and trailhead area in 2001. (Photograph by Tom Taubler; courtesy of the City of Scottsdale.)

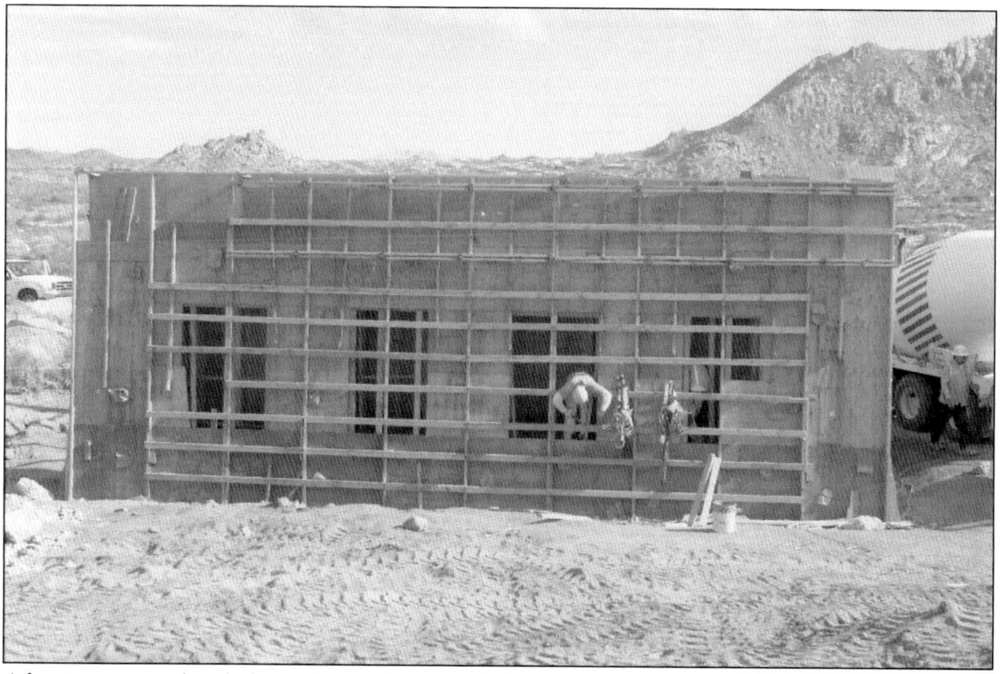

After it was completed, the park's headquarters building included office space for City of Scottsdale staff and volunteers. The building also includes restrooms and a drinking fountain. (Photograph by Tom Taubler; courtesy of the City of Scottsdale.)

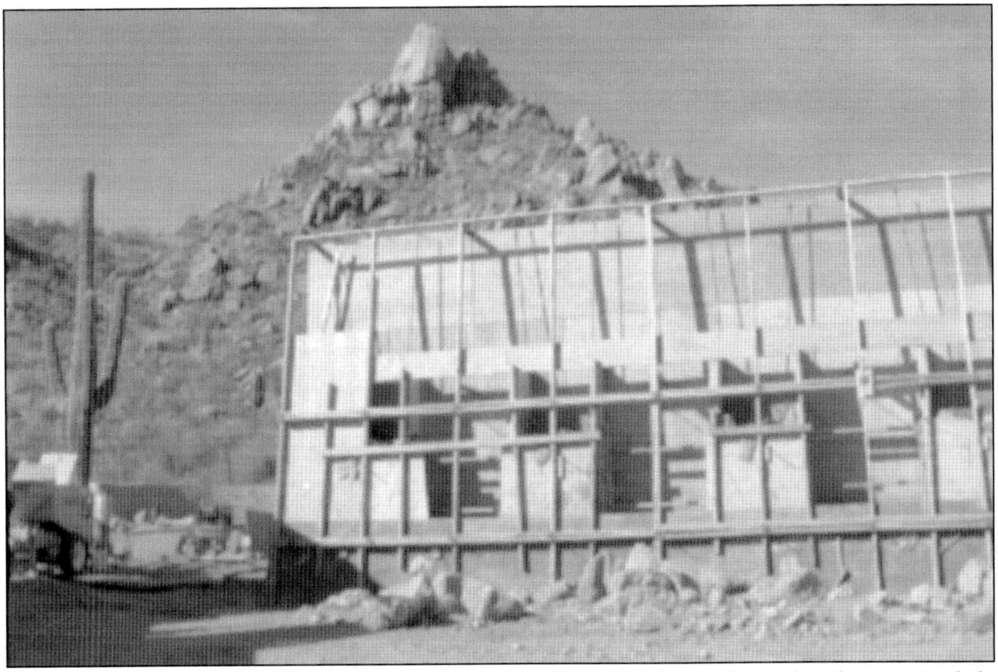

The ramada, pictured here during construction in 2001, provides a shady, cooler place to sit while visiting the park. There are several picnic tables available for the public's use. (Photograph by Tom Taubler; courtesy of the City of Scottsdale.)

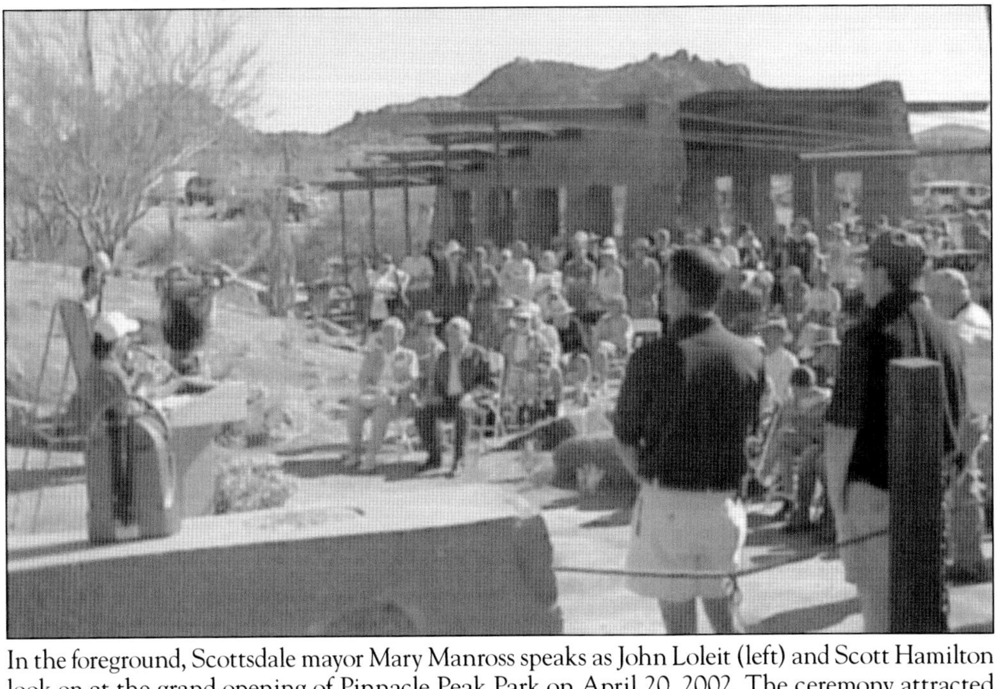

In the foreground, Scottsdale mayor Mary Manross speaks as John Loleit (left) and Scott Hamilton look on at the grand opening of Pinnacle Peak Park on April 20, 2002. The ceremony attracted more than 1,200 visitors. Loleit later credited Gary Meyer and Scott Hamilton, planners with the city, with doing most of the heavy lifting that preceded the opening. (Photograph by Bob Baile; courtesy of the City of Scottsdale.)

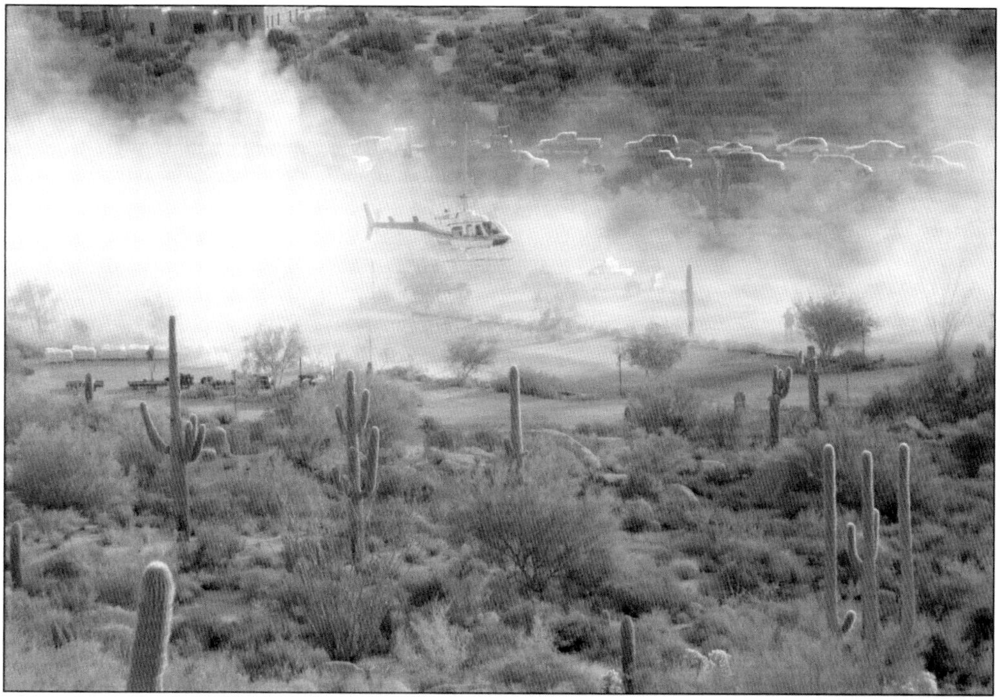

Because of Pinnacle Peak's steep and rugged terrain, helicopters are often used to airlift supplies to work sites on the mountain. The park's parking lot served as a heliport and supply depot. The Rotary Club of Pinnacle Peak paid for the use of helicopters for projects in 2002, 2004, and 2007. (Courtesy of Frank Biondo.)

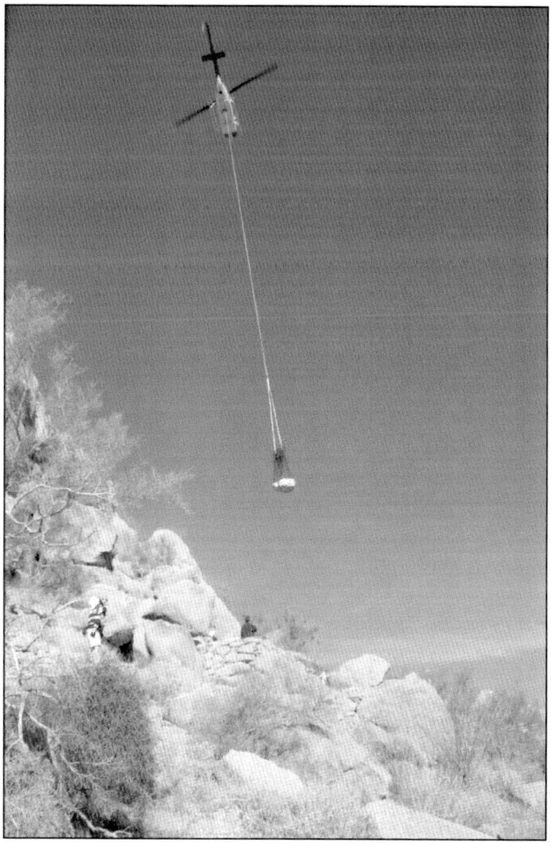

After the cargo has been attached, the helicopter ferries it to the work site on the mountain. (Courtesy of Frank Biondo.)

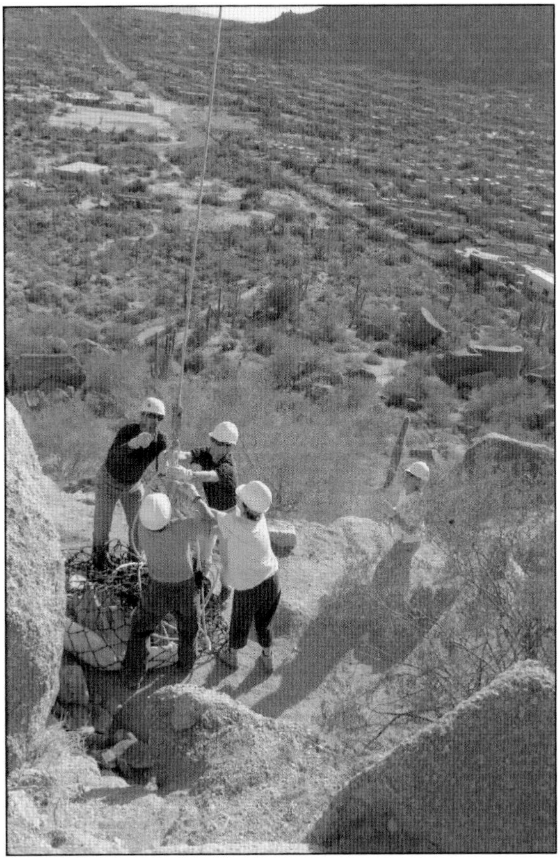

The trail crew on the mountain receives supplies from the helicopter and detaches the cargo bag. Pictured are Clair Miller (second from left) and John Loliet (fourth from left) of the City of Scottsdale assisting unidentified volunteers during the 2007 trail stabilization project. (Courtesy of Frank Biondo.)

In 2007, the City of Scottsdale's Clair Miller (far left, wearing gray shirt) and John Loleit (third from left) work with unidentified volunteers to unpack materials that had been transported to the mountain by helicopter. (Courtesy of the City of Scottsdale.)

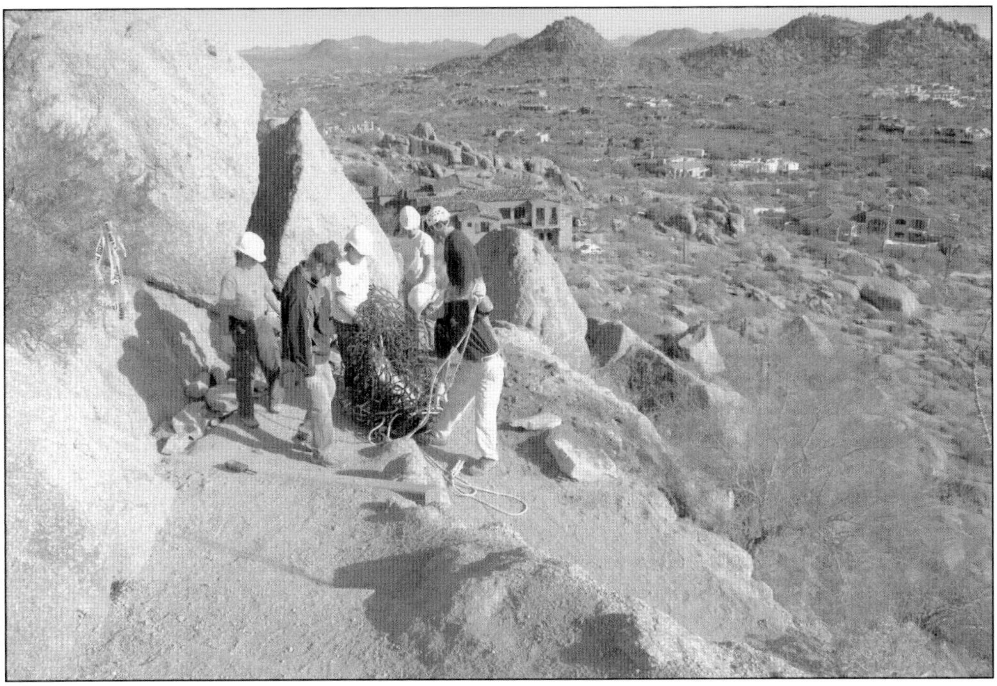

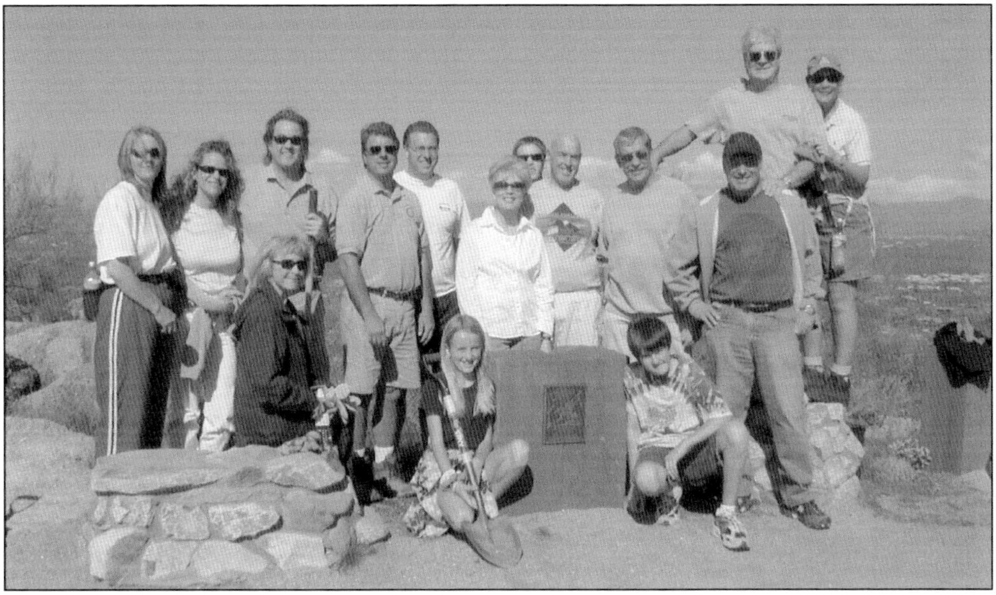

In 2004, members of the Rotary Club of Pinnacle Peak celebrated the completion of the Grand View Overlook. Pictured from left to right are (seated) Gaye Leo, Mackinsie Carson, and Keegan Carson; (standing) Kim Carson, Kate Eastburn, Daniel Eastburn, Brian Carson, Mark Miele, Robin Craig, unidentified, Gary Cohen, Dave Hammond, Lee Scher, Rhody Esmay, and Pat Cohen. (Courtesy of the RCPP.)

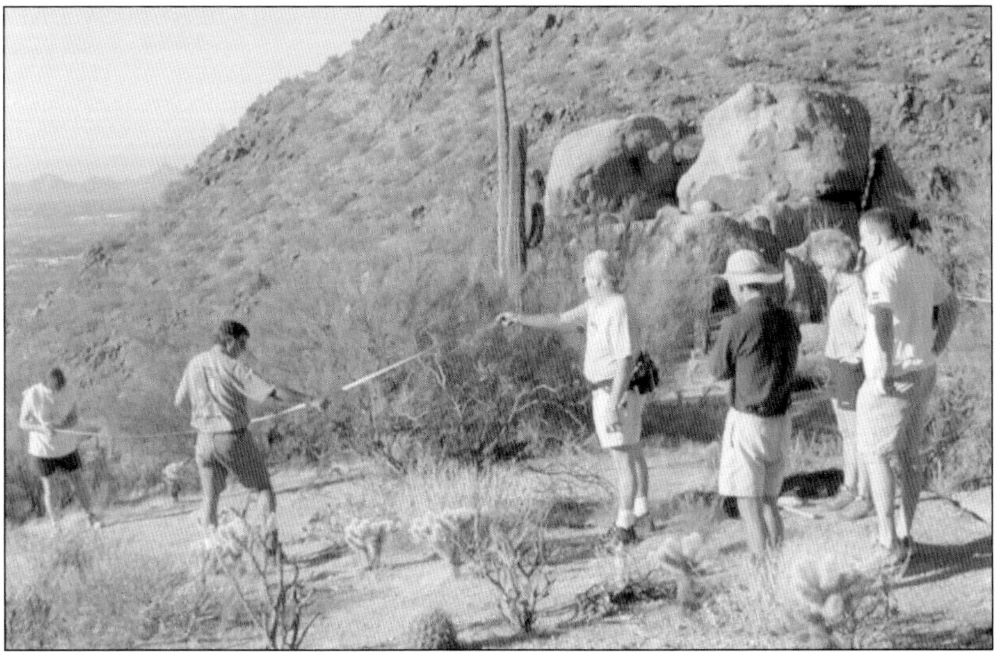

The Rotary Club of Pinnacle Peak invested more than $65,000 in park improvements, including the use of a helicopter for construction of the Grand View and Owl's Nest Overlooks and a trail maintenance project. Laying out the location of Grand View Overlook are, from left to right, Daniel Eastburn, Brian Carson, Rhody Esmay, John Loleit, Robin Craig, and Josh Winston. (Courtesy of the RCPP.)

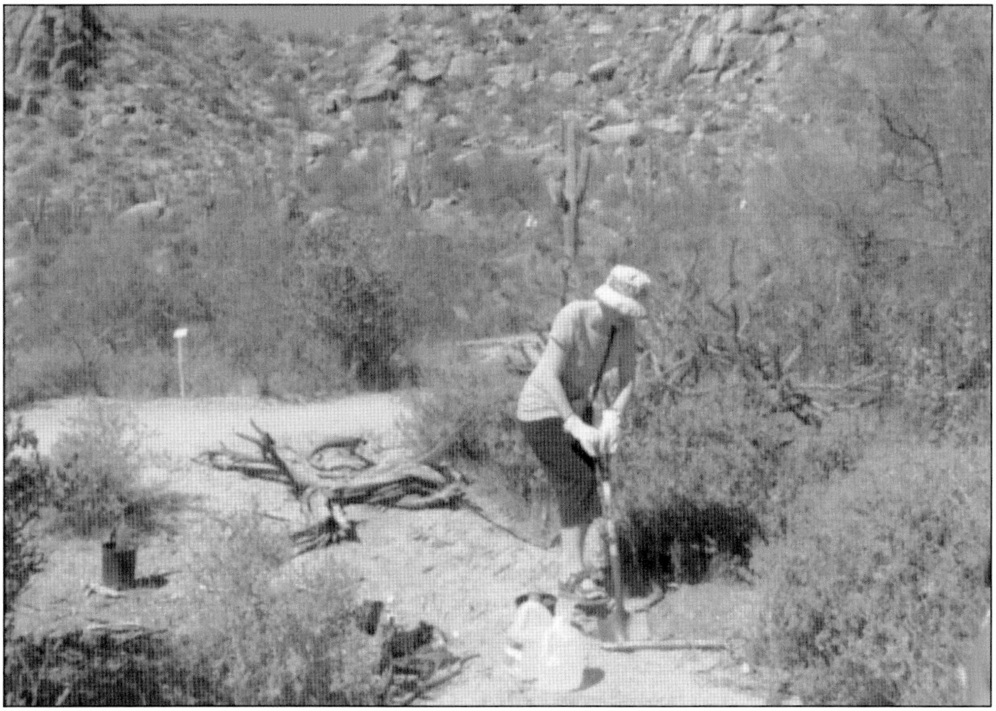

Much of the successful development and operation of the park is owed to volunteers. Groups like the Boy Scouts of America, Volunteers for Outdoor Arizona, the Access Fund, and the Arizona Mountaineering Club (AMC) completed many projects in preparing for the park's opening. This unidentified volunteer was staying at a nearby resort. Upon visiting the park, she asked to help. (Photograph by Kathy Mascaro; courtesy of the City of Scottsdale.)

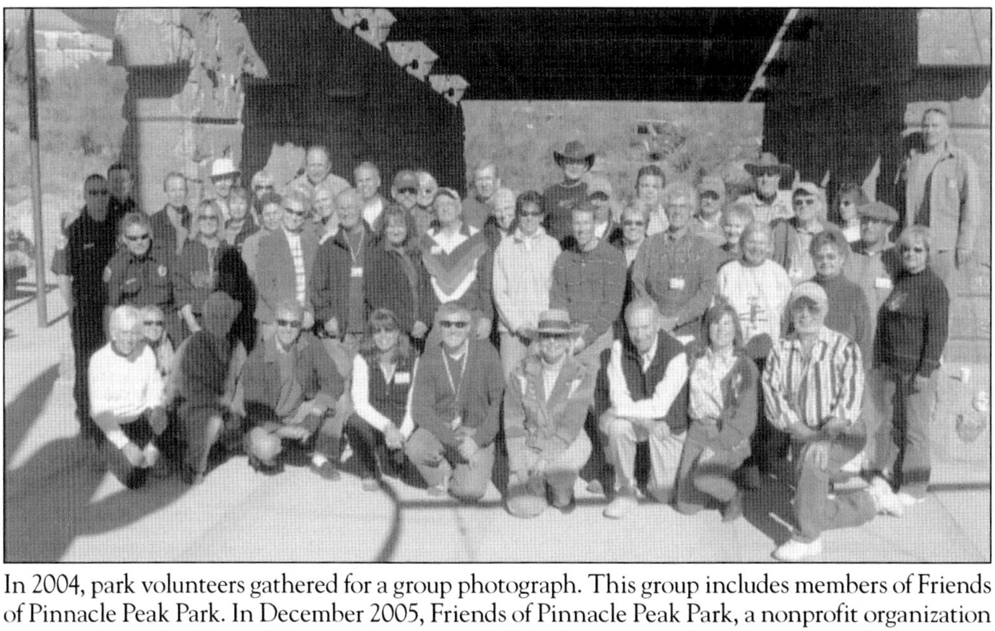

In 2004, park volunteers gathered for a group photograph. This group includes members of Friends of Pinnacle Peak Park. In December 2005, Friends of Pinnacle Peak Park, a nonprofit organization separate from the City of Scottsdale, was established to accept donations for park programs, preservation, and various educational activities. (Courtesy of the FPPP.)

Six

Hiking Pinnacle Peak

Pinnacle Peak Park's trail generally follows the historic trail that was used to hike or ride to Reata Pass from the west. The original trail was further down the northern slope of Red Face Mountain, passing through what is today's Estancia community. Also, the old trail did not climb as high on Pinnacle Peak; it traversed the saddle between the mountains on its way to Reata Pass.

Most visitors come to Pinnacle Peak Park to hike, and Scottsdale took the needs of hikers seriously in developing the new trail. The trailhead is made of stabilized decomposed granite, which is native to the area. The granite blends into the landscape, reduces heat retention, and provides a smooth tread. In accordance with Scottsdale's firm environmental and native plant ordinances, as few native plants as possible were disturbed during construction. When landscaping was required, indigenous species were used.

The eastern trailhead, which is located next to the park headquarters, has exhibits that provide information about the park. There are small signs near the trail's beginning to provide information about the plants and animals that hikers might encounter. Distance markers are placed at 100-foot intervals for the entire one-and-a-quarter-mile length of the trail.

The trail has several climbs and descents. Beginning at an elevation of 2,570 feet at the park headquarters, it gradually gains elevation. Through a series of switchbacks, it traverses about halfway up Pinnacle Peak. The trail then wraps partly around Pinnacle Peak to reach its maximum elevation of 2,889 feet. A series of switchbacks then take the hiker to the saddle, which was used by the old trail separating Pinnacle Peak from Red Face Mountain.

The trail traverses part of the way up Red Face Mountain, and as the hiker walks uphill for the second time, the landscape changes. The rock outcroppings above the trail have a more angular shape than elsewhere in the park. The soil is a dark, reddish color, and fewer saguaros are present. After crossing Red Face Mountain, the trail drops to 2,366 feet at the western boundary of the park, where there are no facilities or parking.

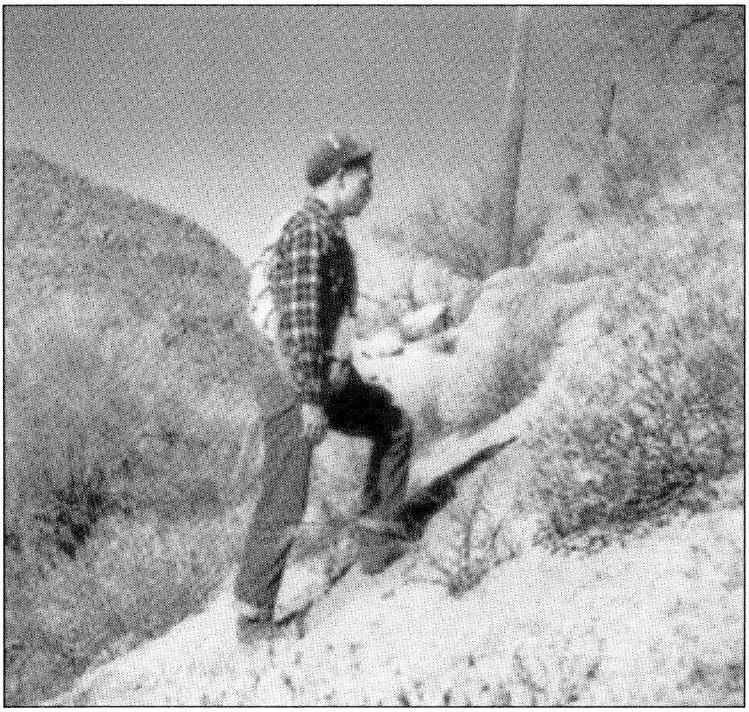

In 1947, Ed George and Bill McMorris, members of Arizona's first organized climbing group, made the first recorded ascent of Pinnacle Peak. This photograph of McMorris hiking up the slope of Pinnacle Peak was taken in the spring of 1948 when some of the Katchinas returned to Pinnacle Peak to make a film for the Boy Scouts of America. (Courtesy of the Katchina Archives.)

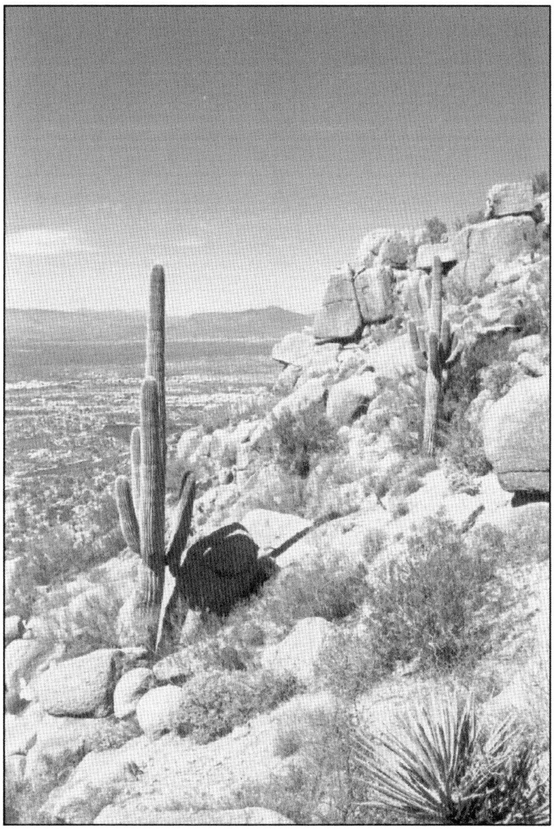

Pinnacle Peak was a popular hiking destination long before Pinnacle Peak Park opened. Curious about the status of the development of Estancia, North Scottsdale resident Howard Myers took this photograph during a hike in 1997. (Courtesy of Howard Myers.)

Pinnacle Peak Park volunteer Trish Costello provides information about the park to a visitor. (Courtesy of the City of Scottsdale.)

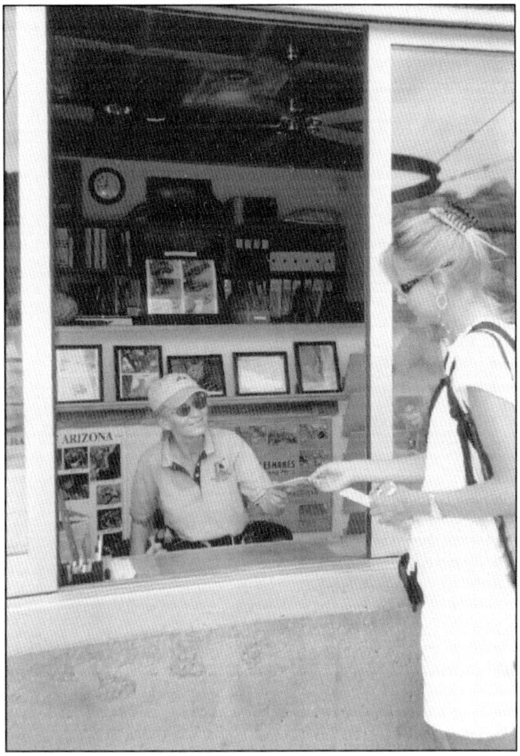

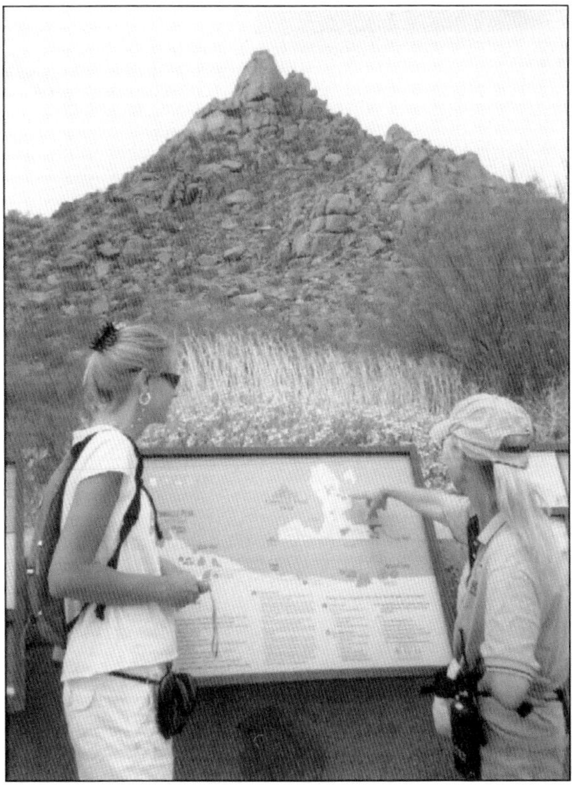

Park volunteer Trish Costello uses a map at the trailhead, which is near the park headquarters, to describe the trail for an out-of-state visitor. (Courtesy of the City of Scottsdale.)

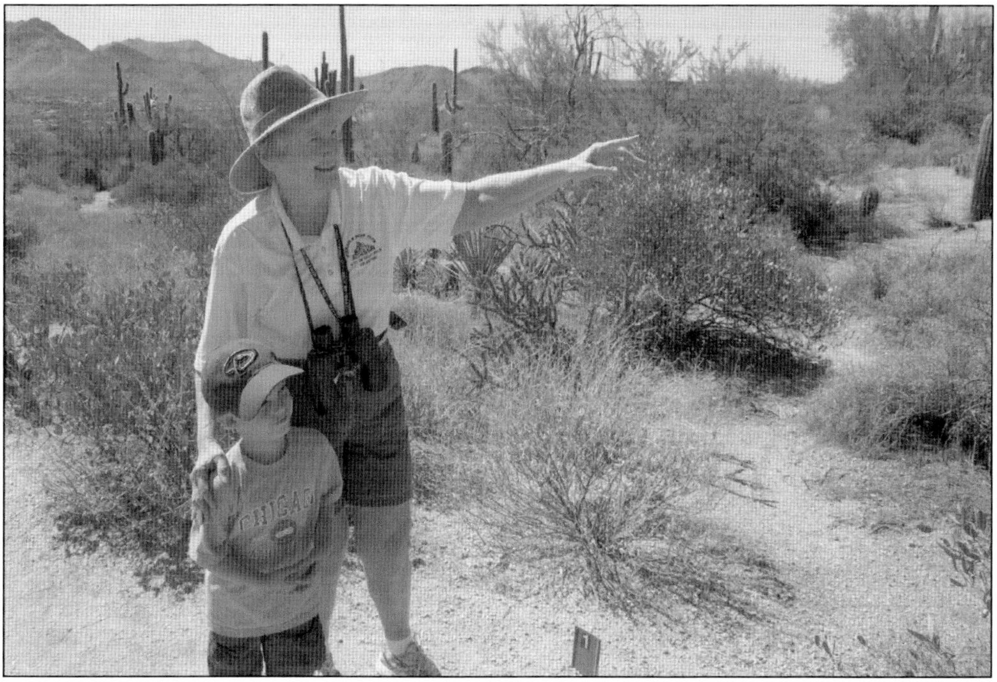

Pinnacle Peak Park visitors often see volunteers either on or near the trail. Here, volunteer Sue Fay points out a park landmark to an unidentified young visitor. (Courtesy of Frank Biondo.)

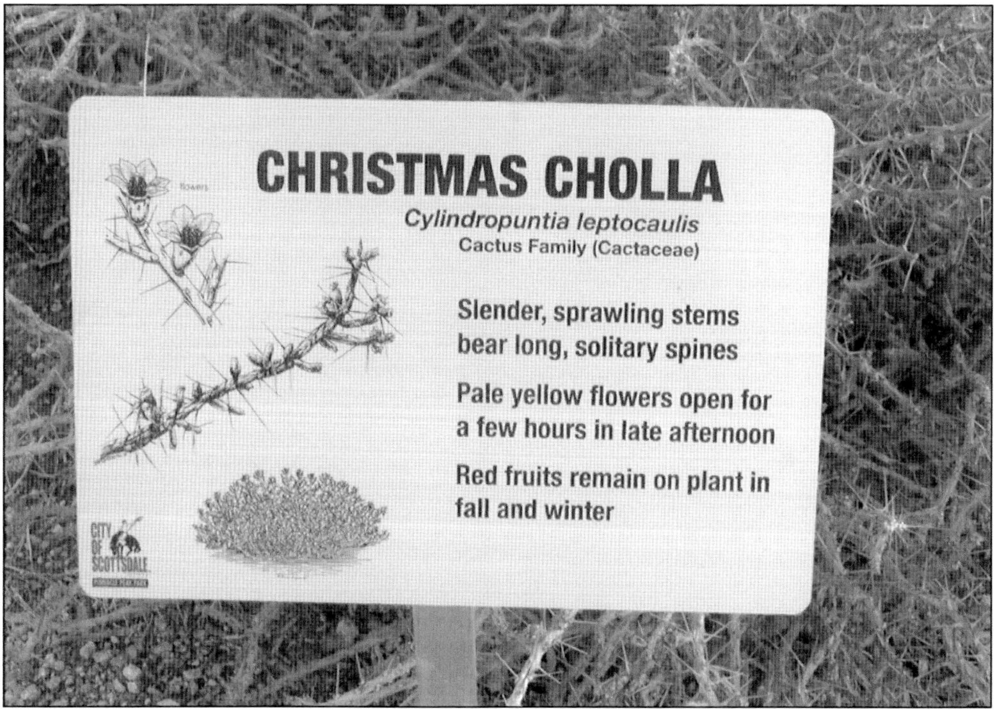

Most hikers begin their hike at the eastern trailhead near the parking lot and park headquarters. The first part of the trail is relatively flat, and Scottsdale has installed small signs that provide information about flora and fauna found in the park. (Courtesy of the City of Scottsdale.)

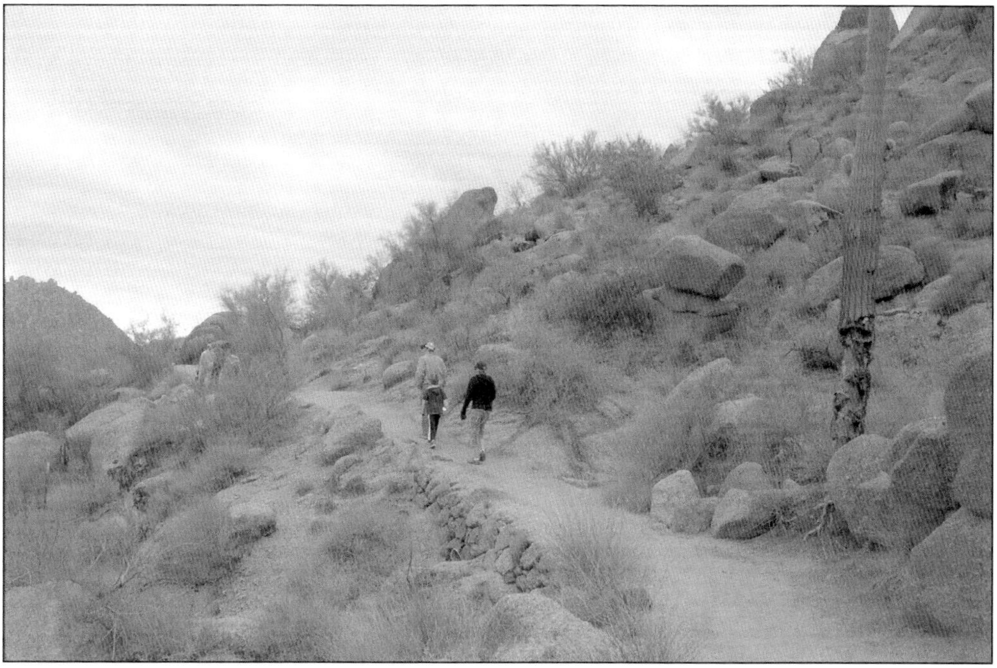

It is not unusual to see families hiking together at Pinnacle Peak Park. Distance markers along the way are helpful in gauging how far hikers have travelled, and there is always the option to reverse direction and hike back to the starting point. (Courtesy of the City of Scottsdale.)

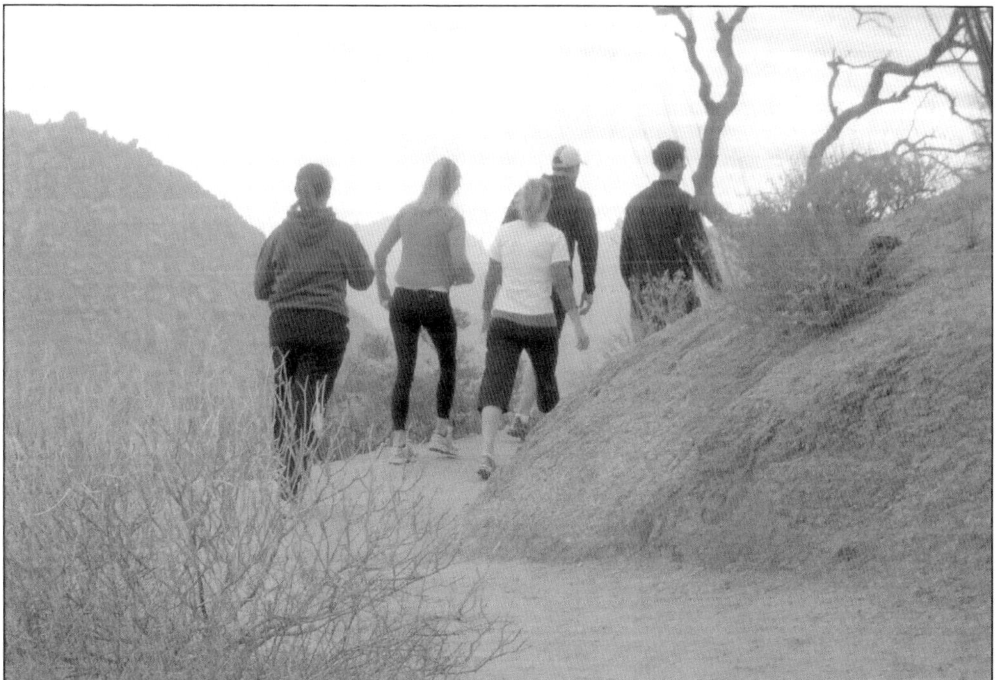

Unidentified hikers approach one of the numerous switchbacks along the trail. The trail is wide enough to accommodate hikers travelling in opposite directions and to enable faster hikers to pass others moving at a slower rate. (Courtesy of the City of Scottsdale.)

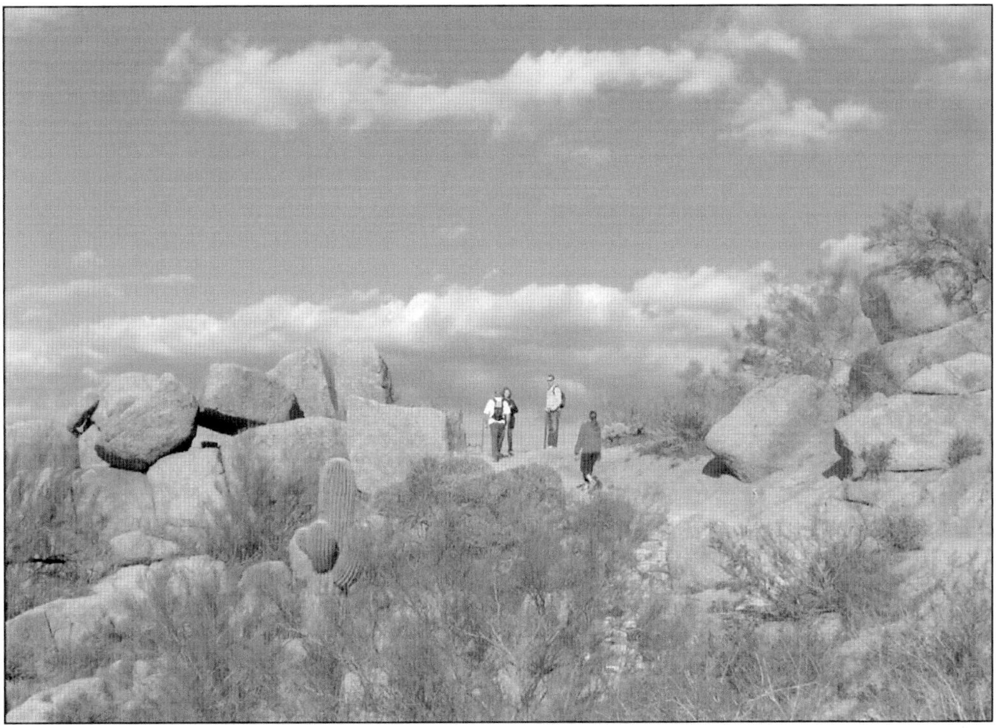

Unidentified hikers wait for their friends at the top of a rise amidst a field of large boulders. (Courtesy of Howard Myers.)

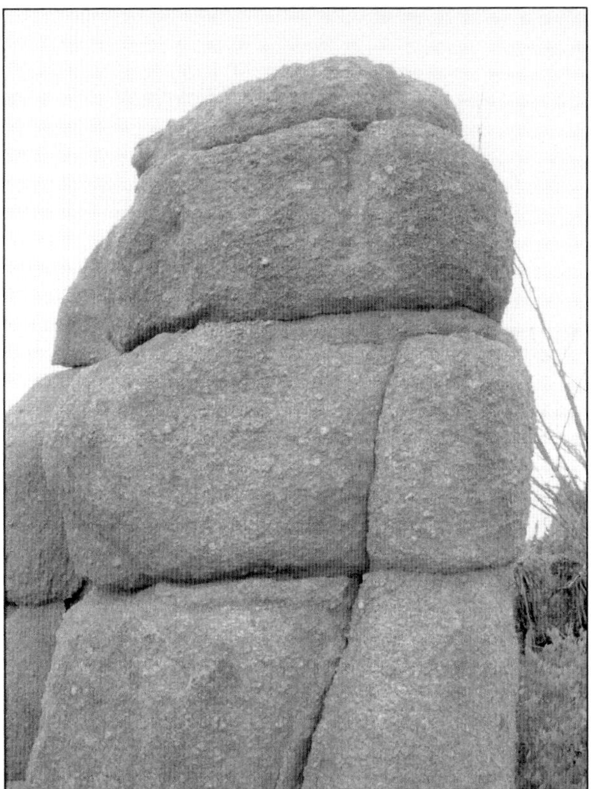

There are many oddly shaped boulders and rock formations either adjacent to or visible from the trail. While hiking the trail at Pinnacle Peak Park, visitors enjoy looking for the imaginary shapes of animals and other objects among the rocks. (Courtesy of FPPP.)

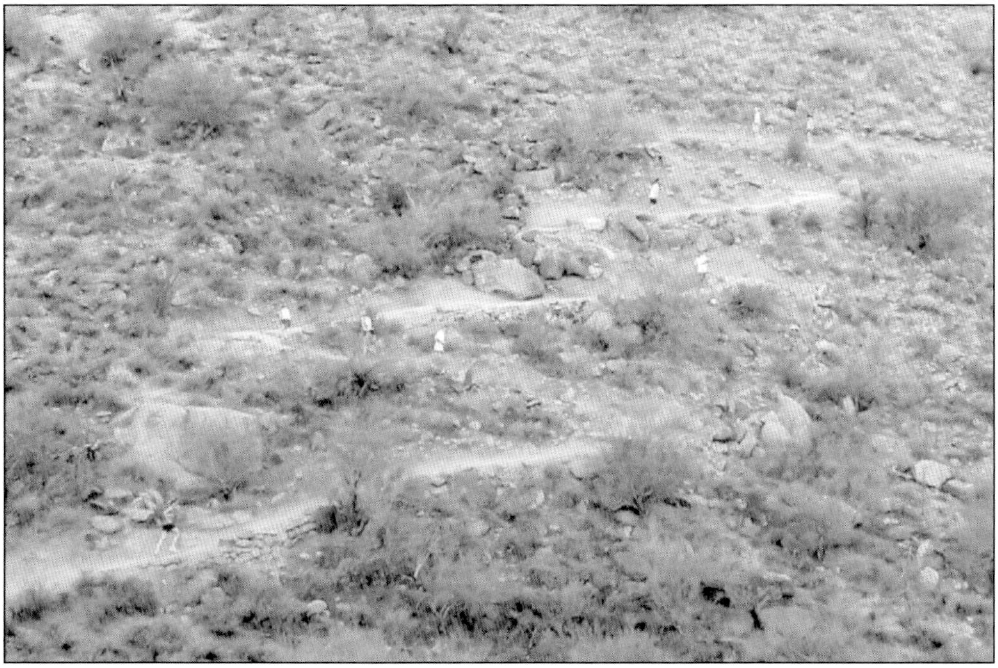

In this photograph, an unidentified jogger can be seen making his or her way up one of the switchbacks on Red Face Mountain. Jogging is allowed on the park trail. (Photograph by Kathy Mascaro; courtesy of the City of Scottsdale.)

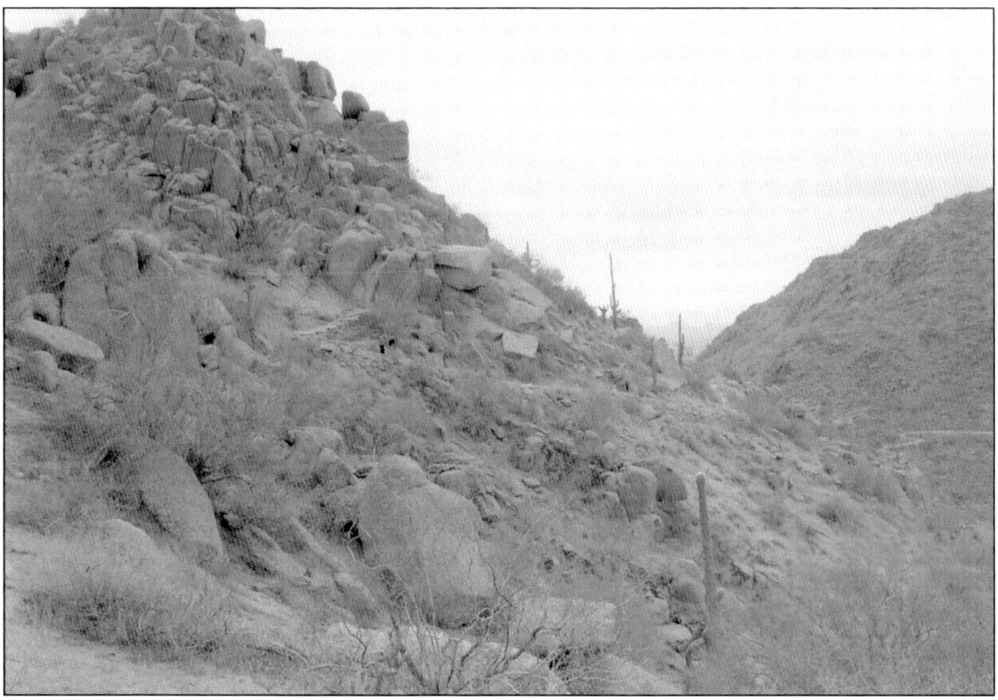

The hikers and the trail are difficult to see as they blend into the rugged landscape on the western side of Pinnacle Peak summit. This portion of the trail is just east of the saddle that separates Pinnacle Peak from Red Face Mountain. (Courtesy of FPPP.)

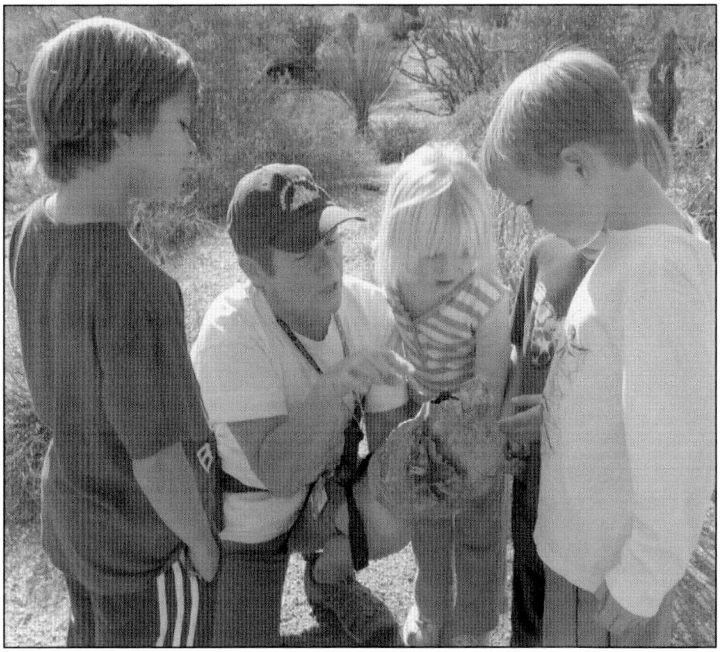

Pinnacle Peak Park holds interpretive hikes on a regular basis. In this photograph, park volunteer Beverly Angeli-Burch captures unidentified young visitors' attention as she provides information about an interesting item she found along the trail. (Courtesy of the City of Scottsdale.)

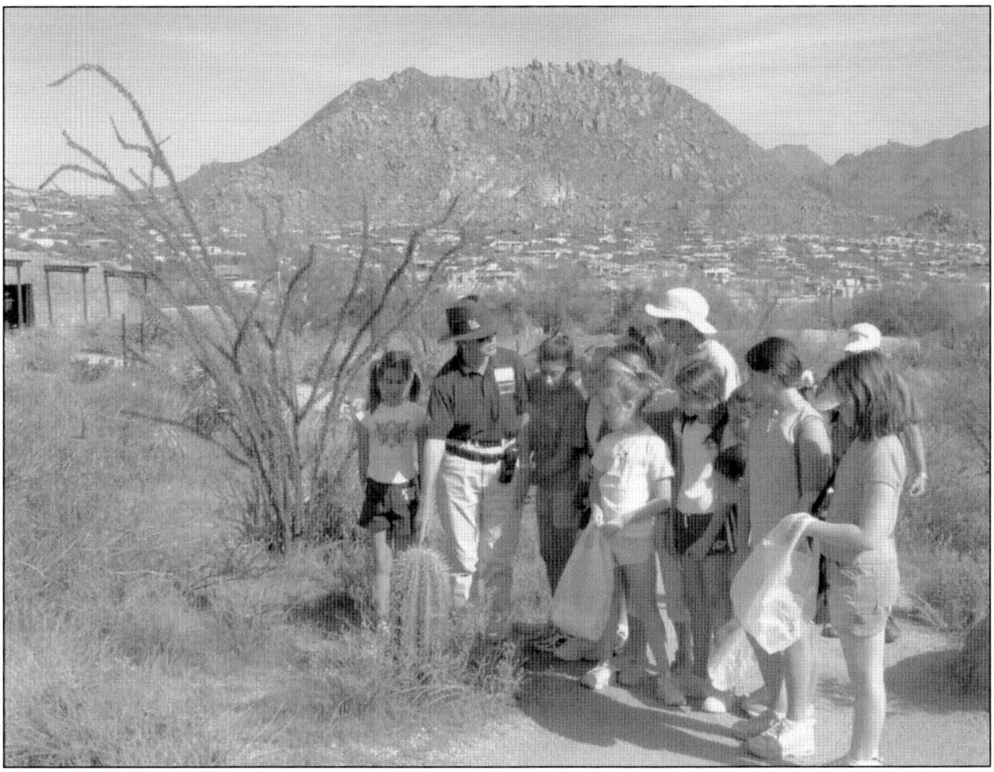

Park volunteer Diane McCoy Berney could be describing the difference between barrel and saguaro cacti as she points to the straight spines of a young saguaro cactus. The spines of a barrel cactus are hooked and have a reddish color. The children are also learning about community service by picking up litter during their visit. (Courtesy of the City of Scottsdale.)

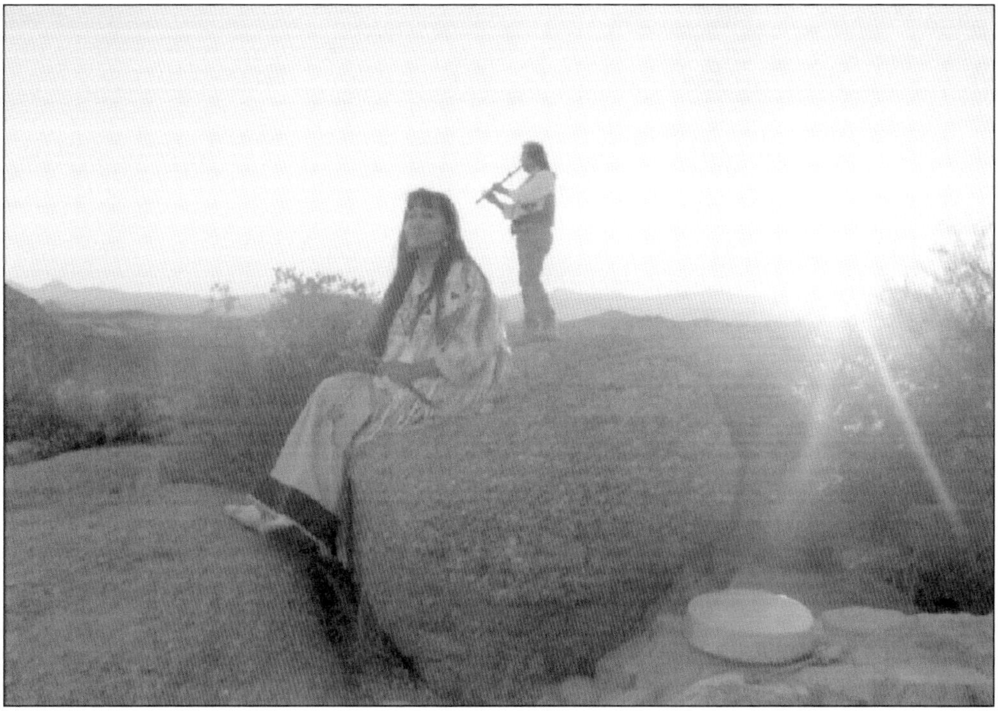

Groups sometimes hold special programs at Pinnacle Peak Park. In this 2004 photograph, an unidentified Native American plays a flute to participants in an organization's cultural awareness program. (Courtesy of Frank Biondo.)

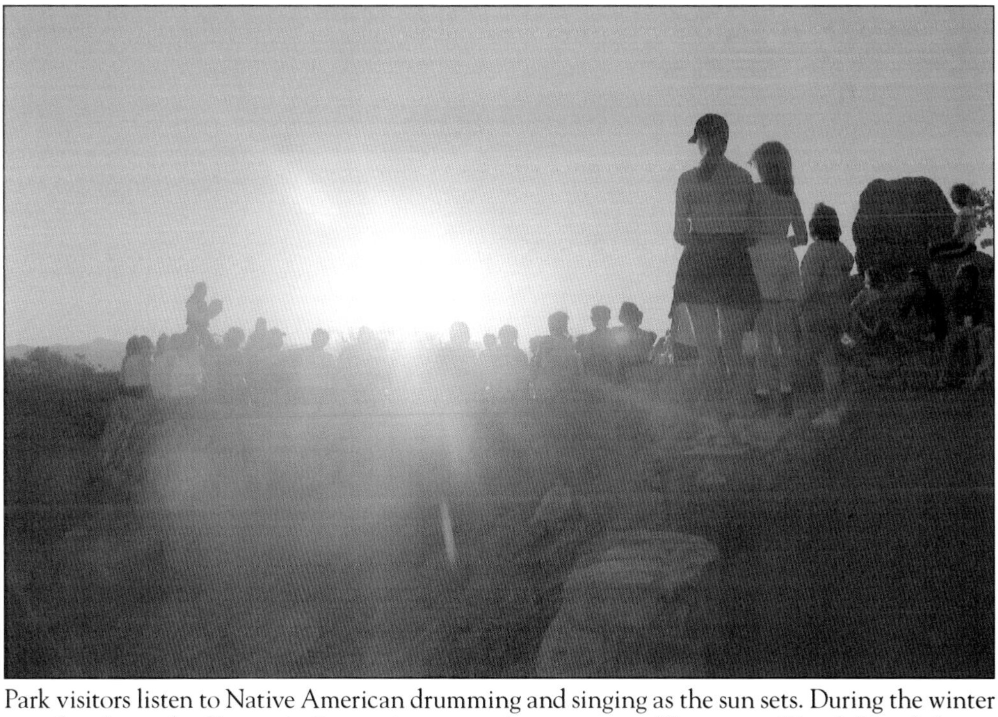

Park visitors listen to Native American drumming and singing as the sun sets. During the winter months, the park offers periodic evening stargazing programs. (Courtesy of Frank Biondo.)

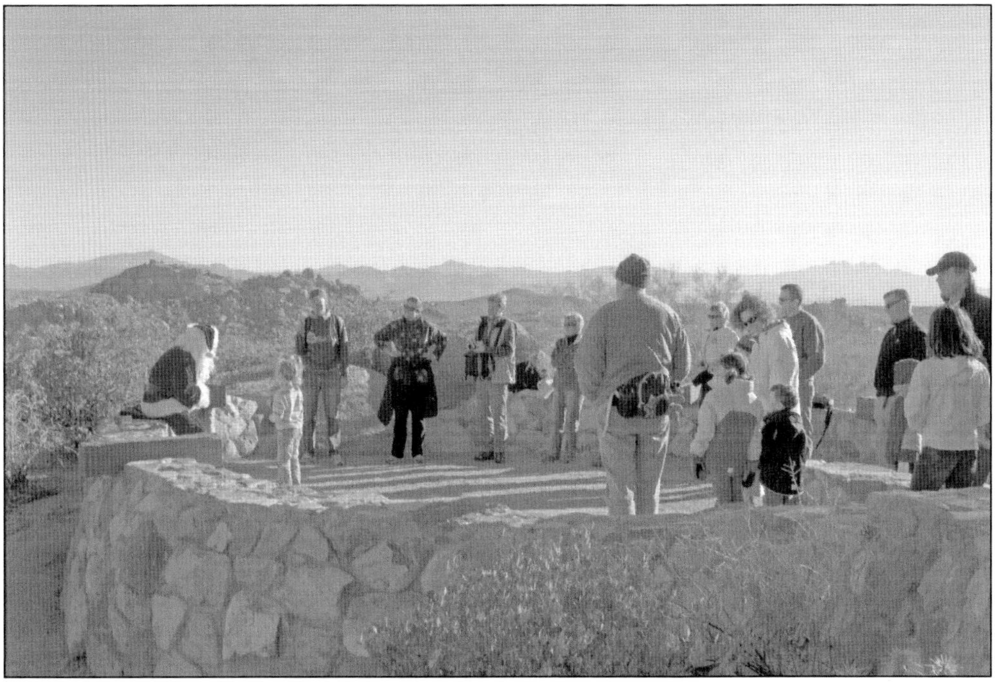

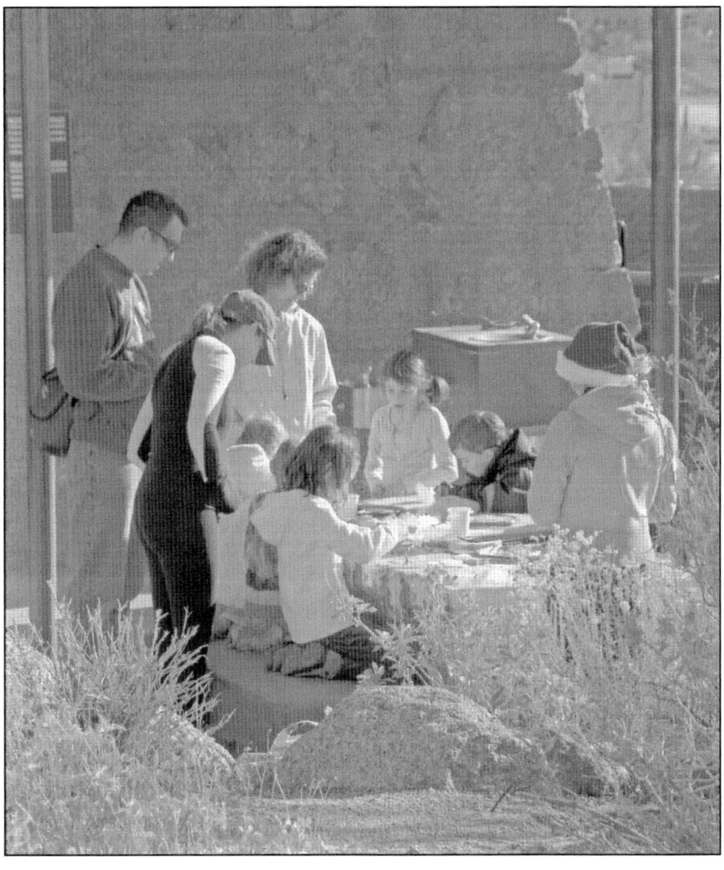

During December, the park conducts Jingle Hikes to give children an opportunity to meet Santa. In this photograph, hikers visit with Santa, played by park volunteer Bob Rosenberg, at Grand View Overview. (Courtesy of Frank Biondo.)

A family puts the picnic tables near the park headquarters to good use following a hike. On warm days, the shaded ramada, which is also near the headquarters, can provide a welcome relief from the sun. (Photograph by Kathy Mascaro; courtesy of the City of Scottsdale.)

Seven

Riding Pinnacle Peak

It seems likely that groups of Yavapai and Apache were the first to visit Pinnacle Peak on horseback. Later equestrians included curious soldiers, prospectors, cowboys, and pioneers. From the early days of prospecting and ranching, the equestrian lifestyle has been important to many residents.

During the 1950s and 1960s, local guest ranches featured trail rides as an important part of their offerings to eastern tourists. In the 1950s, Rancho Vista Bonita Guest Ranch (located on the southwest corner of Pinnacle Peak and Pima Roads) offered its guests three daily meals, an individual cabin, and horse privileges—all for $12.50 per day. Surely, many of those guests made the short ride to Pinnacle Peak.

Scottsdale equestrians, including members of the Arizona Horseman's Association, were leading advocates for the creation of Pinnacle Peak Park. Proponents requested the creation of parking spaces for horse trailers near the park headquarters and a multipurpose trail for both horseback riding and hiking. In addition to responding to these requests, the City of Scottsdale also connected the park trail to the city's trail system.

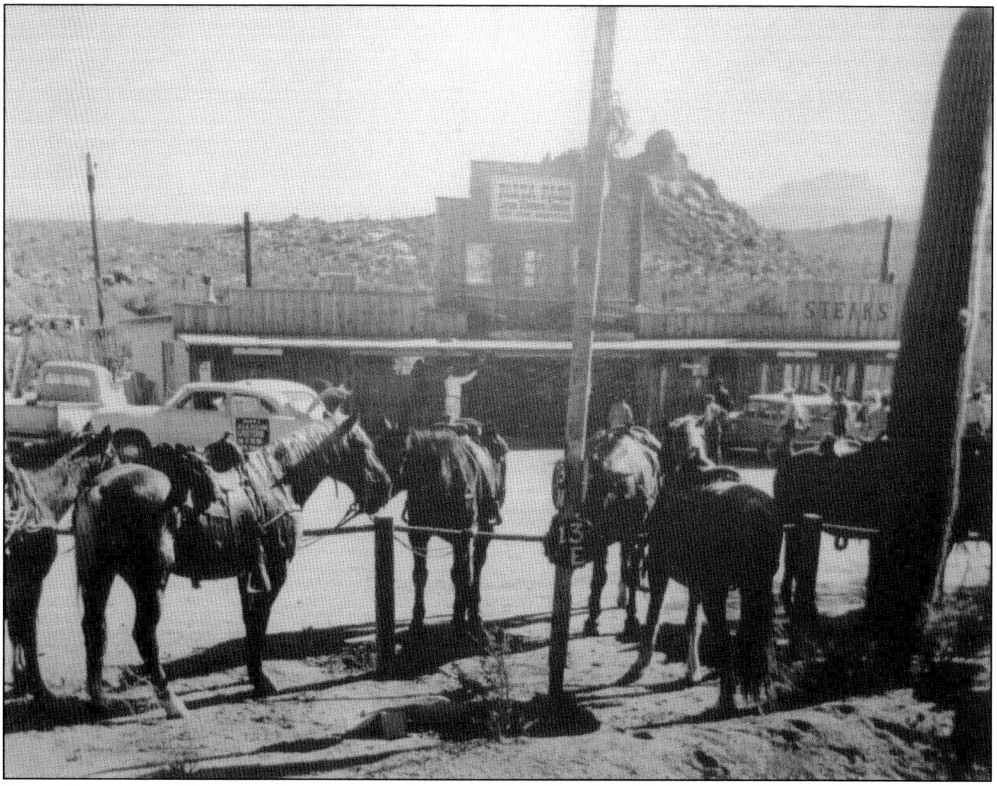

Reata Pass was a favorite restaurant and watering hole for local cowboys. This 1959 photograph shows horses waiting for their owners, who are inside Reata Pass Steakhouse enjoying a meal. This photograph was a favorite of the founder, George R. Cavalliere. (Courtesy of Joyce Eller.)

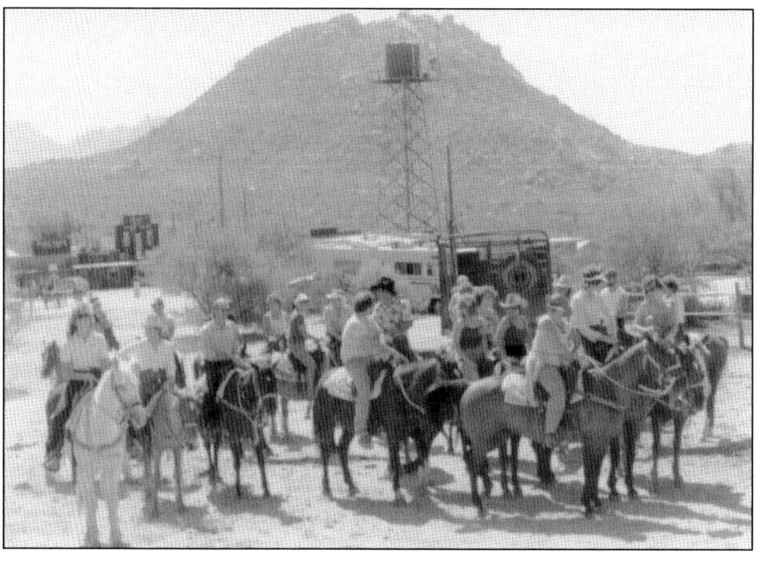

Long before Pinnacle Peak Park opened, Pinnacle Peak and its nearby cowboy restaurants were favorite destinations of groups, families, and individuals on trail rides. This photograph, taken at Reata Pass Steakhouse, shows tourists on a trail ride in the 1960s. (Courtesy of Joyce Eller.)

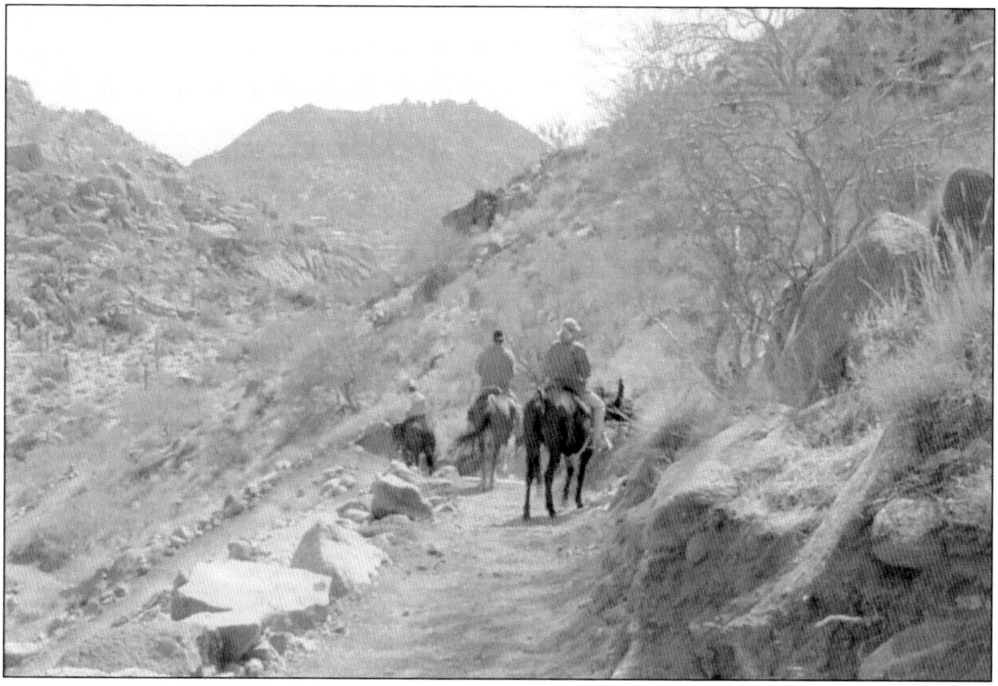

A few weeks before the park's official opening on April 20, 2002, North Scottsdale residents John Aleo (left), Tony Nelssen (center), and Marg Nelssen rode their horses on the trail. Tony Nelssen, who served on the City of Scottsdale Parks and Recreation Commission, had been asked by the city to organize the test. (Courtesy of the City of Scottsdale.)

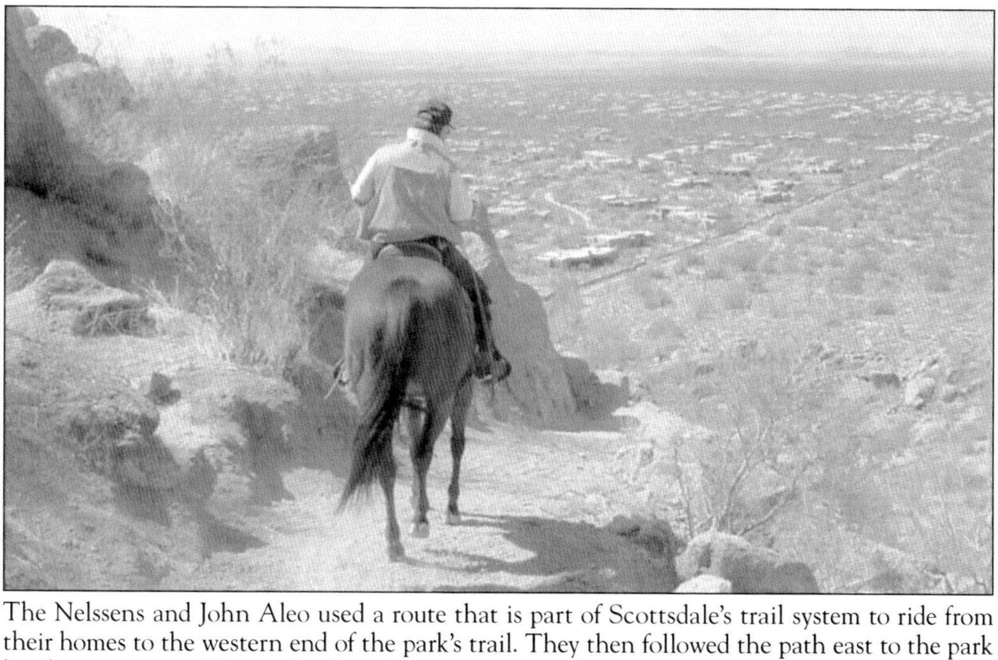

The Nelssens and John Aleo used a route that is part of Scottsdale's trail system to ride from their homes to the western end of the park's trail. They then followed the path east to the park headquarters near Alma School Parkway. This photograph shows Aleo on the return trip. In the distance on the right side of the picture, Jomax Road can be seen stretching to the west. (Courtesy of the City of Scottsdale.)

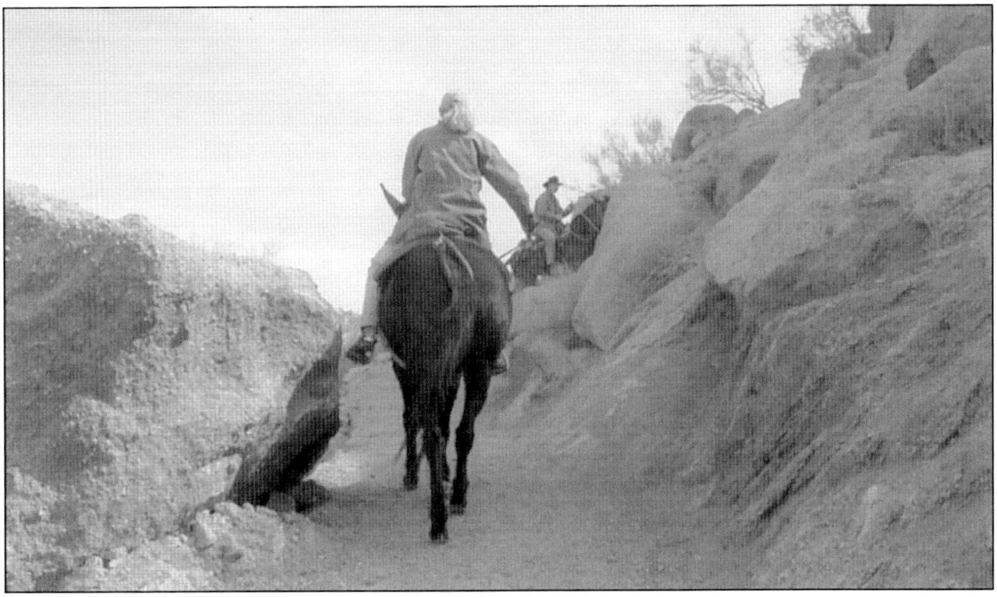

The test ride made by Aleo and the Nelssens resulted in several safety improvements. In this photograph, Marg Nelssen follows Tony Nelssen to a switchback. Tony pioneered the Great Sonoran, a group that championed environmentally conscious development guidelines. The Great Sonoran served as a prototype to Scottsdale's environmentally sensitive design guidelines. (Courtesy of *The Peak*.)

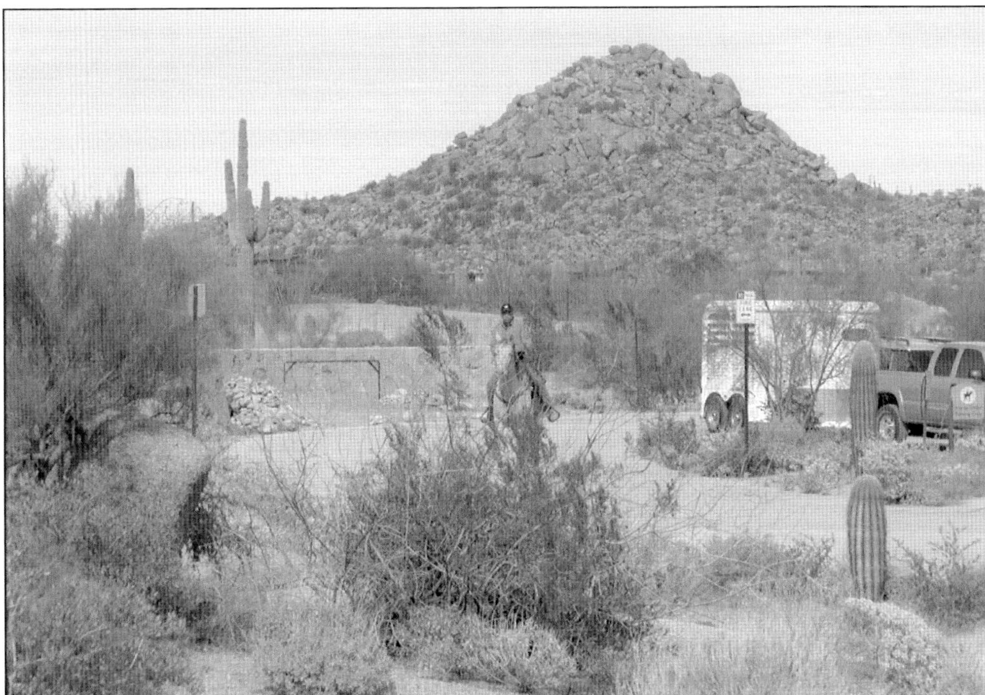

A horse and rider begin their ride from the parking lot near park headquarters on the eastern end of the trail. Several parking spaces for horse trailers are available in the lot. There is no parking lot at the western end of the trail. (Photograph by Bob Baile; courtesy of the City of Scottsdale.)

Two unidentified riders and their horses travel uphill as they head west toward Pinnacle Peak. The park headquarters building can be seen in the background. Riders and their mounts have rights-of-way on the trail. (Photograph by Bob Baile; courtesy of the City of Scottsdale.)

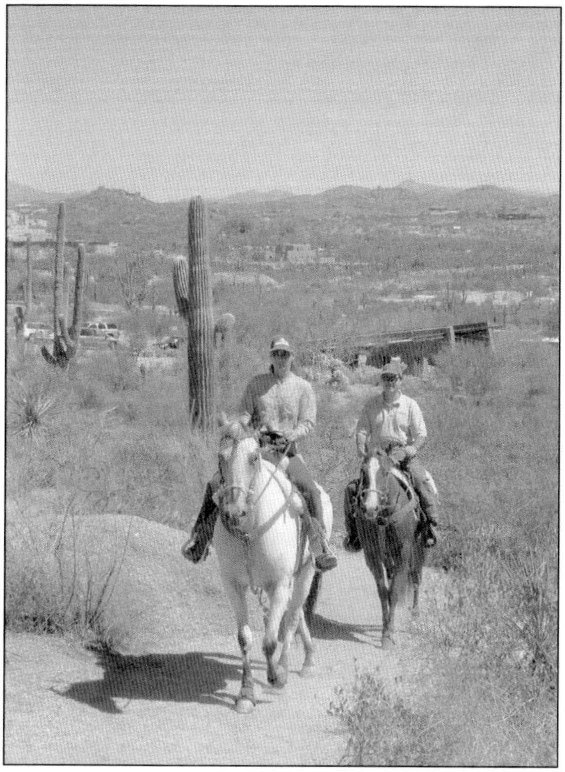

This unidentified rider and her mount are difficult to see as they follow the trail through the rugged, boulder-strewn landscape. Equestrians report that the trail provides a spectacular ride, but the presence of hikers and runners can be a distraction for the horses. (Photograph by Bob Baile; courtesy of the City of Scottsdale.)

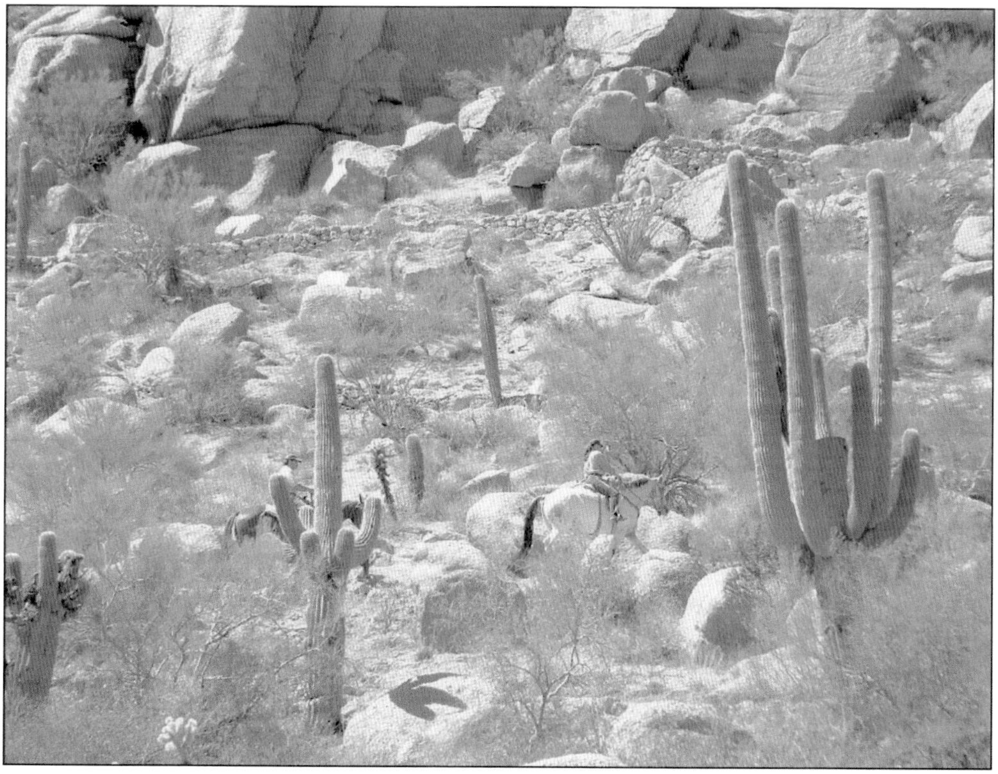

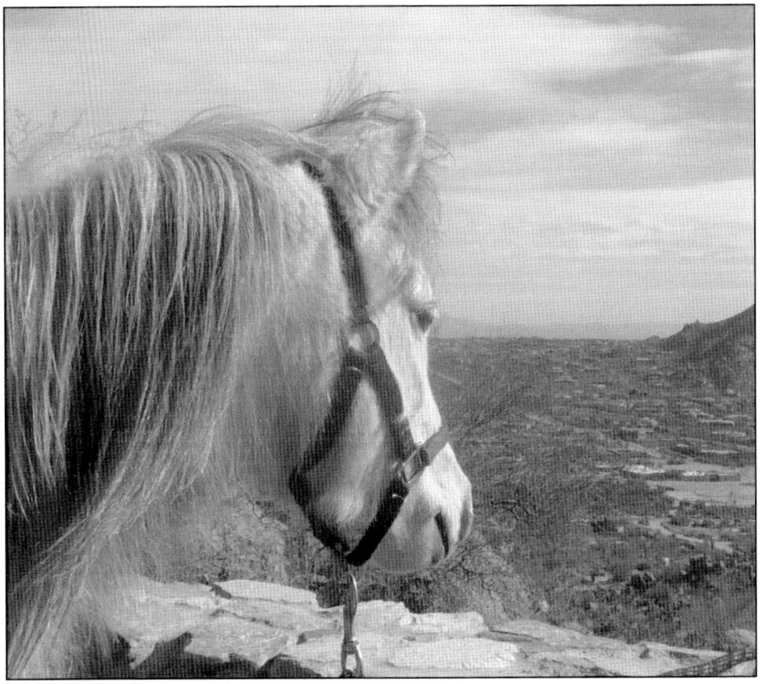

Earl the Trick Pony enjoys the scene from Grand View Overview. Earl, who performs at community events in the Pinnacle Peak area, visited the park in 2000 with his owner, Gina Mure. (Photograph by Gina Mure; courtesy of *The Peak*.)

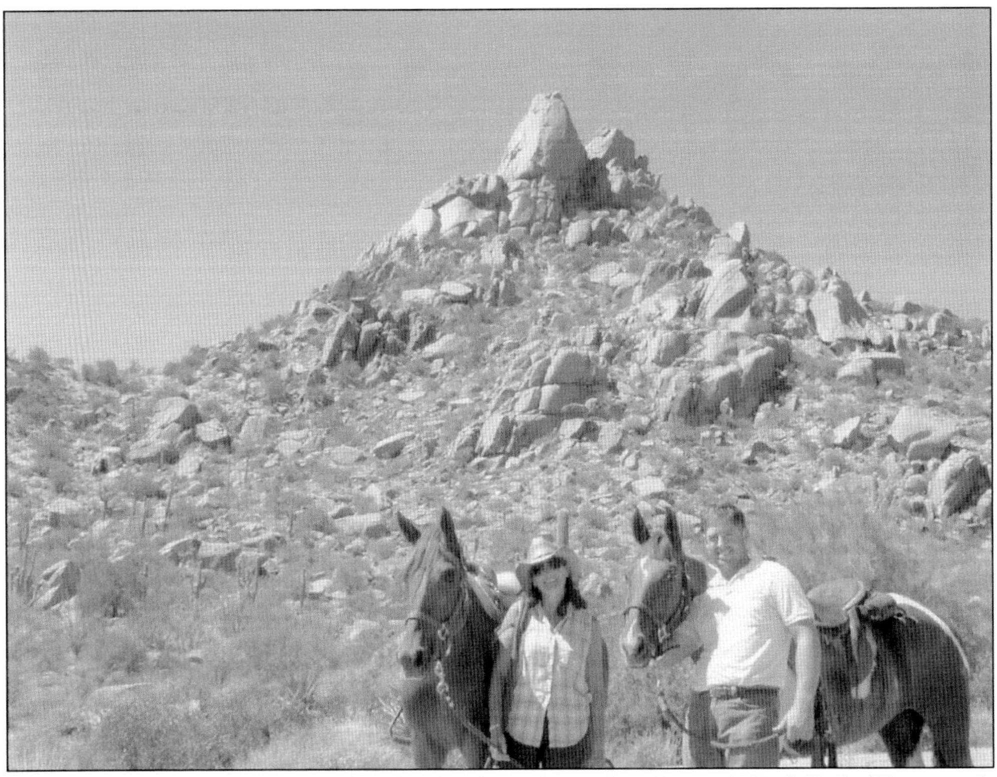

This unidentified couple is all smiles after finishing their ride at Pinnacle Peak Park. (Photograph by Bob Baile; courtesy of the City of Scottsdale.)

Eight

Climbing Pinnacle Peak

The first known ascent of Pinnacle Peak was made by members of the Katchinas, the first organized rock-climbing club in Arizona. In 1944, the group was trained by Ray Garner. Garner was the explorer advisor of the Katchinas and Explorer Post No. 1 of the former Theodore Roosevelt Council Boy Scouts of America in Phoenix. He was also a pilot, professional cinematographer, and mountain guide at Grand Teton National Park. Garner taught the Scouts technical mountain-climbing techniques. Most of the training was conducted on Camelback Mountain in Phoenix.

During 1944, the Katchinas climbed all of Four Peaks in one day, and despite some interruption from World War II, they had also pioneered more of the basic climbing routes on the head of Camelback Mountain. The Katchinas also pioneered climbing in other desert mountain ranges, including the Superstitions, the Kofas, Saddle Mountain, and Eagle Tails. The Katchinas made climbs in the McDowell Mountains and were the first to climb Tom's Thumb, which was known to them as "the Dork."

In addition to climbing, the Katchinas made movies. One of these movies was filmed on Pinnacle Peak for the Boy Scouts of America. The Katchinas remained active through the 1950s. The Arizona Mountaineering Club (AMC) was organized in 1961 and was a strong supporter of the creation of Pinnacle Peak Park.

Most park visitors are not rock climbers, but with luck, visitors may be able to watch experienced climbers in action from the hiking trail. Climbers get to enjoy a quality climbing experience and an unparalleled scenic view.

According to Greg Opland's rock climbing guide, *Phoenix Rock II*, Pinnacle Peak "has been the crown jewel of granite rock climbing areas" since the 1960s. The City of Scottsdale allows rock climbing at the park for experienced climbers with appropriate equipment.

The 200-foot granite peak and two other climbing areas, Cactus Flower and Y-Crack Boulder, are available for rock climbing whenever the park is open. Together, these areas offer a wide selection of traditional crack and bolted routes. Climbing areas can be accessed from marked climbing trails.

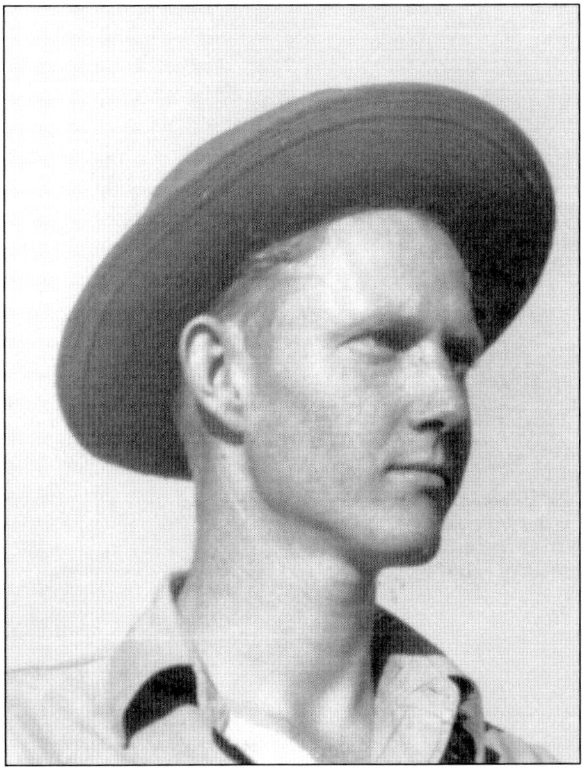

The first known ascent of Pinnacle Peak was made on Saturday, December 13, 1947, by Katchinas Ed George (pictured in this late 1940s photograph) and Bill McMorris. The entire Katchina group, fully expecting to make the first ascent, had planned to climb on the next day, but George and McMorris beat the rest to the punch and carried out the practical joke they had planned. (Courtesy of the Katchina Archives.)

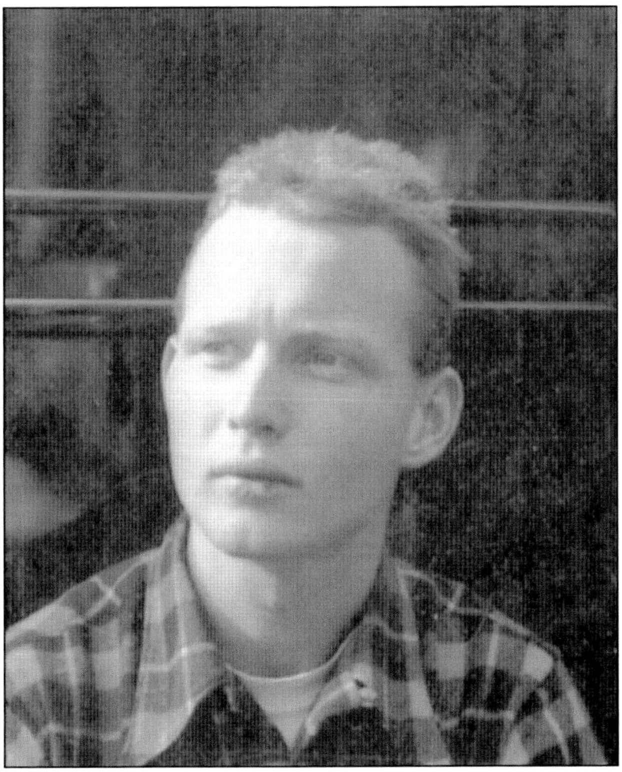

Bill McMorris scrawled a note, purportedly by a little girl on a second-grade Sunday school class picnic. The note and orange peels were placed in a cairn piled up on the summit. This photograph of McMorris was taken in the 1948. (Courtesy of the Katchina Archives.)

On December 14, 1947, the full Katchina group, Ray Garner, Win Akin, brothers Ben and Lee Pedrick, Charles Lidner, Dick Hart, Ed George, and Bill McMorris, travelled to Pinnacle Peak. At the summit, they found the cairn, note, and orange peels. The plot quickly unraveled. In this photograph, Lee (left) and Ben Pedrick relax on the summit. (Courtesy of the Katchina Archives.)

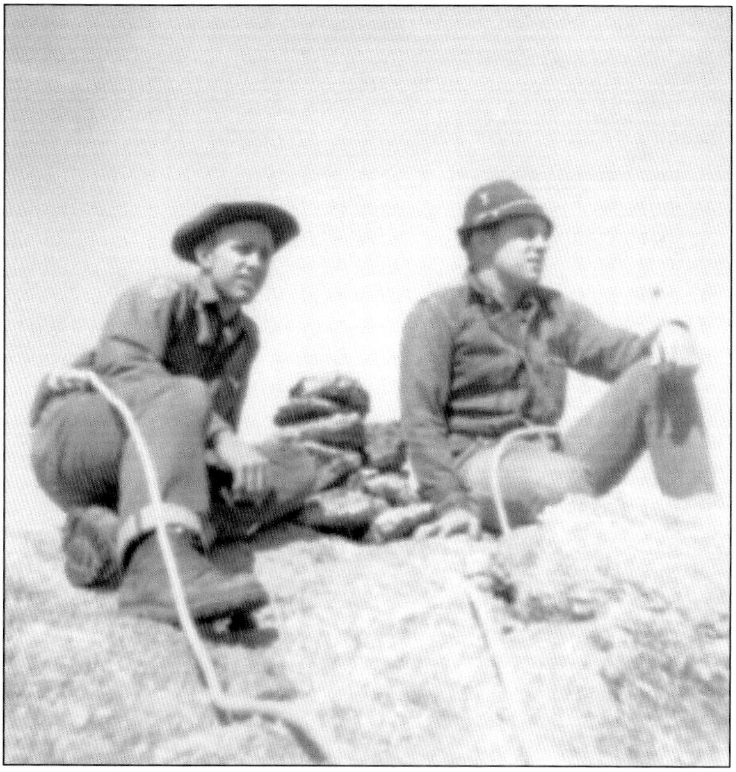

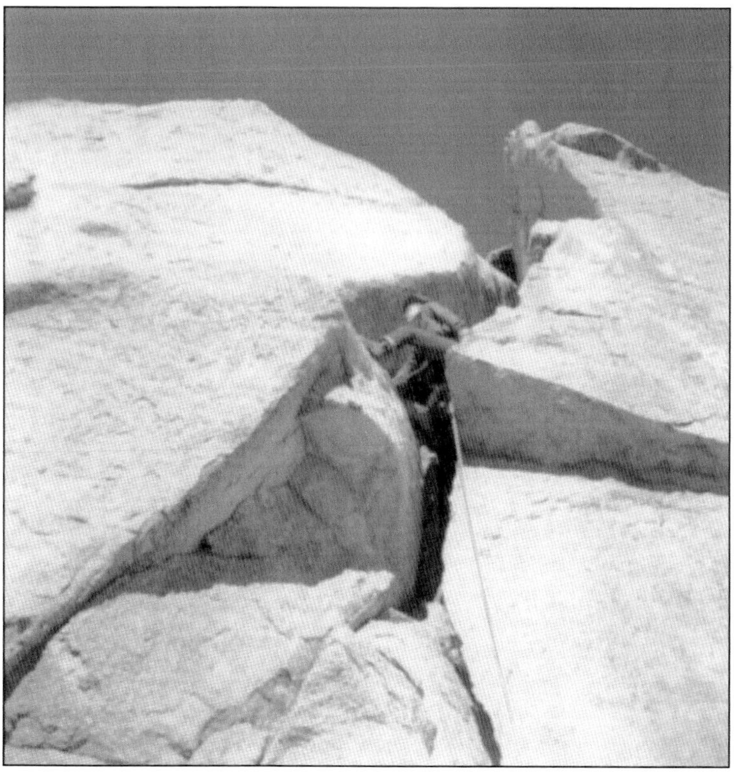

In the early spring of 1948, Ray Garner made a film for the national office of the Boy Scouts of America. In this still from the film, Lee Pedrick is climbing the route that was used by Bill McMorris and Ed George to make the first ascent in 1947. (Courtesy of the Katchina Archives.)

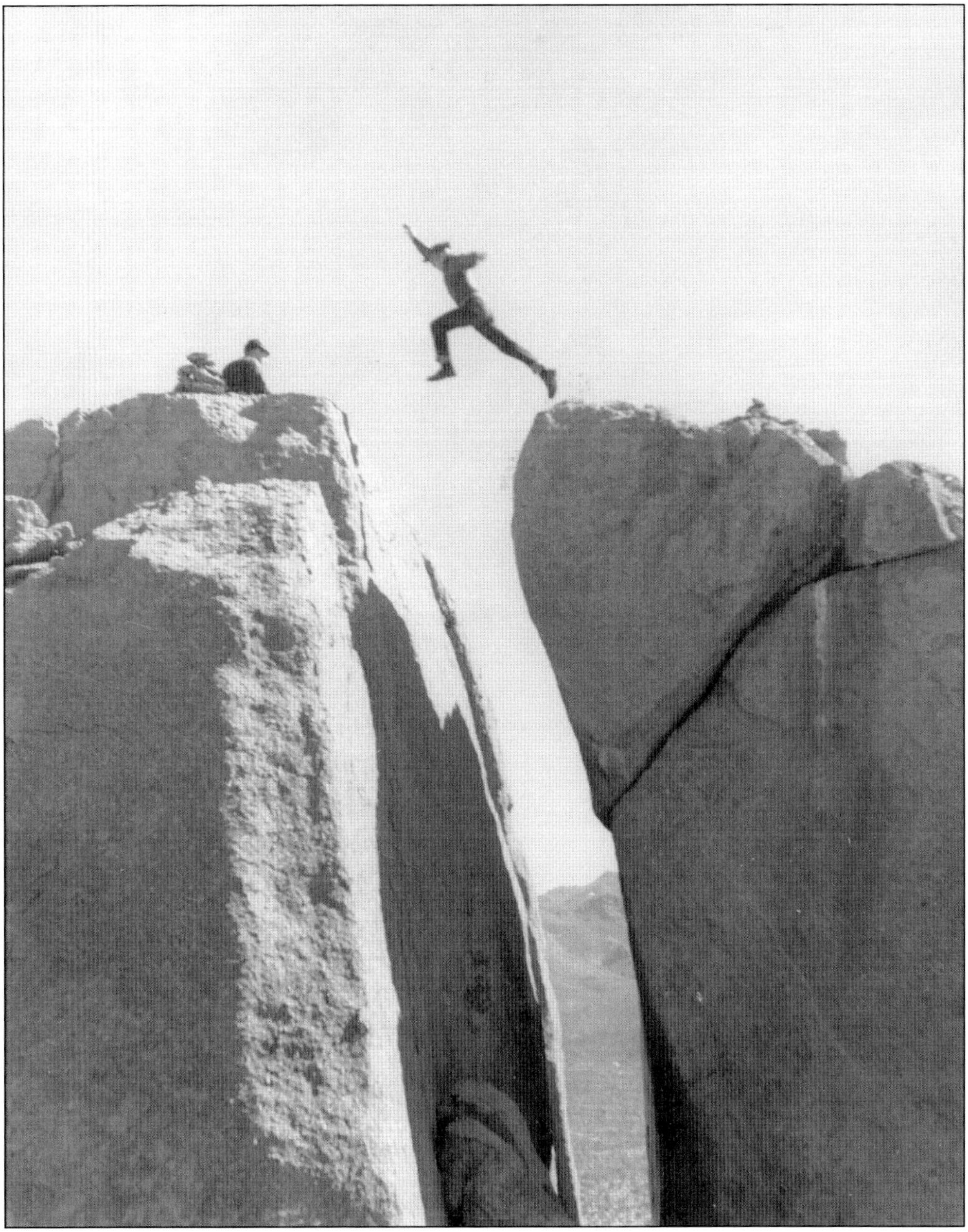

Pinnacle Peak's summit is slit by a five- or six-foot-wide chasm. During the 1948 filming session, Ray Garner took this photograph of Lee Pedrick jumping between the split pinnacles, belayed to his brother Ben. (Courtesy of the Katchina Archives.)

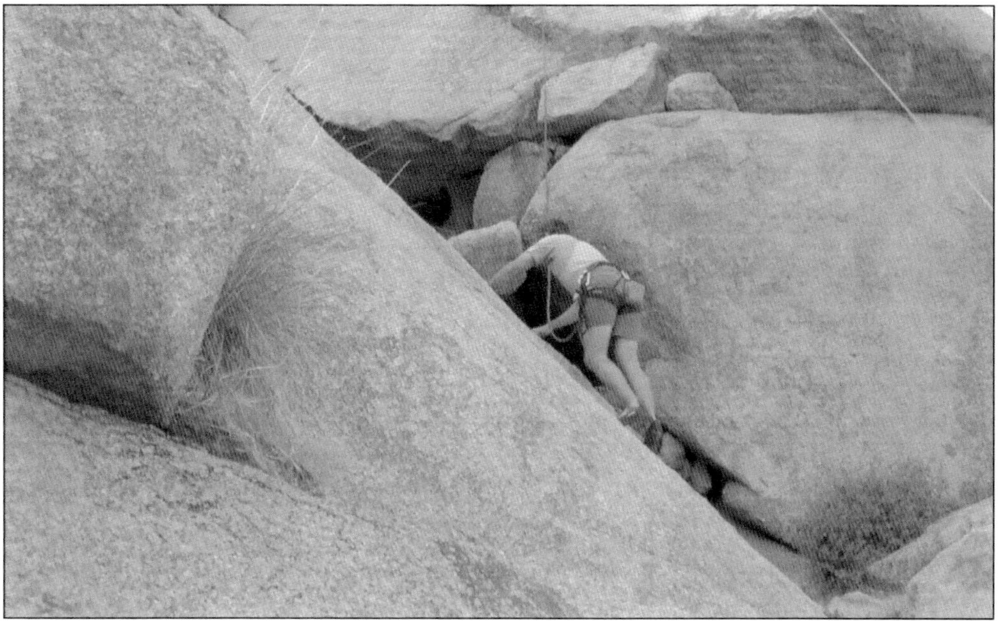

Erik Weihenmayer climbed Pinnacle Peak in November 2005. He is the only blind man to reach the summit of Mount Everest, a feat he accomplished in 2001. He has also climbed the highest mountain on each of the seven continents and authored several books. (Photograph by Bob Baile; courtesy of the City of Scottsdale.)

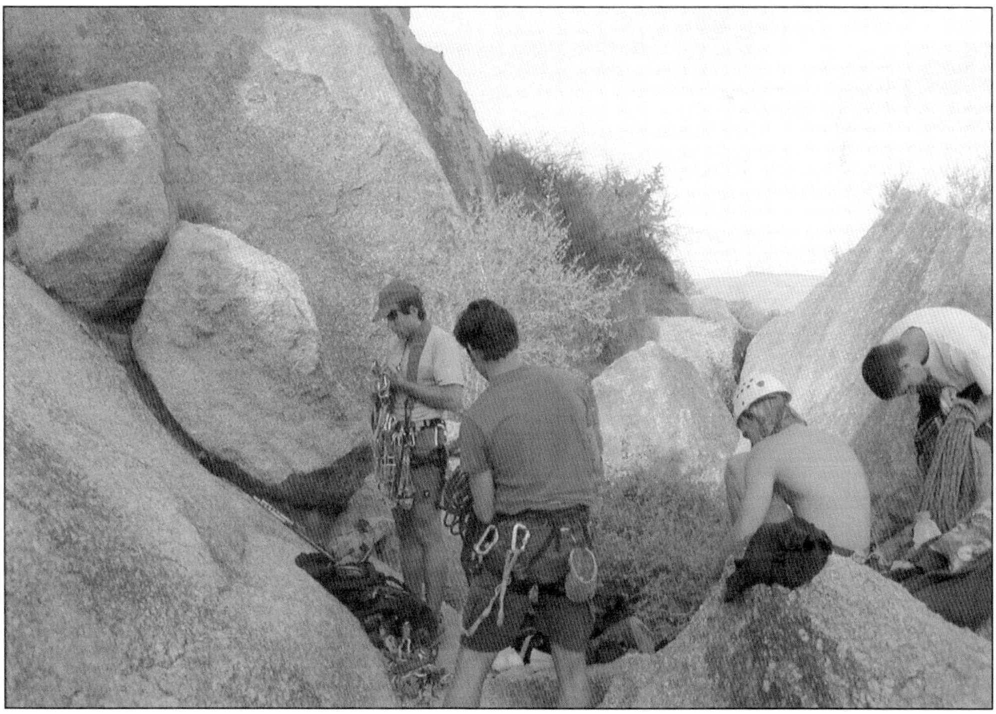

Prior to beginning their climb, Weihenmayer and three other climbers prepared and checked their equipment. Climbers must have appropriate experience and equipment to climb at Pinnacle Peak Park. (Courtesy of the City of Scottsdale.)

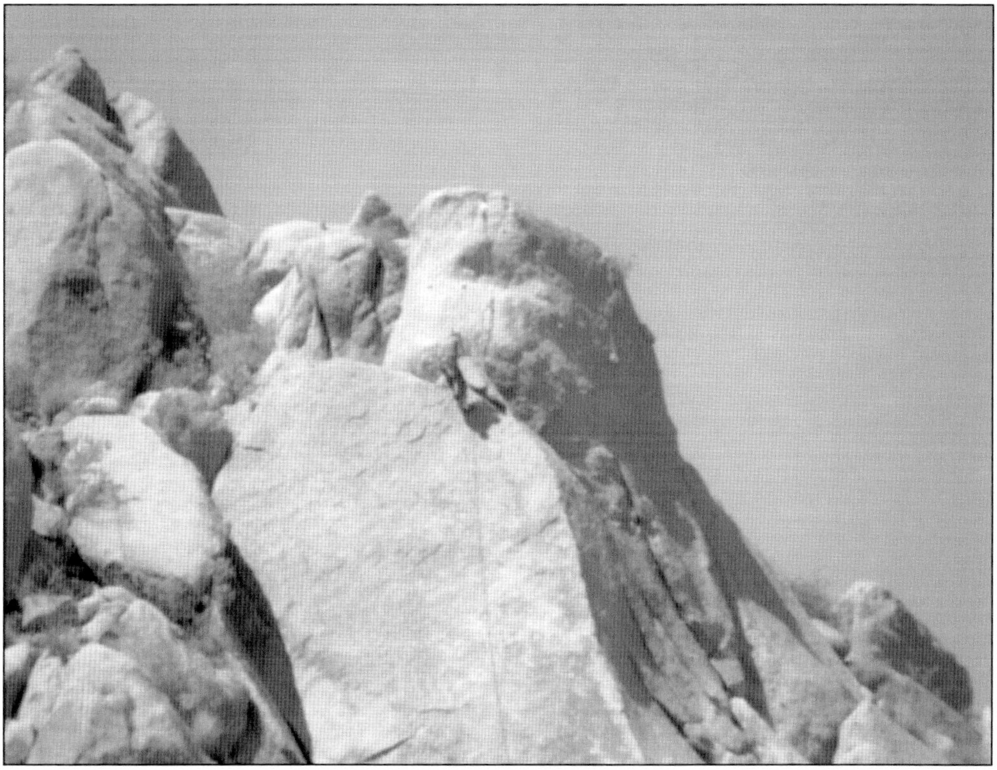

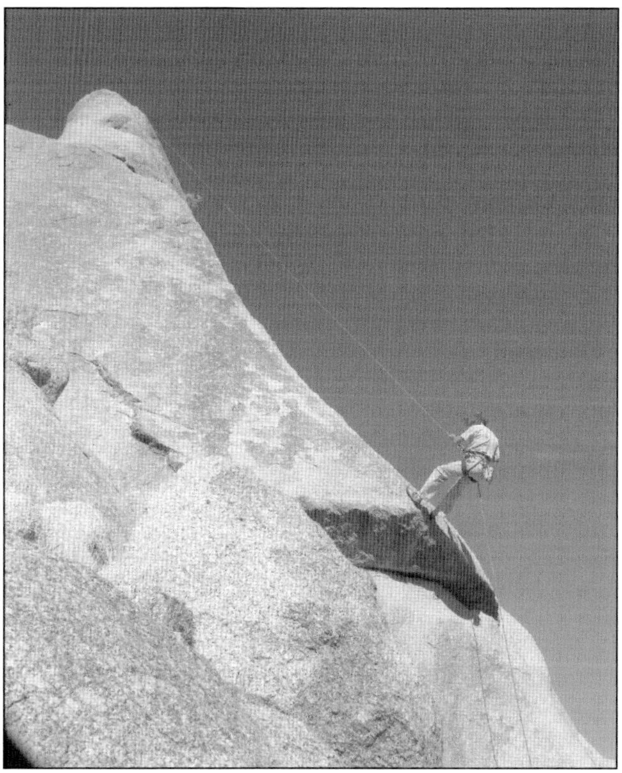

Loafer's Choice Slab is clearly visible from the trailhead of Pinnacle Peak Park. The slab offers several different climbing routes. *Phoenix Rock II* by Greg Opland provides information about the many climbing routes available at the park, including their locations, characteristics, and degrees of difficulty. (Photograph by Kathy Mascaro; courtesy of the City of Scottsdale.)

Paul Diefenderfer, president of Friends of Pinnacle Peak Park, rappels down Dead Meat, a moderate to difficult climbing route on Loafer's Choice Slab. (Courtesy of Frank Biondo.)

Climbers tackle one of the routes in the park's AMC Boulder area. The routes, which were named by past climbers, have interesting names such as Reunion, Varicose, Mickey Mantle, Mean Streak, and Delayed Flight. (Photograph by Kathy Mascaro; courtesy of the City of Scottsdale.)

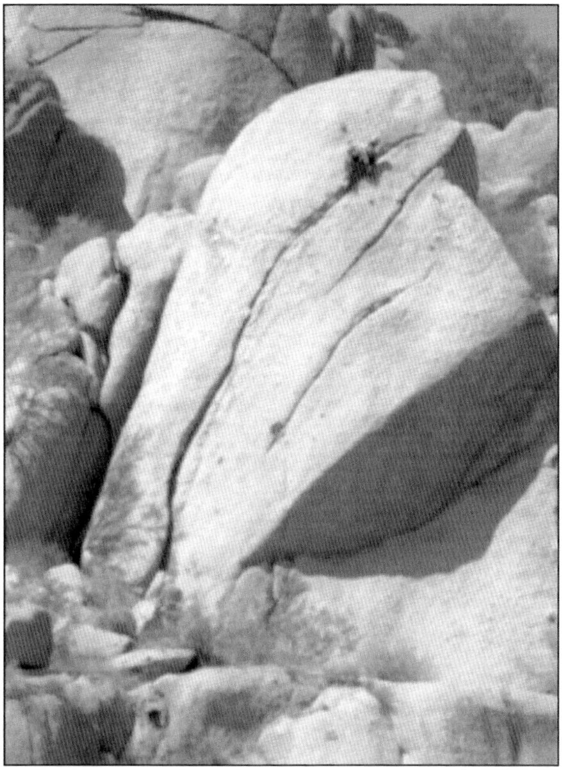

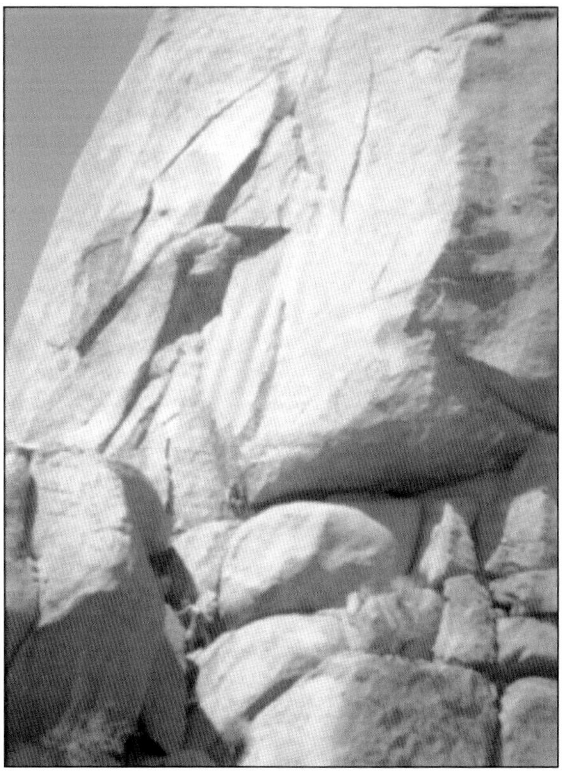

Climbers are dwarfed by the size of Pinnacle Peak as they take the South Crack route to the summit. According *Phoenix Rock II*, "South Crack is a classic beginning route to the top of Pinnacle Peak!" (Photograph by Kathy Mascaro; courtesy of the City of Scottsdale.)

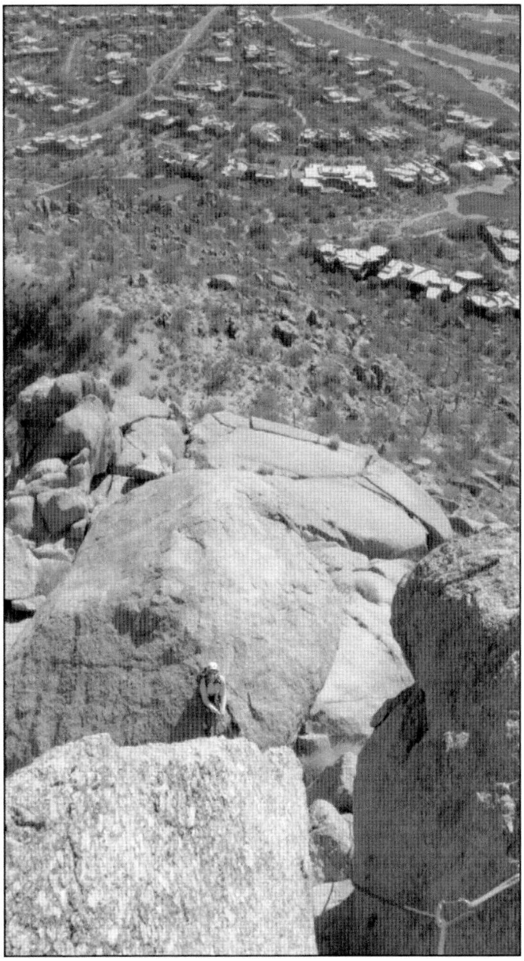

The Arizona Mountaineering Club (AMC) was a strong advocate for the creation of Pinnacle Peak Park. In this photograph, Kim McClintic belays her husband, David, from the Sun Deck Boulder on the South Crack route to the top of Pinnacle Peak. The McClintics are AMC members. (Photograph by David McClintic; courtesy of the AMC.)

Kim McClintic is standing on the summit of Pinnacle Peak. The smile on her face reflects the sense of satisfaction that many hikers, riders, and climbers feel during a visit to Pinnacle Peak Park. (Photograph by David McClintic; courtesy of the AMC.)

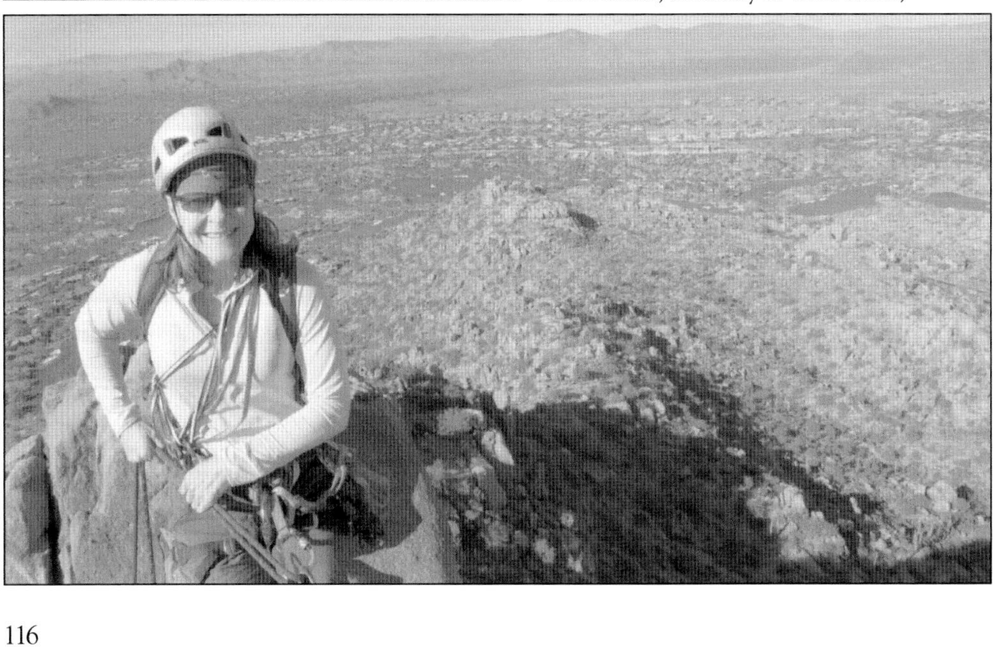

Nine

Pinnacle Peak Flora and Fauna

Many visitors to Pinnacle Peak Park return home with memories of the interesting animals and diverse plants that they encountered in the park and neighboring areas. The park's interpretive signs and educational programs are designed to enhance these memories by providing information about the unique flora and fauna that live in the Upland Sonoran Desert.

It only rains about seven inches per year in the Pinnacle Peak area, but the many species of trees, shrubs, and cacti have adapted to survive the lack of water. The trees found in the Pinnacle Peak area include the foothills palo verde, ironwood, and mesquite. In addition, local shrub varieties include catclaw acacia, triangle-leaf bursage, and chuparosa. Cacti varieties include saguaro, barrel, buckhorn cholla, ocotillo, and fishhook pincushion. Lupine, brittlebush, and desert marigold produce wildflowers from mid-February to mid-April. Pinnacle Peak's diverse, drought-tolerant vegetation provides food, shelter, and protection for many species of mammals, reptiles, insects, and birds.

With patience and an attentive eye, visitors can spot different types of bats, rabbits, and small rodents. Larger mammals include coyotes, javelina, and bobcats. And although they are not as common as the others, mule deer can also be observed around Pinnacle Peak.

Varieties of geckos, lizards, and snakes thrive in the park's rocky environment. The Pinnacle Peak area has five types of rattlesnakes: diamondback, speckled, black-tailed, Mohave, and tiger. Other reptiles include the venomous Gila monster, the Sonoran Desert tortoise, and the Sonoran Desert toad.

An adventurous visitor to the Pinnacle Peak area may lift a rock or dead piece of wood and cause at least one scorpion, spider, centipede, millipede, or beetle to scurry to safety. Depending upon the season, other insects, such as butterflies, moths, bees, ants, and termites, can be observed.

Visitors are also likely to see turkey vultures or a hawk circling overhead or a great horned owl silently flying toward an unknown destination. Varieties of doves, roadrunners, ravens, hummingbirds, woodpeckers, wrens, finches, and other birds add to an abundance of life that many humans find astounding.

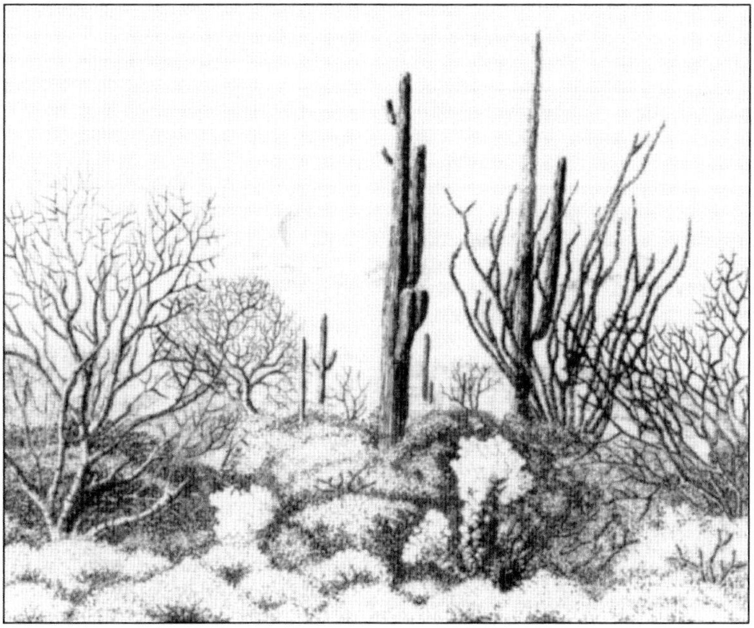

The flora and fauna of the Upland Sonoran Desert, combined with Pinnacle Peak's dramatic landscape, have captured the attention of many artists, including Walter Bohl. An internationally acclaimed painter, Bohl lived on the western slopes of Pinnacle Peak in the 1950s and 1960s. He titled this 1957 work *Our Desert*. (Courtesy of Liz Stapleton Ogden.)

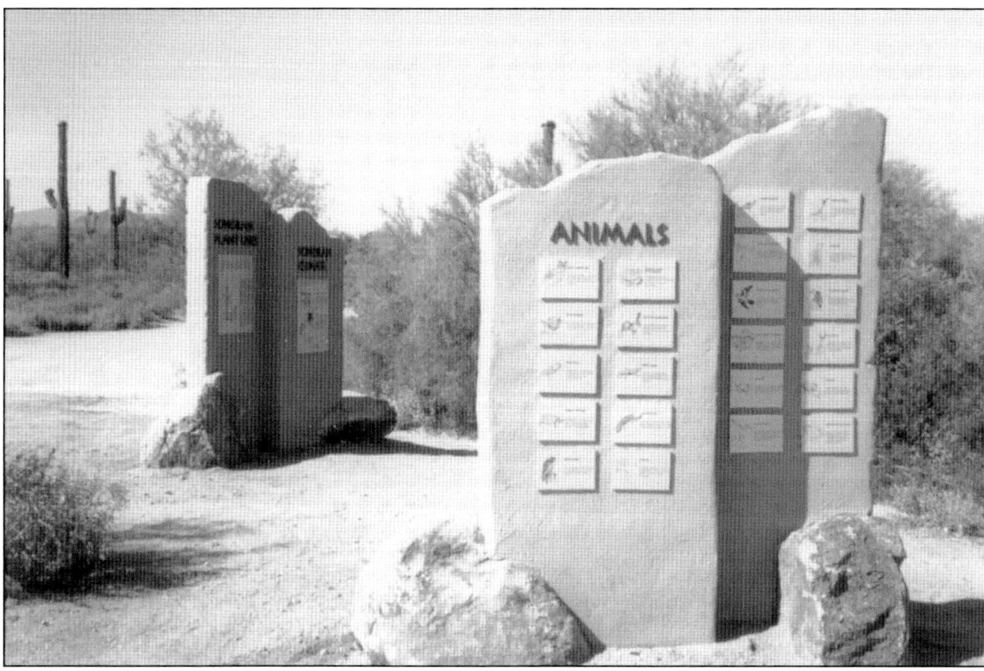

In 1995, local artists Marg Nelssen and Judy Conklin created drawings of the best-known species of flora and fauna that live in the Upland Sonoran Desert. These drawings were incorporated in the Desert Foothills Scenic Drive exhibits that are located on the east side of Scottsdale Road, north of Pinnacle Peak Road. (Courtesy of FSD.)

Advocating and working for the protection of local flora and fauna is part of the heritage of Pinnacle Peak and the surrounding area. In 1963, residents created the Desert Foothills Scenic Drive to protect the desert. They installed the sign pictured here and redwood signs to identify species of flora alongside Scottsdale Road. (Courtesy of FSD.)

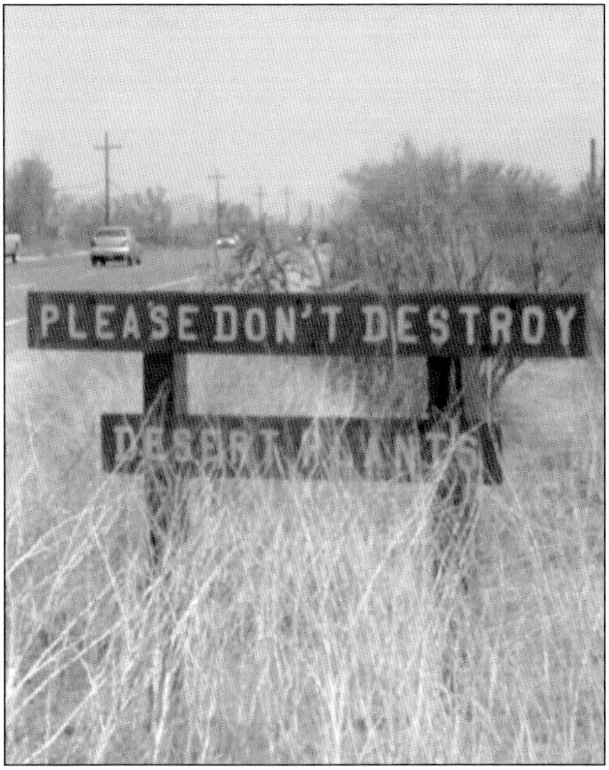

Many Scottsdale residents donate their time to help protect and maintain the flora at Pinnacle Peak Park. Cacti provide beauty and educational value, but they also serve a more practical purpose at the park. The sharp spines of strategically placed cholla help protect the park and visitors by deterring hikers from leaving the trail. (Photograph by Kathy Mascaro; courtesy of the City of Scottsdale.)

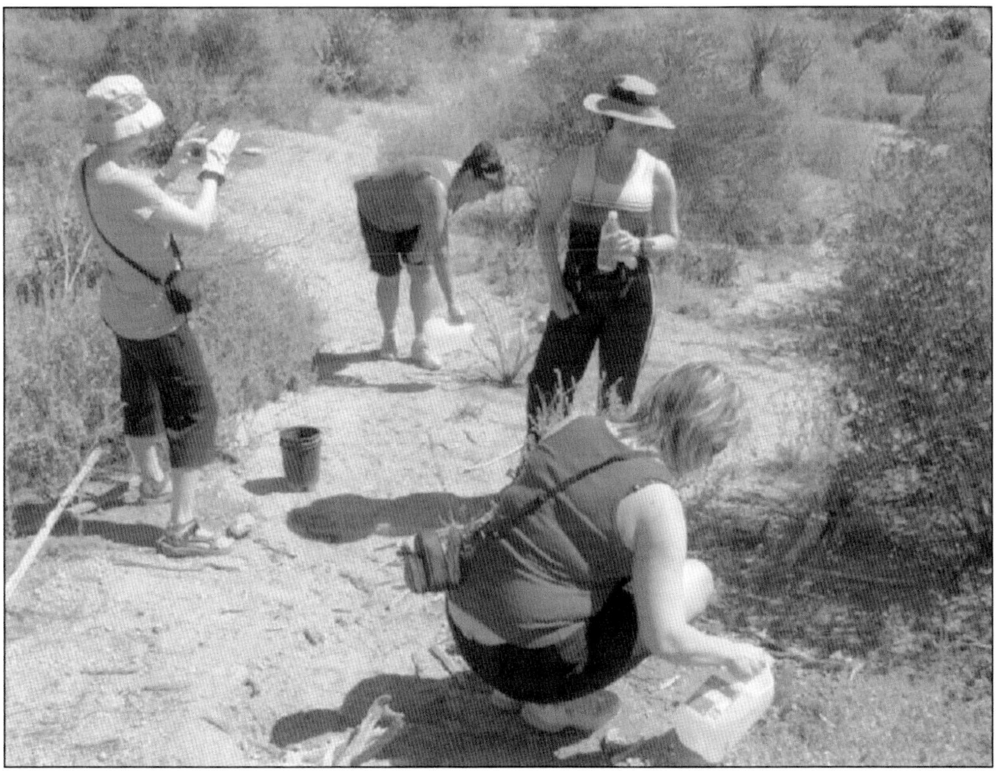

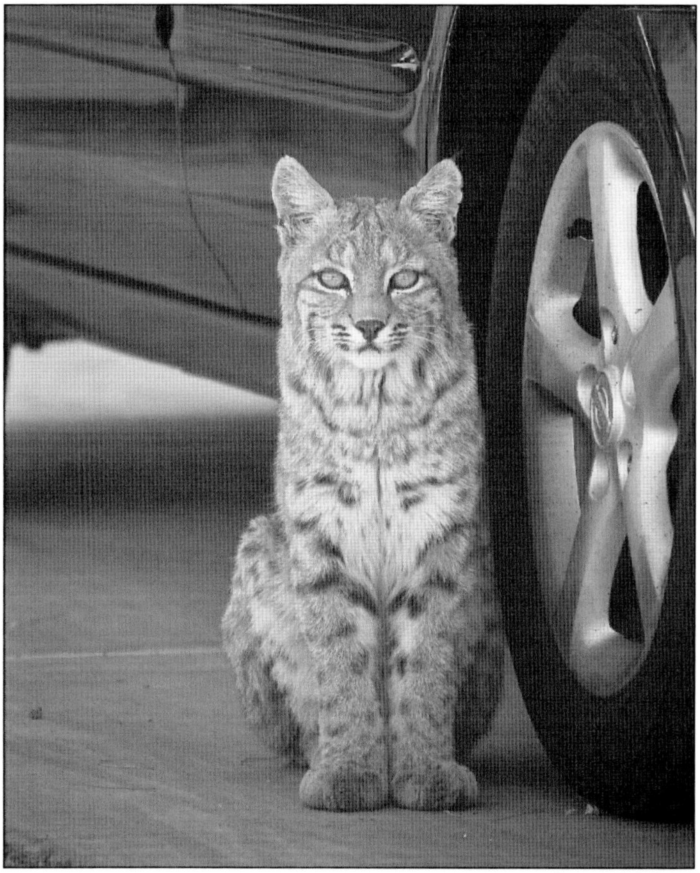

That's not a large house cat waiting to go for a ride in the family car. It's a bobcat that ran down a nearby North Scottsdale street, stopped, and posed for this photograph. Of the large mammals, bobcats are seen most often at Pinnacle Peak Park, usually in the early morning or late afternoon. (Courtesy of Kim Perina.)

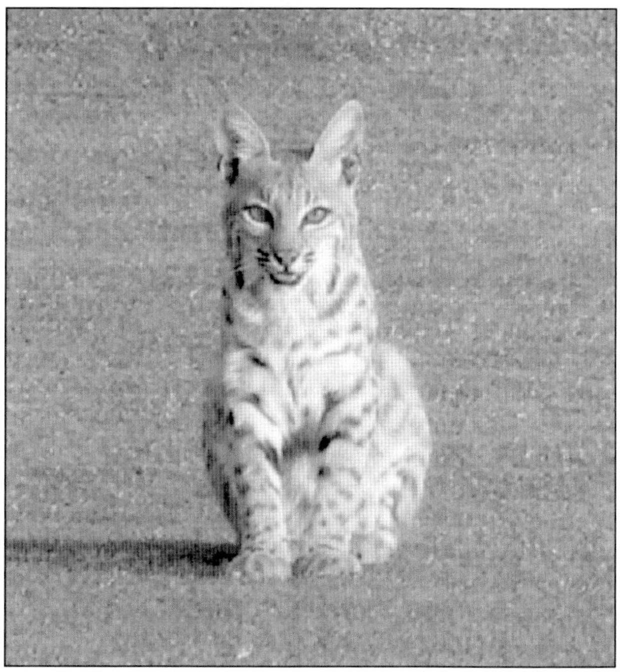

Bobcats hunt small prey, including rabbits. Although they are good climbers, they prefer to hunt on the ground. Secretive, shy, and mostly nocturnal, bobcats prefer thickly vegetated areas and are not often seen by people. Evidently, this bobcat has learned that a grassy fairway at Troon North Golf Course is a good place to find a meal. (Courtesy of Kay Suchomel.)

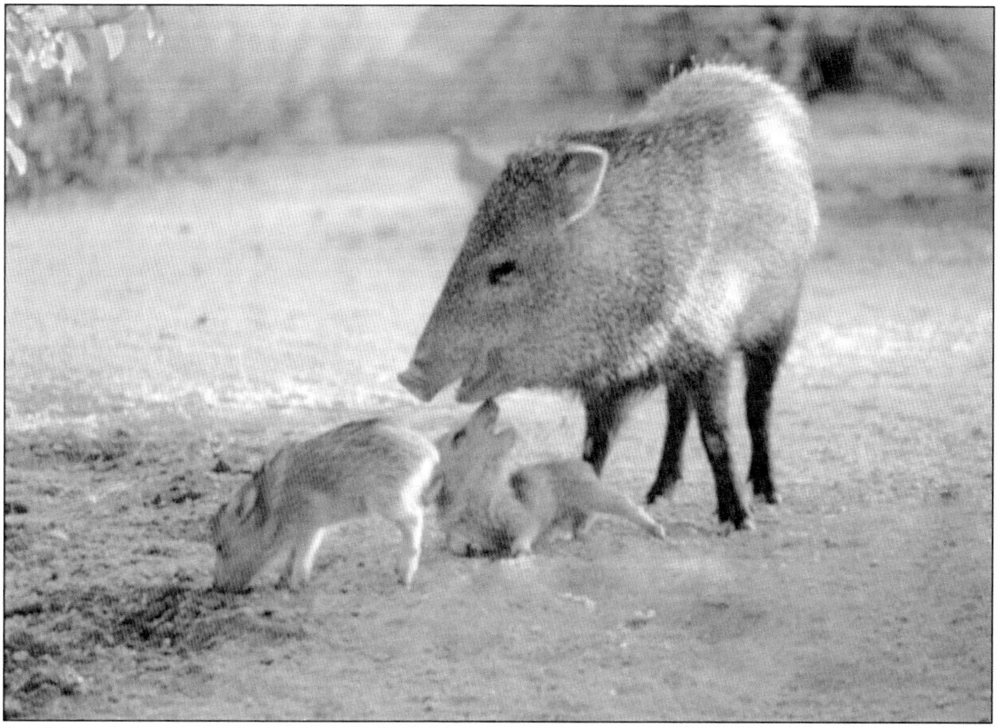

Javelinas are not wild descendants of pigs that escaped from early settlers. These grunting, poor-sighted collared peccaries are indigenous to the American Southwest and Central and South America. Javelinas enjoy dining on succulent plants; prickly pear cactus is one of their favorite foods. They travel in herds of up to 20 animals, and some find a meal by visiting residential areas and tipping over City of Scottsdale refuse barrels. (Courtesy of Dennis Liddell.)

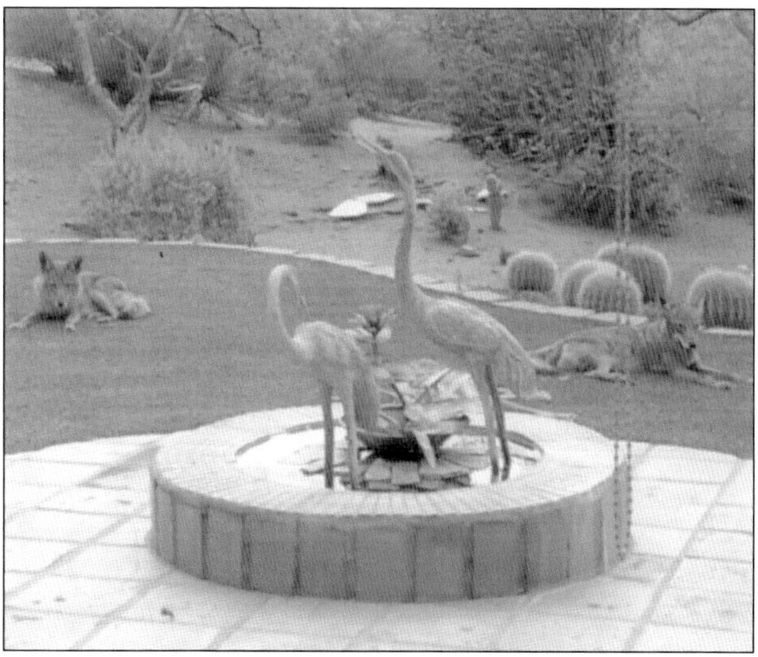

Local coyotes have learned to share their world with man. They can be heard at night either howling or yipping and barking as they race through the open desert. It is not unusual to see them crossing roads in the area or cutting through neighborhoods. It is unusual to see them lounging next to the backyard pool. (Courtesy of Connie Intenso.)

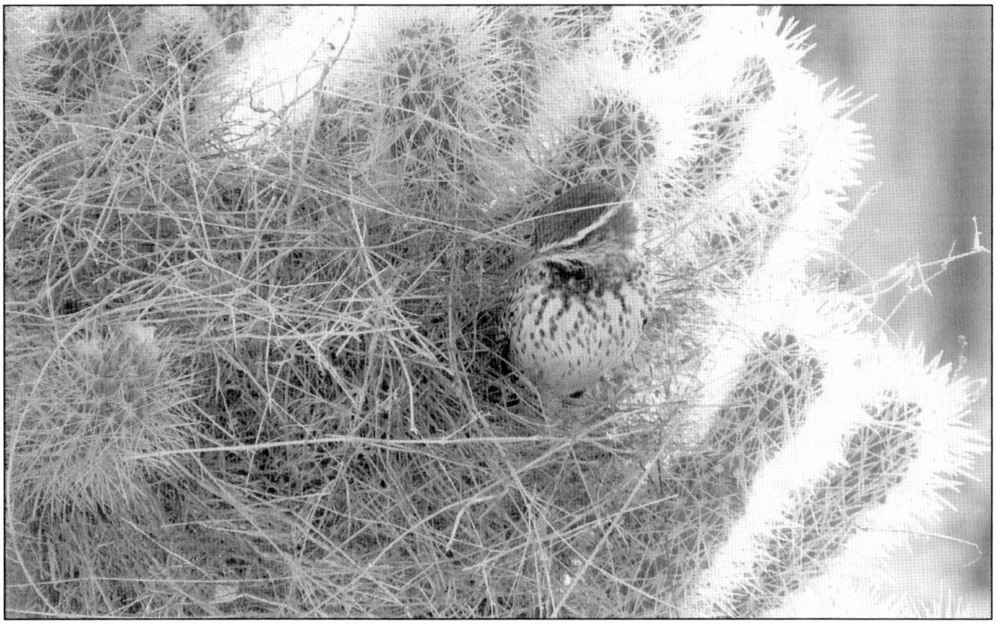

Arizona's state bird, the cactus wren, is the largest of the North American wrens. Wren pairs build football-shaped nests in cholla cacti year round. One nest is used for breeding and another for roosting. Chicks stay with their parents for about 50 days. This photograph was taken at Pinnacle Peak Park. Cactus wrens enjoy exploring open garages and harassing pet cats and dogs. (Photograph by Mark Johnson; courtesy of the City of Scottsdale.)

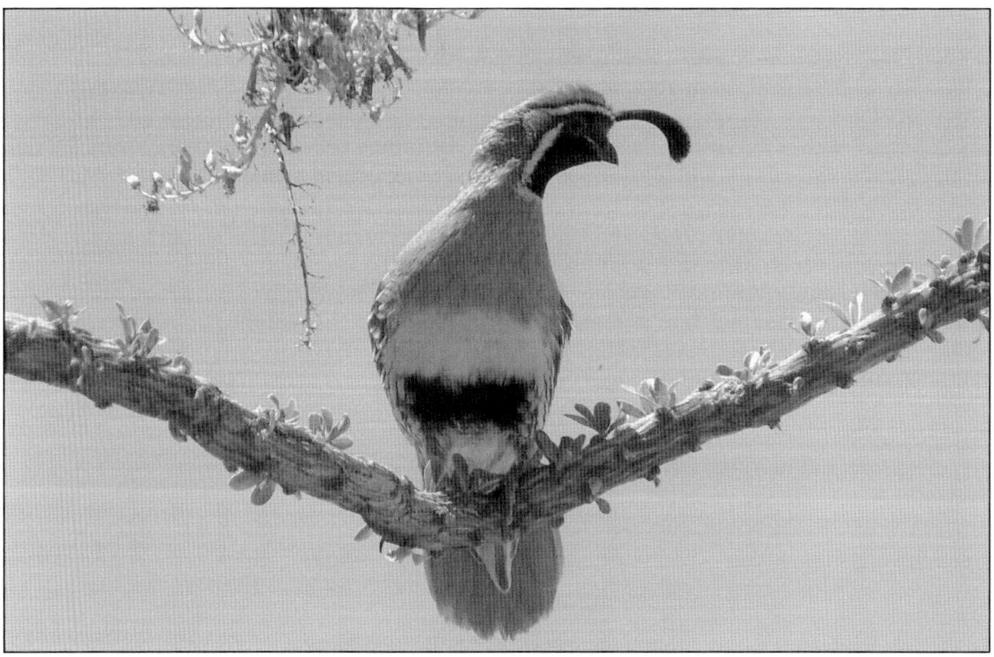

These pigeon-sized quail are usually around in good numbers. It is not unusual to have a group of 6 to 12 birds scratching in a yard in search of food. Just as is pictured here, one male typically perches on a plant or paces on a nearby wall, ready to sound the alert at the first sign of danger. (Courtesy of Heinz Kagerer.)

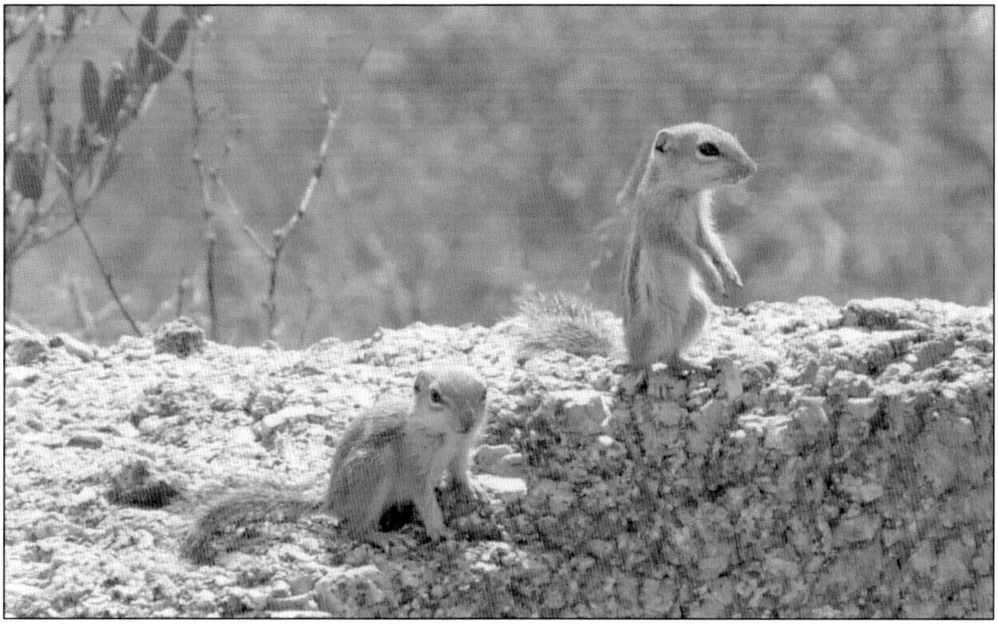

Some visitors to Pinnacle Peak Park mistake the little Harris's antelope squirrel for a chipmunk. However, antelope squirrels live in the rocky deserts, while chipmunks prefer higher elevations. Harris's antelope squirrels are often seen running around the desert sniffing out seeds in the ground and digging them up. These young squirrels were photographed at the park. (Photograph by Mark Johnson; courtesy of the City of Scottsdale.)

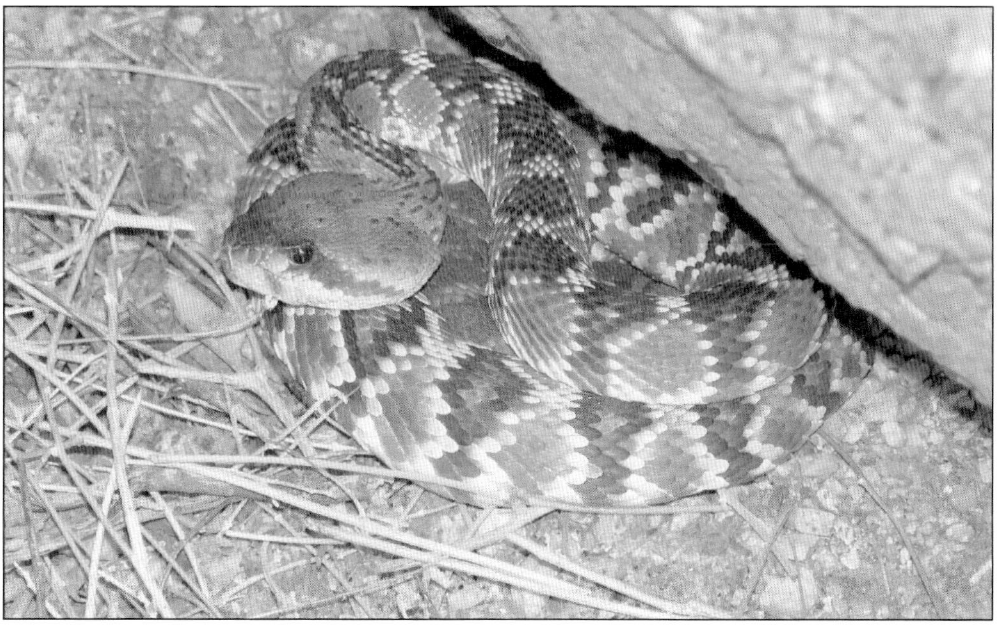

This black-tailed rattlesnake was photographed at Pinnacle Peak Park, but development, flooding, and increased populations can cause snakes and other animals to leave their usual habitats and enter into human neighborhoods. Scottsdale residents can call the fire department, which will safely capture an intruding rattlesnake and transfer it to nearby open space. (Photograph by Mark Johnson; courtesy of the City of Scottsdale.)

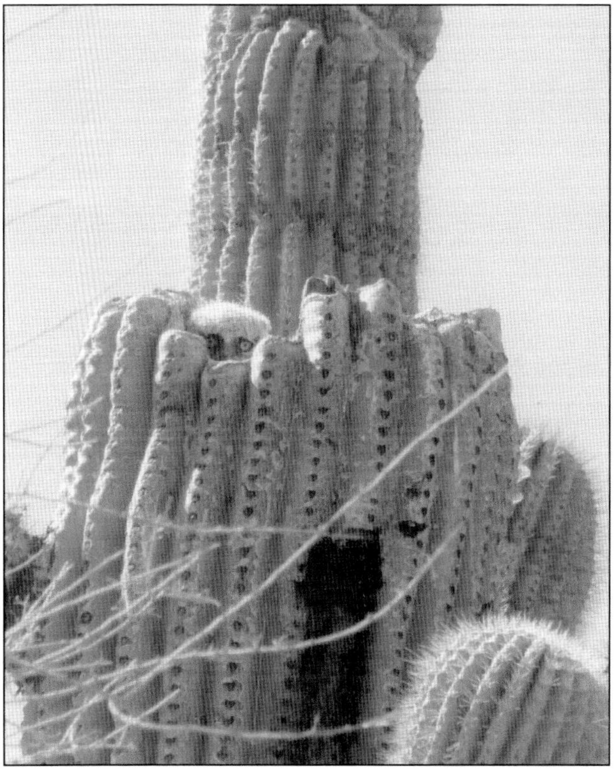

Instead of building their own nests, great horned owls prefer to take up residence in nests built by other large raptors, such as the Harris hawk. Pinnacle Peak area residents commonly see great horned owls perched in trees or on rooftops. The low-pitched, hooting calls of the owls can be heard at night. When the owl chick shown here becomes independent, its parents will force it out of their hunting area. (Courtesy of Linda Whitehead.)

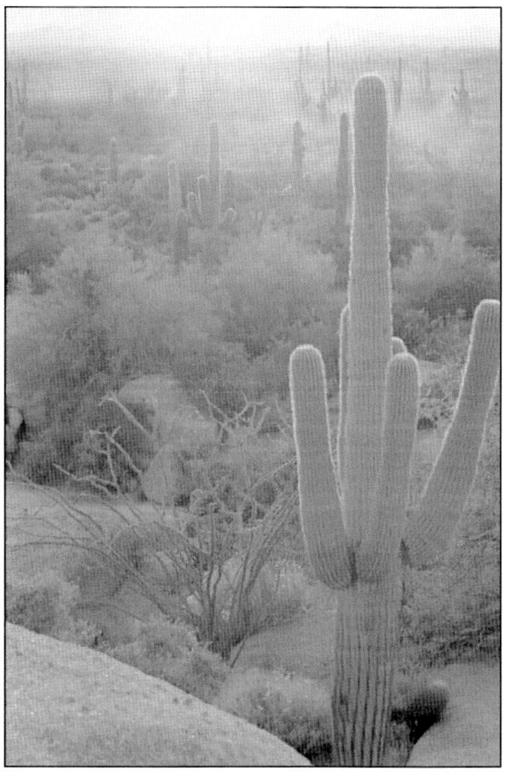

The saguaro is the signature plant of the Sonoran Desert, Arizona's state flower, and the largest cactus in the United States. This group of saguaros is found on the western slope of Pinnacle Peak, on the land that was homesteaded by Kenyon Turner Palmer. Since the saguaro can live for 200 years, some of these cacti were likely to have been Pinnacle Peak residents before Palmer's arrival in 1933. (Courtesy of Kathy Howard.)

About the Author

Les Conklin is the president of the Greater Pinnacle Peak Association (GPPA) and publisher and editor of the association's community magazine, *A Peek at the Peak*. *The Peak* won the Society of National Association Publishing's EXCEL Award in the editorial category in 2009 and 2007. A veteran technical, marketing, and business writer, Conklin has had numerous articles published in local, corporate, and industry publications.

A student of history, Les founded Friends of the Scenic Drive, a volunteer organization that restored and maintains the Desert Foothills Scenic Drive, which has been a North Scottsdale landmark since 1963. Conklin also founded and is the primary organizer of Cookout at the Ranch. Started in 1996, the cookout is North Scottsdale's largest preservation benefit.

Since he and his family moved to what is now North Scottsdale in 1983, Les has been active in the community. He has served on the boards of directors of the McDowell Sonoran Conservancy, the Pinnacle Peak Rotary Club, and the Monte de Paz Homeowners Association. He has also served on the City of Scottsdale's McDowell Sonoran Preserve and Pride commissions.

Conklin was a pioneer in the software industry. During his professional career, which spanned 43 years, he traveled extensively and held management and consulting positions in marketing, sales, business development, Web development, and business writing. At age 29, he cofounded Synergetics Corporation, which developed and sold software products used by the defense, retail, manufacturing, banking, insurance, health care, and other industries. Conklin served as the project leader for development of electronic business systems, including configuration management software for Apollo I.

The Greater Pinnacle Peak Association, founded in the Pinnacle Peak area of Scottsdale, Arizona, in 1977, is a nonprofit organization dedicated to the preservation of the natural environment and the enhancement of quality of life in the North Scottsdale Sonoran Desert. GPPA supports desert preservation, wildlife conservation, the arts, education, and community service through its publications, initiatives, student grants, and by assisting local nonprofit organizations. GPPA began as the Greater Pinnacle Peak Homeowners Association (GPPHA) and remains dedicated to representing the interests of the neighborhoods in the Pinnacle Peak area.

Bibliography

Bartlett, Michael with photographs by Tony Roberts. *The Estancia Club*. Scottsdale, AZ: Pinnacle Development Group, 2007.

Carefree, Cave Creek Foothills: Life in the Sonoran Sun. Cave Creek, AZ: Foothills Community Association, 1990.

Carlson, Frances. *Cave Creek and Carefree, Arizona: A History of the Desert Foothills*. Scottsdale, AZ: Encanto Press, 1988.

Fudala, Joan. *Historic Scottsdale: A Life from the Land*. San Antonio, TX: Historic Publishing Network, 2001.

———. *Scottsdale*. Charleston, SC: Arcadia Publishing, 2007.

Gilman, Patricia. *Pinnacle Village: An Overview of the Spring 1988 Excavations*. Tempe, AZ: Arizona State University Office of Cultural Resource Management Anthropological Field Studies, 1993.

Harris, Rick. *Easy Field Guide to Rock Art Symbols of the Southwest*. Phoenix, AZ: American Traveler Press, a division of Primer Publishers, 2008.

Opland, Greg. *Phoenix Rock II*. Evergreen, CO: Chockstone Press, 1996.

Palmer, Kenyon Turner (K.T.). *For Land's Sake: The Autobiography of a Dynamic Arizonan*. Flagstaff, AZ: Northland Press, 1971.

Patterson, Alex. *Rock Art Symbols of the Greater Southwest*. Boulder, CO: Johnson Books, 1992.

The Plants and Animals of Pinnacle Peak Park. Scottsdale, AZ: City of Scottsdale, 2008.

Schroeder, K. J. *Troon North Archaeological Project, Maricopa County*. Scottsdale, AZ: Roadrunner Publications in Anthropology No. 1, 1993. (Report prepared for Pinnacle Paradise, Inc.)

Trimble, Marshall. *Arizona, A Cavalcade of History*. Tucson, AZ: Rio Nuevo Publishers, 2003.

Index

Consistent with our mission to preserve history on a local level, this book was printed in South Carolina on American-made paper and manufactured entirely in the United States. Products carrying the accredited Forest Stewardship Council (FSC) label are printed on 100 percent FSC-certified paper.

MADE IN THE USA